SIMON RICKARD is a passionate plant wonk and gardener. He is best known as the former head gardener at the Diggers Club, in which role he oversaw the magnificent gardens of Heronswood and the Garden of St Erth until 2009. Until 2012 he collaborated with restaurateur Annie Smithers, designing and operating her kitchen garden in country Victoria.

These days, Simon works as a garden designer, gardening coach and garden communicator. He leads garden tours for Botanica World Discoveries, and gives lectures and workshops for bodies such as the Stephanie Alexander Kitchen Garden Foundation, the University of Melbourne School of Land and Horticulture, Open Gardens Australia and the Australian Landscape Conference, as well as local horticultural societies and sustainability groups around the country.

Somehow, Simon finds time to live out a parallel existence as a freelance baroque bassoon player.

This is Simon's second book.

www.simonrickard.com

HEIRLOOM VEGETABLES

A GUIDE TO
their history and varieties

SIMON RICKARD

LANTERN

an imprint of
PENGUIN BOOKS

For my grandmothers:

Marj, who Dug for Victory,

and Win — poor as a church mouse, rich as a queen.

CONTENTS

INTRODUCTION

I first fell in love with heirloom vegetables when I took up a gardening position at the Diggers Club's flagship garden, Heronswood, on Victoria's Mornington Peninsula in 2001. Twelve years later I find myself back at Heronswood, watching the rain bucket down over Port Phillip Bay from the comfort of Heronswood house's bay window (what better place?). I am meant to be outside photographing pumpkins but there's no chance of that in this weather. Being back in the old house where I spent nearly four happy years living as resident head gardener has given me cause to reflect on why I wanted to write this book.

Heirloom vegetables were a revelation to me. Right off the bat they appealed to my sense of aesthetics and my love of the quirky and, above all, they appealed to my tastebuds. But the more I got to know heirlooms the more I began to appreciate them for their stories. It turns out that their stories are our stories, too. Thousands of years of human history are written in their genes if we only know how to look for it. Vegetables are human creations. They are domesticated organisms that only exist within the sphere of humans. They depend on us for their furtherance. But domestication is a mutual process and we humans also depend on our vegetables to a much greater extent than most of us realise. These are the stories I wanted to tell: to reveal how far humans and vegetables have travelled together through the ages and what we've done for one another along the way. This book is, in part, a social history of vegetables. Or, you might say, a human tale told through vegetables.

I also wanted to explore vegetables' fascinating family relationships. Vegetable families are as interesting as any in the human world. Their members include many well-loved ornamentals and herbs, as well as weeds and poisonous plants. Examining the relatives of vegetables throws into sharp relief just how much the domestication process has changed them over the centuries.

I should say that as a survey of the actual cultivars of heirloom vegetables in existence, this book barely scratches the surface. There are 4300 distinct potato cultivars alone – enough to fill several volumes – let alone tomatoes (up to 75 000) and eggplants (your guess is as good as mine). Far from trying to be exhaustive, I have mostly limited myself to varieties which are available in this country and which might be useful to a twenty-first-century Australian backyard gardener.

The how-to-grow chapter of this book is fairly brief. There was not room to be prescriptive about each and every vegetable variety. However, I felt it was important to include some general cultural pointers based on my own first-hand experience. These days too many gardening books are written by authors with no real experience of their subject matter. As for gardening blogs, one can't help but feel that they are more often than not a case of the blind leading the blind. I sincerely hope this book goes some way towards dispelling some of the specious misinformation that is endlessly recycled on the internet and which is now finding its way into books. Happily there are still some excellent books on how to grow vegetables available. I have listed some of them at the back of this book for readers hungry for more information.

I did not intend for this book to degenerate into a polemic on the ownership and politics of food. However, these issues have become so closely bound up with the heirloom vegetable revival that a little pontificating was unavoidable. I do not claim to be the absolute arbiter of any such matters and I welcome readers to agree or disagree with any or all of my opinions. It is only by calmly thinking through and talking about these vexed issues, and questioning the motives of those who so desperately want to exercise ownership over the global food supply, that we will make progress.

I hope that heirloom vegetables are as much of a revelation to you as they were to me. As you get to know them better in the pages of this book, I also hope that you will be inspired to grow your own heirloom vegetables and, having tasted them, fall in love with food, gardening and nature anew.

HOW TO USE THIS BOOK

•

The main purpose of this book is to tell some of the interesting stories about heirloom vegetables, and to reveal their family affiliations. As in all good stories, the plot jumps around a bit. And just as in all families, the interrelationships can get a little messy. Accordingly, you won't find the vegetables in this book listed in alphabetical order from Artichoke to Zucchini. However, you will find the different varieties, or cultivars, of each kind of vegetable listed alphabetically.

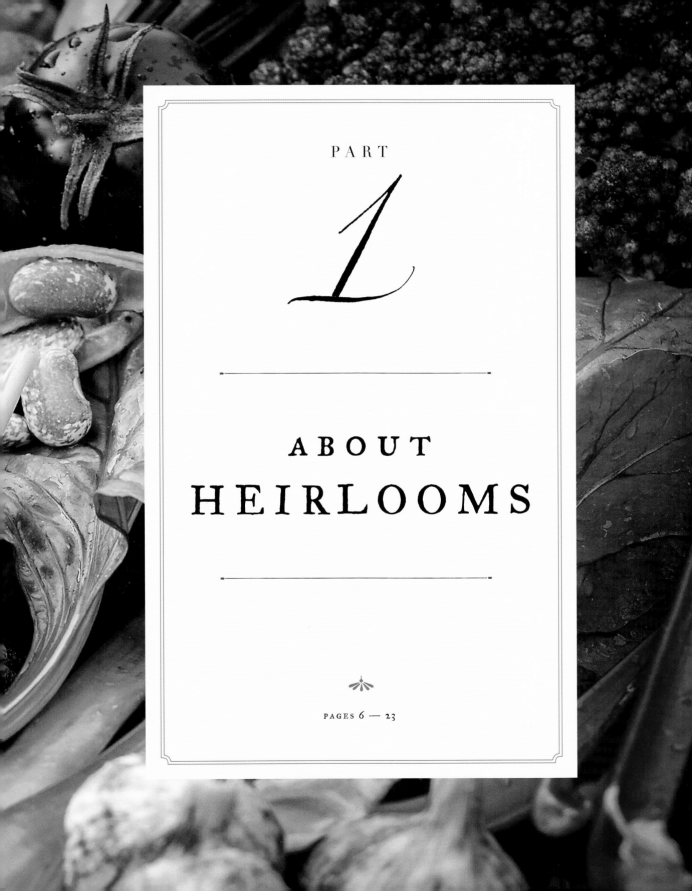

ABOUT
HEIRLOOMS

Heirloom vegetables have been enjoying a renaissance since the 1980s. With their often unusual appearance, surprising flavours and multifarious culinary uses, heirlooms have become the darlings of the horticultural and foodie sets. They have breathed new life into gardening and cookery, encouraging a whole new generation to take up those noble pursuits.

These days, heirloom vegetables are so frequently encountered at farmers' markets and on the tables of fine dining establishments that it is hard to imagine we nearly lost them completely. Yet until their revival three decades ago, these precious horticultural jewels teetered on the edge of extinction.

Since the 1950s our society has abdicated responsibility for its food supply to agribusinesses and middlemen. It was their business models which came to dictate which vegetable varieties farmers would be allowed to grow and which varieties people would be able to eat. Such decisions were taken out of the hands of food producers and consumers. As a result, vegetable breeding businesses became obsessed with homogeneity. Seed companies bred dozens of new hybrid vegetables each year but, far from giving consumers more choice, they began to converge on a single point of uniformity.

Many of us remember the days, not so long ago, when you could buy any kind of tomato as long as it was red, round and tasteless, any kind of lettuce as long as it was 'Iceberg', and any kind of cucumber as long as it was eight inches long and the prescribed shade of dark green. Driven by the commercial imperatives of the middlemen, all newly bred vegetables had to look the same and taste the same so that consumers wouldn't be alarmed, or distracted from the job of *buying*, as different varieties came and went from the supermarket shelves during the course of the season. There was no room for individuality in this brave new world of super-market dominance. Under this paradigm, vegetables became little more than units for selling, no longer a source of sustenance, let alone of enjoyment.

Then heirloom vegetables came along and reawakened our jaded eyes and palates. Far from being alarmed, we were fascinated by them. Heirlooms reminded us that food could be a complete sensory experience. Heirloom vegetables were beautiful to behold and delicious in unique ways; they had unusual names and inter-esting stories to tell about their provenance or culinary use. Heirloom vegetables snapped us out of our stupor. They woke us up to what was happening to our food under our very noses.

The critics pronounced heirloom vegetables 'edible nostalgia'. They brushed them aside as pretty but irrelevant fripperies belonging to a sentimental era when trifling concerns such as flavour were more highly valued than the unassailable certitudes of profit and efficiency. Perhaps there is an element of truth in that crit-icism. But really, is it so bad to feel a sense of passion about food, even if it doesn't measure up to the hard-edged mandates of economic rationalism? I have never heard anybody accusing fine wine of being a ludicrously outdated Phoenician drink made from rotten grape juice, yet that is exactly what it is. Nobody is denouncing cheese as an antiquated Neolithic recipe for preserving milk, redundant in this age of refrigeration. To argue that the existence of modern hybrid vegetables renders heirloom vegetables obsolete strikes me as a bit joyless. It's like asserting that there is no longer a need for roast dinners in a world that has protein shakes.

By the last quarter of the twentieth century the dominance of hybrid vege-tables was so complete that in many cases heirloom strains were being kept alive by single committed individuals, who grew the plants out and saved their seeds year after year. Heirlooms were on the verge of extinction. It is thanks principally to the work of Americans Diane Ott Whealy and Kent Whealy, who founded the Seed Savers' Exchange in the USA state of Iowa in 1975, that gardeners and cooks were made aware of how much we stood to lose. Through seed savers' networks, a mechanism was established to locate and save endangered heirloom varieties. Since then, hundreds of heirloom varieties have been reintroduced to horticulture. Maintaining thousands of years' worth of human cultural heritage in the form of heirloom vegetables has become the work of individuals and organisations around the world, including in Australia, with organisations like the Seed Savers Network and the Diggers Club.

So what exactly are heirloom vegetables and why are they special? Loosely speaking, heirloom vegetables are varieties which pre-date WWII. As the name suggests, heirloom vegetables have been handed down through families or communities for generations. Just like your nanna's wedding ring or your granddad's fob watch, or a beloved local custom like the Birdsville Races or the Melbourne Cup, heirloom vegetables are cherished as precious cultural touchstones. They *mean* something to the people who grow and eat them.

These bean seeds demonstrate the staggering genetic diversity of heirloom vegetables.

Heirloom vegetables are more than just sentimental keepsakes, however. Migrants leaving troubled lands for a better life overseas have always taken their heirloom vegetables with them. Heirlooms have travelled the world as seeds sewn into the hems of clothes, stuffed into children's soft toys or in paper envelopes hastily shoved into pockets. Jews fleeing the pogroms in Russia took their favourite pickling cucumbers to the USA. Ukrainians escaping civil unrest took their precious tomatoes. Chinese gold diggers brought their leafy Asian greens to the Victorian goldfields. Poor Italian labourers who came to work on the Snowy Mountains hydroelectric scheme brought *nonno*'s best eggplant seeds. Heirloom vegetables have always represented food security to people who have fallen on uncertain times. They provide a link with family and community in the old country and symbolise the ability to make a new life in the new country.

After WWII the face of agriculture changed. Wartime technologies paved the way for the mechanisation of farm labour, the rollout of large-scale irrigation schemes, and the development of artificial fertilisers and pesticides (both legacies of wartime chemical production). These new technologies enabled farming on an increasingly large scale. Breakthroughs in the emerging science of genetics revolutionised plant breeding. Agronomists bred specialised crops, capable of bearing extraordinarily high yields when grown under the intensive irrigation and fertilisation regimes made possible by the industrialisation of agriculture. It was the dawn of the Green Revolution.

The Green Revolution has had many positive effects. It is widely credited with averting famine in India in the 1960s. It gave developing nations a means for self-nutrition and self-reliance. However, the Green Revolution also had some unintended consequences. One is that it tethered world food production to an unending supply of cheap oil. Oil is required as a fuel for both mechanised farm labour and for transporting crops to distant markets. Oil is also the raw material needed for making the artificial fertilisers and pesticides upon which high-yielding crop varieties (HYVs) rely in order to give optimum results. It has been said, not without a kernel of truth, that industrialised agriculture is the process of turning oil into food.

The HYVs and intensive farming techniques of the Green Revolution have been so successful that they have increased crop yields many times over. Wonderful, I hear you say. If you are relying on your crops to eat, then high yields are undoubtedly good. If you are growing your crops to sell, however, then abundance is not necessarily such a good thing. It has long been a point of pride among farmers to grow as much produce as they possibly can. However, our market-driven economy is geared for scarcity, not surplus. Surpluses drive prices down. So, ironically, the bigger the yields farmers produced with the new crops and techniques of the Green Revolution, the less their product was worth. The only way farmers were able to make a living under such circumstances was to get bigger and bigger, to grow more and more, and swallow up competitors. Family-run smallholdings gave way to industrial mega-farms. Agriculture came to be driven by economic rationalism, which dictates that crops must be grown in vast, uniform monocultures in the name of maximising profit and minimising cost. Food came to be considered a commodity, like gold or iron ore: just another resource to be extracted from the earth in ever increasing amounts. The age of big agribusiness had arrived.

In such an age it might seem that heirloom vegetables are just quaint relics of the past. I would argue that they are more important than ever before. To understand why, we need to look more closely at their genetics.

Heirloom vegetables are, by definition, open pollinated (OP for short). Open pollination occurs when the pollination of flowers is taken care of by nature; by bees or the wind, sometimes with a little help from humans. It is usually thought of as including self-pollination, too. Open pollination results in a high degree of genetic variability within a population of seedlings. Just as you look different from your siblings, so the individuals in an open-pollinated (OP) vegetable population have slightly different characteristics from their siblings, even though they come from the same parent stock. Some individuals in an OP population will be taller, some shorter, some will crop earlier, others later, some will have bigger fruits, others smaller. Most will be of average quality, a few will be really good and a few will be duds.

From this inherently variable OP population, growers select the best individuals from which to save seeds so that their genes are passed on to the next generation. Once again the best individuals are selected from that generation for seed saving, and so on. Growing OPs is a process of constant selection and refinement as the pool of genes inherent in the population is reshuffled at each generation by open pollination. By selecting the best plants in the population over many generations, a strain is developed which has relatively stable physical characteristics, and which is adapted to local conditions.

Heirloom vegetable varieties have been selected over many generations with two aims in mind. First, they have been selected for their culinary attributes: their flavours, textures and usefulness for specific purposes in the kitchen, such as bottling, drying, and eating fresh. Naturally, different cultures have their own culinary preferences, and this in itself has driven an enormous amount of diversity. For example, the French like small, crisp radishes for eating fresh while the Japanese like huge, solid radishes for pickling and cooking. On the other hand, the French like enormous pumpkins while the Japanese prefer pumpkins that fit in the palm of your hand.

For cooks, this means that there is an heirloom variety perfectly suited to any recipe you can name. Take eggplants, for example. If you are making Greek stuffed eggplants, there is no better variety than the Greek heirloom 'Tsakoniki'. For Japanese *nasu dengaku* you'd want Japanese 'Kamo' eggplants. For Thai curries it has

The Japanese prefer their radishes big and their pumpkins small.

to be tiny Thai pea eggplants. For ratatouille and baba ghanoush, 'Long Purple' is your variety. It's the same story with tomatoes. For drying, 'Principe Borghese' is the best, 'San Marzano' is a great variety for making passata and 'Lemon Drop' is good for garnishing salads, while a single slice of 'Mortgage Lifter' is big enough to cover a slice of bread. For cooks interested in seasonal produce with a strongly regional flavour, heirloom vegetables have a lot to offer.

The second attribute for which heirlooms have been selected is to grow well under particular climatic conditions. For example, the onion Tropeana Rossa Lunga was selected in Sicily to thrive in the hot, dry conditions there, while Ailsa Craig was selected in Scotland to cope with that country's cool, wet summers. This means that there is an heirloom variety suited to just about any set of local conditions. Jaune Flamme is a tomato that ripens reliably in cool summer districts. Gold Rush is a lettuce that resists bolting in hot, dry climates. Modern hybrid vegetables are by their nature one-size-fits-all (or, perhaps more accurately, one-size-fits-none).

Another useful feature of heirloom vegetables is that they tend to crop over an extended period compared with modern hybrid varieties. This is very useful for home gardeners who don't need massive gluts of produce, but rather small amounts of produce, harvested over a long period. For example, heirloom sprouting broccolis crop over a two-month period, whereas hybrid broccolis are bred to crop all in one hit, with commercial harvesting in mind. Heirloom tomatoes are mostly 'indeterminate', or vining, plants, meaning that they continue to crop over many months, unlike their hybrid counterparts, which are bred to be compact bushes that crop all at once to make mechanical harvest more efficient.

Tom Thumb is a determinate hybrid tomato, bred to crop all at once.

The intrinsic genetic variability of heirloom strains means that they are quite robust. If one plant in an OP population is prone to a particular disease, there's a good chance that the plants growing on either side of it will be resistant. By saving the seeds from the resistant plant, you can develop your own locally adapted strain, suited to your particular growing conditions.

Genetic diversity is crucial to global food security, especially in a world affected by relatively rapid climate change. Heirloom vegetables represent a vast repository of genetic information which we cannot afford to lose. Thousands of years of human history are written in their genes, not to mention millions of genetic recipes for making plants fit for human food. Hidden in heirloom vegetables are genetic recipes for tolerating drought, heat, flood, saline soils and disease. We might need to access those genetic recipes some day, so best not lose them.

In 2008 the Svalbard Global Seed Vault was opened. Built by the Norwegian government for the use of the entire world, the vault is a state-of-the-art, nuclear-bomb-proof facility carved into the bedrock on the Arctic island of Spitsbergen, just 1300 kilometres south of the North Pole. The vault has room to hold 4.5 million seed samples, a genetic library of human food plants kept safe and sound in the permafrost at −18°C. In fact the Svalbard Global Seed Vault is just a backup copy of this gene library. Its accessions are duplicates of germplasm held by institutions around the world, pointing to the importance of maintaining genetic diversity. Just as migrants have always taken their heirloom vegetable seeds with them into an unknown future, so the world must do the same.

By now you are getting a feel for what heirloom vegetables are. Another way of defining what heirlooms are is to contrast them with what they are *not*. What they are not is F1 hybrids. An F1 ('filial one') hybrid is the first generation progeny of a deliberately controlled cross between two known parents. The parents are carefully inbred OP strains. However, unlike an OP, if you save the seeds from an F1 hybrid, the resulting progeny will not be like its parent. In horticultural parlance we say that F1 hybrids 'do not come true to type'. Because of this characteristic, F1 crosses need to be artificially remade each and every generation.

You might ask how F1 hybrids have come to dominate agriculture if they don't come true to type? Why grow them at all if they have to be recreated from scratch each time you want to grow them? There are several reasons for this. The first few concern the horticultural characteristics of hybrids. F1 hybrids display a phenomenon called *heterosis*, or hybrid vigour. This makes them notably strong growing. Unlike open pollinated strains, F1 hybrids are very uniform in their outward appearance, their growth habits and their genetic expression. All individuals in an F1 hybrid population grow at the same rate, crop at the same time and look identical. These characteristics are critically important in industrialised agriculture. The other reason for hybrids' dominance is purely commercial: F1 hybrids are able to be patented. More on this later.

F1 hybrid crops have been custom bred for industrial agriculture, driven by criteria such as ease of mechanical harvest, marketability, transportability and storability. F1 hybrid breeding is all about metrics: How many? How big? How heavy? How soon? Qualitative considerations such as flavour and culinary merit have largely fallen off plant breeders' radars since the 1950s. It's almost as if breeding for 'flavour' is some kind of dewy-eyed fantasy that has no place in the brave new world of the Green Revolution. Or, at the very least, it should play second fiddle to commercial breeding criteria. Food crops have come to be treated less as a source of nutrition and enjoyment than a raw material for turning into money.

Comparing hybrid tomatoes with their heirloom counterparts clearly demonstrates the differences between F1 hybrid and OP vegetables in general. Hybrid tomatoes are bred to bear their fruits more or less simultaneously, so that the entire crop can be harvested mechanically. They are bred to have thick, leathery skins and hard flesh so that they will withstand mechanical harvesting, being packed into crates, long-distance transport and lots of handling, without significant loss in appearance. They are tomatoes whose *raison d'être* is to be bought, sold and thrown around a lot. In other words, they have been bred to suit the needs of middlemen, not for the enjoyment of consumers.

The attributes of F1 hybrid tomatoes are, in fact, the exact opposite of what consumers want. We want tomatoes which are soft, juicy and tasty, produced over an extended harvest season. Whether or not tomatoes are able to stand up to the rigours of long-distance transport and extended storage is of no interest whatsoever to people whose primary interest is in *eating* them. Heirloom tomatoes have been bred for eating and enjoying. They have been selected for their intense flavours, succulent textures, mouthwatering perfumes and beautiful appearance, as well as to crop over an extended period. From the point of view of home gardeners and gourmets, heirlooms are superior to F1 hybrids in every way.

FACTS AND FALLACIES

•

At this point it's probably a good idea to dispel a few myths about heirloom vegetables. A common misunderstanding about heirlooms is that they are 'pure' and untouched by the hand of man – exactly as Mother Nature intended them. Nothing could be further from the truth. Heirloom vegetables are *entirely* the work of human hands. True, nature originally created the prototypes of vegetables but humans have spent thousands of years customising them and pimping them up. Vegetables bear little resemblance to their wild ancestors. Corn is a good example of this. Ancestral corn has ears the size of your little finger, with kernels hard enough to break your teeth. It was only through human intervention that the big, juicy, sweet cobs we know today were created.

The calabash gourd is one of the oldest domesticated vegetables.

A second myth about heirlooms is that they are not hybrids. Most vegetables can trace their ancestry back to more than one wild species, which, by definition, makes them hybrids. The swede is a hybrid of *Brassica oleracea* and *B. rapa*. The potato is a hybrid of *Solanum stenotomum* and *S. sparsipilum*. Heirloom vegetables are not F1 hybrids like their modern supermarket counterparts. They are advanced-generation hybrids; that is, strains which have been back-crossed repeatedly over many generations until they breed true.

One could easily get the impression from some of the literature surrounding heirlooms that F1 hybrids are somehow intrinsically 'evil'. They are not. ISA Brown chickens are F1 hybrids. That is, they are a deliberate cross between specially inbred strains of Rhode Island Red chickens and Rhode Island White chickens. Similarly, the mule is an F1 hybrid between a horse and a donkey. Look into a mule's soulful eyes and you will know that F1 hybrids are not evil. It is what people use F1 hybrids for that deserves some scrutiny and debate. More on this later.

A third myth about heirloom vegetables is that they are not genetically modified. It is true that heirlooms are not genetically modified in the same way that *transgenic* organisms are; the so-called GMOs (for example, a cotton plant which has had a gene from a bacterium inserted into it so that it produces the insecticidal compound normally made by that bacterium within its own cells). But neither are heirloom vegetables 'plants as nature intended them'. Returning to our examples of the swede and the potato, those vegetables are not only hybrids but also *polyploids*. That means they have more than the normal two sets of chromosomes just about every other living organism on the planet has to make do with. Instead of being *diploid* like you and me, with two sets of chromosomes, half inherited from mum and half from dad, potatoes and swedes are *amphidiploid* or *allotetraploid*, meaning they have four sets of chromosomes – *all* of mum's and *all* of dad's – squeezed into the one organism. You may be even more surprised to hear that bread wheat is *hexaploid*, meaning it has six sets of chromosomes: three times the number that naturally occurring organisms have. If that's not monstrous and unnatural I don't know what is.

The fact of the matter is that humans have been manipulating plants' genes for ten thousand years. True, genetic freaks such as potatoes and wheat appeared spontaneously as impossibly rare natural mutations. But freaks such as these would not necessarily have survived in nature without human intervention. Humans were intelligent enough to seize these rare genetic opportunities. Our ancestors found the one weird potato plant with extra large tubers growing in the field of wildlings, and kept its tubers back to see what would happen. They noticed the strange new grain with large, non-shattering seed heads, and saved its seed for next year. Humans propagated spontaneously occurring mutant plants, refined them and bent them to their will. Thus began selective breeding and domestication. Domesticated crop plants are referred to as *cultigens*. They are plants which have evolved not by the forces of *natural* selection (which are referred to as *indigens*) but by *human* selection. Heirloom vegetables are cultigens, created by humans, not by nature. They do not exist in nature, only in the human sphere.

It is worth pointing out that OP vegetables are not without their problems. Poorly maintained strains can suffer from inbreeding depression, resulting in weak seed with poor germination, and in inferior strains which lack vigour or stray too far from type. However, these faults are caused by human error rather than any intrinsic weakness in open-pollinated varieties *per se*. Unfortunately, lacklustre strains of OP seeds are increasingly prevalent in the marketplace. As interest in heirloom vegetables grows, it is not always attended by good breeding technique and seed saving practices. This turns some gardeners off growing heirlooms, perhaps unfairly.

PUBLIC vs PRIVATE OWNERSHIP

•

Heirloom vegetable varieties are open source. They are part of humankind's collective cultural history, just like our diverse languages, customs and musical traditions. Heirloom seeds come true to type, so they can be saved by anyone. They have been passed down through generations, given to friends and family and shared with strangers. They belong to all of humankind.

F1 hybrids are fundamentally different. They do *not* belong to everyone. They are privately owned. They are the patented intellectual property of corporations. If you save seed from an F1 hybrid the resulting progeny won't come true to type. This ensures that you have to go back to the seed company year after year to buy their patented F1 seed. The same is true of ISA Brown chickens. They do not breed true to type, so you cannot breed your own at home. If you want true ISA Browns that lay 300 eggs per year you must source chicks from a licensed breeder who remakes the ISA Brown cross each and every generation using the specially inbred parent strains, and pays a royalty for the right to do so.

F1 hybrid vegetables are cash cows for agribusinesses because they can be patented, and their seeds sold for a premium price. There is nothing wrong with wanting to make a profit, of course. Patenting hybrids is just another way for a company to make a buck. But at what point does profit-making become profiteering?

A couple of years ago Diggers Club founder Clive Blazey interviewed a Dutch tomato grower who paid his seed supplier $483 000 per kilogram for top-of-the-line hybrid glasshouse tomato seeds. To put that in perspective, heirloom tomato seed costs around $440 per kilogram and gold is a snip at a mere $55 000 per kilogram. Clearly there's big money to be had in patenting hybrid plants.

Patenting is said to drive research and development. No doubt there is an element of truth in that. However, tens of thousands of crop varieties have been bred over the centuries, before the patenting system was even dreamed of. Plant breeding is perfectly capable of continuing in the absence of patenting. Indeed, non-patented crop varieties are still are being bred today in not-for-profit sectors of the plant breeding industry.

Today, patents are granted not only for hybrids but for genes themselves. This gives corporations exclusive rights to the use of particular genes – ownership of them, for all intents and purposes. Until very recently, genes belonged to everyone, and no one. Today, they are being claimed in the name of private interests and hoarded away.

One can't help but be reminded of the Enclosures of British history. Under the Enclosures Acts, public lands were essentially grabbed by powerful private individuals, using a combination of force and cunning, and locked away for their exclusive use. The Enclosures denied ordinary people the right to graze their livestock, collect wild food, cut hay or otherwise derive a living from those lands, which had been their right for centuries prior. It was a ruthless land grab. Today, there is a gene grab underway.

Ownership of the world's food supply is increasingly being concentrated into fewer and fewer hands. Almost all of the seed companies in the world are now owned by just a handful of gigantic agribusinesses. These oligarchs get bigger and more powerful each year. They continue to buy up smaller seed companies one by one, acquiring their genetic resources and patents as they go. What, one wonders, is the logical endpoint of this situation? Will all our food be owned by a single, gigantic monopoly? If that sounds like a far-fetched conspiracy theory, it's not. We are already perilously close to that very situation. Is it such bad thing? Well, let's just say that last time I checked, monopolies (or, indeed, oligarchies) do not necessarily feel a sense of obligation to act in the interests of the greater public good. You don't become a monopoly by performing acts of altruism. And let us not forget, it is not flat-screen TVs or luxury cars we are talking about. It is the most basic of human needs: food. Research and development of crop plants, and by extension patenting, ultimately need to be in the public interest.

Recent decades have seen the development of new *transgenic* gene technologies, commonly called GM (genetically modified) technology or GMOs (genetically modified organisms). As mentioned earlier, humans have been manipulating the genes of plants in various ways for ten thousand years. Genetically manipulated organisms have been used in research, medicine, industry and indeed agriculture for quite some decades. However, the new transgenic GM technologies, in which genes are extracted from one organism and inserted into another, strike the public as something very different and are the cause of considerable anxiety. It is normal for new technologies to cause anxiety. Even the humble telephone caused a great deal of alarm when it was first invented, so it is perfectly understandable that fear exists about the ramifications of GM technology.

Personally I'm happy to keep an open mind on the science of GM. I cannot help but feel that gene technologies will bring enormous benefits in the future. Where I take issue with the GM industry is its corporate behaviour. Gene tech companies have lobbied aggressively to get their products into the marketplace, in spite of conspicuous consumer antipathy toward them. The premise on which GM crops have entered the human food chain is that they are 'substantially equivalent' to traditionally bred crops. The argument goes that GM crops are essentially identical to non-GM crops and therefore do not need to be labelled differently from them. This may or may not be true. But surely it is still our right as consumers to have that choice. GM crops have entered our food chain by stealth and we are being denied a choice about whether we want to eat them or not. I cannot think of a single other product that is permitted to be foisted on consumers in this way. Nor can I think of any other product that has been thrust so hard on consumers in the absence of any appetite for it whatsoever. Why is this so?

Gene tech companies seem to want things both ways. They want to patent, protect and charge a premium price for their GM products, which presupposes that they are substantially different in some way, yet at the same time they want their products to be considered 'substantially equivalent', thereby going unnoticed in the marketplace. This kind of corporate behaviour doesn't inspire a great deal of trust among consumers. But then, if you are an oligarch with effective control over an entire industry, why should you care about consumer trust?

It seems to me that there are two separate issues surrounding GM which have become conflated in the public mind. First, the science of GM technologies, and secondly, the corporate ethics of the GM industry. The science of GM – which may prove very beneficial in the future – is being tarnished by legitimate concerns over the corporate ethics of the GM industry. These two issues need to be teased apart in the public mind, or we risk throwing the baby out with the bathwater. If most independent evidence leads to a consilience around the benefits of GM technologies outweighing the risks, then we should be willing to take scientists at their word, just as we should take them at their word about the dangers of anthropogenic climate change. However, if we are not comfortable about being forced to buy the products of a technology that we are not yet ready to accept, we should have a right to exercise that choice.

Vegetables are masterpieces of human ingenuity. Their pasts and futures are in our hands.

Concerns about the ethics, safety and morality of our food are part of the reason why heirlooms are making such a strong resurgence. Heirlooms might not be an 'antidote' to those concerns, but at least they stand for something. For now, at least, heirloom vegetables sit outside the industrial agriculture edifice. They resist ownership and corporatisation. They represent the democratisation of food. They stand for the fact that growing and eating food is as much about human relationships as it is about making money. They represent the power of the producers and consumers of food to join forces to exclude greedy third parties from their transactions. They represent, just as they have for countless human generations, the power to shape our own future – perhaps one which is more equitable and inclusive.

Heirloom vegetables are exquisitely beautiful, sublimely delicious, fascinating and unique; one can easily run out of superlatives when describing these masterpieces of human ingenuity. Far from being moribund museum pieces, heirloom vegetables are still being created by a vibrant network of individual breeders and organisations around the world. Vegetables and people have come a long way together, and I believe we have a lot further yet to go.

WHAT'S IN A NAME?

•

The names of heirloom vegetables are endearingly whimsical and frequently tell a story about the plant. Often we can divine something about its colour, shape, provenance, growth habit or eventual use just by looking at the name of a vegetable: Long Black Spanish Radish, Queensland Blue Pumpkin, Bloomsdale Long Standing Spinach, Amish Paste Tomato.

By contrast, modern F1 hybrid vegetables tend to be given an identifying number before they get a name. Later on they might be lumbered with some turgid marketing handle, usually more trademark than name: 'Profitmaster 2020', 'AdvanX' or 'GroBigga'; that sort thing. You get the distinct impression that focus groups, marketing committees and advertising agencies have been at work. Or possibly just someone who can't spell.

Perhaps the claims against heirlooms of being 'edible nostalgia' have an element of truth to them. But honestly, who wouldn't rather eat a tomato called 'Radiator Charlie's Mortgage Lifter' than one called 'BHN-1021'? Or a pumpkin called 'Pink Banana' over one called 'JWS 6823 PMR' (I kid you not)?

Here are some of the quirkier heirloom vegetable names to whet your appetite for what is to come:

Blond Blockhead Lettuce

Take note: that's 'blond' without an 'e' – the *masculine* form of the word. This heirloom lettuce is noted for its handsome, thick heads. Enough said.

Drunken Woman Frizzy Headed Lettuce (*Cappuccio Ubriacona Frastagliata*)

This unusual Italian butter head lettuce has heavily ruffled and savoyed, pale green, red-tipped foliage. It looks like a lettuce that's put its finger in a power socket.

Collective Farm Woman Melon

A no-nonsense post-Soviet name for a sublime Ukrainian melon. This melon was originally sourced from a *woman* from a Ukrainian *collective farm*. Not from a farm's *collective woman*. Careful where you put the emphasis.

Amish Nuttle Bean

What is a 'nuttle', I hear you ask? Well, nothing actually. It's a corruption of the Pennsylvania Dutch word *Gnuddel* which means, ahem, 'turd'. This charming term refers to the appearance, not the taste, of this old Amish drying bean which, it has to be said, does bear an unsettling resemblance to freshly extruded rabbit pellets in a pod.

Cherokee Trail of Tears Bean

This bean has a sad story. In the winter of 1838–39 the indigenous Cherokee people of the USA were forcibly removed from their country. They were made to walk from North Carolina to Oklahoma. Four thousand Cherokee people died of exposure, hence the name given to the forced march, the Trail of Tears. Like refugees before them and since, the Cherokee took precious seeds on their journey into the unknown, including this bean, which is still grown today.

Makes the Daughter-in-Law Cry Potato (*Pusi Qachun Waqachi*)

An ancient Peruvian potato with so many indentations and knobs that it is all but impossible to peel. The story goes that young women were required to peel these potatoes in front of their fiancé's mother. If the young woman wasn't careful enough to peel them without destroying the flesh, then she probably wouldn't be a good wife either.

FAMILY
PORTRAITS

PAGES 26 — 307

When I see an old family portrait of people long dead, I can't help but wonder about their lives. What sort of people were they? Where did their family come from originally? Where are their descendants now?

I wonder the same things about vegetables. Like a faded black and white photograph of once-living, breathing people hanging on a museum wall, it is easy to forget that vegetables are living things. It is so easy to take them for granted. We treat them as manufactured commodities, soulless objects which magically reappear on supermarket shelves as quickly as we can consume them. We eat them grudgingly because they are good for us, not because we like them. When we sit down to a meal it doesn't cross our minds that the vegetables in front of us belong to families, full of interesting relationships, each member with its own story to tell. But they are. And just like human families, plant families have their share of glamorous cousins, embarrassing uncles and annoying throwbacks nobody likes. Occasionally there is even a scandalous family secret.

In this section we will explore vegetables' family relationships. We will find out who is related to whom, compare family likenesses, meet some long-lost cousins and dish the dirt on the black sheep of the family. We will find out about the family's relationship with humans, how long we've known each other and what we've done for each other during that time. We will also meet just a tiny handful of the dizzying array of heirloom cultivars available and delve a little into their fascinating back stories.

CHAPTER ONE

THE

Pea

FAMILY

The pea or legume family is an enormous one, with over 19 000 species. It is the third biggest family of flowering plants after the orchids and the daisies. Referred to as the Fabaceae (literally the 'broad bean family') or the Leguminosae (the legumes), this family is of enormous economic importance to humankind. It contains dozens of important food crops, flavourings, food additives, stock feeds, soil-improving crops and ornamental plants as well as some significant weeds. Australia's floral emblem, the golden wattle (*Acacia pycnantha*) is a legume, as is South Australia's resplendent Sturt's Desert Pea (*Swainsona formosa*).

STURT'S DESERT PEA

Members of the legume family are instantly recognisable by their bean-like seed pods and divided foliage. However, the flowers can look quite different, so the family is divided into three subfamilies according to their floral structure. The Mimosoideae subfamily has fluffy flowers – the wattles and mimosas. The Caesalpinioideae has big, tropical-looking flowers, like bauhinias and poincianas. The Faboideae subfamily has unique and unmistakeable flowers. One large petal stands erect like a flag at the back of the flower – the 'banner' or 'standard'; two petals point out and forward – the 'wings'; and two are fused together into a 'keel' which faces forwards, enclosing the reproductive parts of the flower. The Faboideae subfamily is the one of most interest to us because it contains peas and beans.

Members of the pea subfamily have a unique floral structure.

The pea family contains some beautiful ornamental climbers. Wisteria is the best known. It is loved for its trusses of perfumed, purple or white spring flowers, and hated in equal measure for pulling down fences, strangling trees and smothering buildings with its strong, woody vines.

Sweet peas are much better behaved. Their heavy, spicy fragrance is one of the joys of spring in cooler parts of the country. It's hard to believe but the most ruffly, feminine varieties of sweet pea were bred by tough coal miners in England's industrial north. After spending their days in the coal pits doing unimaginably hot and dangerous work, these hard men would come home and, with the utmost care and pride, tend their competition sweet pea plants. On competition days the men would pick a few perfect stems, place them in a tall vase and display them competitively against their mates' flowers at – where else? – the pub. No doubt these competitions led to the occasional bar brawl over whose sweet peas were the pinkest or the most heavily ruffled, but I for one am very keen to see a return to competitive flower showing at pubs. Bring it on.

The prize for the most stunning flowering vine in the world also goes to a legume. *Strongylodon macrobotrys*, the jade vine of the Philippines, has flowers of the most luminous, otherworldly shade of turquoise green, borne in gigantic hanging chains so that they can be pollinated by hovering blossom bats. If you are lucky enough to live in the tropics, don't hanker after English sweet peas, grow the jade vine. You'll make your friends in the southern states green with envy.

SWEET PEA

Not all legumes are climbers, of course. One of the most widespread groups of legumes is under our feet a lot of the time: clover. Clovers are easily overlooked but they are a very important group of plants. They are economically important as bee food (producing a distinctively perfumed honey), animal fodder (producing a sweet-flavoured milk), and as a nitrogen-rich green manure. You may think clover is an irritating lawn weed, but the CSIRO has been actively breeding it for decades, developing superior strains to help farmers improve their soils. Lucerne (or alfalfa) is another legume grown as a green manure and stockfeed. It is a waist-high perennial with a very deep taproot that allows it to mine nutrients from the subsoil and bring them to the surface.

A feature of the legume family is the specialised nodules on their roots. These nodules evolved for the express purpose of housing *Rhizobia*: specialised soil bacteria that live in conjunction with a plant host. *Rhizobia* are able to 'fix' nitrogen directly from the air, providing their host plant with nitrogen in a form the plant can metabolise. This nitrogen eventually finds its way back into the soil when the plant dies and decays. This is the reason why legumes are good soil improvers and such an important component of crop rotation regimes. It's not the legumes themselves

JADE VINE

that are doing the soil-improving, but the bacteria to which they give board and lodging.

Lupins are yet another genus of legumes grown as soil improvers, although it was once thought that they depleted the soil, hence their name *Lupinus* – 'the wolf'. Lupins are also grown for their edible seeds and in some varieties their ornamental flowers. Russell lupins are grown for their noble spires of blue, white, red, yellow, peach, purple or black flowers. They are very beautiful indeed, but sadly they are unsuited to growing in most parts of Australia. They need cold winters and cool summers to thrive. In parts of the world with those conditions, such as the Southern Alps of New Zealand and in Scotland, lupins have made quite a nuisance of themselves.

RUSSELL LUPINS

Peas and beans aren't the only food we derive from plants of the legume family. Lentils (*Lens culinaris*) come in several colours and sizes, from the small orange and large olive-green varieties seen in Indian cuisine to the tiny, black-green lentils traditionally grown around the French town of Le Puy. Chickpeas or garbanzo beans (*Cicer arietinum*) are native to the Middle East and are enormously popular from the Mediterranean to India. Their most famous incarnation is as hummus, a more-ish Middle Eastern chickpea puree flavoured with garlic, tahini and lemon juice.

The peanut (*Arachis hypogaea*) is more pea than nut. Originally from Paraguay, peanuts are grown throughout the tropics and are as essential to South East Asian cuisine as chilli. Sadly, peanuts have come to be feared because of the potentially fatal allergy that increasing numbers of people have to them. Peanuts are sometimes called groundnuts due to their unusual fruiting habit. After the yellow flowers are pollinated, the flower stem turns downward and burrows into the soil, where the peanuts develop underground (*hypogaea* is Greek for 'under the ground').

The soybean (*Glycine max*) is a very important legume crop native to Asia. Some varieties of soybean are consumed fresh, such as the brilliant green *edamame* varieties from Japan. However, soybeans are more commonly dried and processed into an ingenious range of products. The best known of these are soy sauce, soy

SOYBEAN

milk and the unfairly maligned bean curd or *tōfu*. *Yuba* is the skin which forms on the top of soy milk and is then hung up to dry. *Nattō*, a goopy, smelly fermented soybean product, is almost unknown outside Japan and even there it is not universally liked. Tempeh is a fermented soybean product from Indonesia with an unusual firm-spongy texture. An Indonesian gentleman once remarked to me that in his country rich people eat meat and poor people eat tempeh, but in Australia the opposite is true.

Aside from their utility as human food, soybeans are an important source of protein-rich stockfeed. The oil and protein extracted from them have endless industrial applications, from crayons to biodiesel. Soybeans are a crop of such importance to industry that they have been a subject of genetic modification. For right or wrong, a gene from a bacterium has been inserted into GM soybeans to make them resistant to the herbicide glyphosate.

Other edible legumes include the mung bean (*Vigna radiata*), used as a dried pulse in South Asia for making dhal, while in East Asia and North Asia they are germinated to produce crisp white bean sprouts. The red or azuki bean (*Vigna angularis*) is a common ingredient in Chinese and Japanese sweets, boiled to form a sweet, red-grey, mealy mash.

Legumes not only give us food but also flavourings and food additives. The rich, mouth-filling sweetness of liquorice comes from the root of a perennial legume, *Glycyrrhiza glabra*. The seeds of fenugreek (*Trigonella foenum-graecum*) are an essential ingredient in curries. The pulpy seed pods of the tamarind tree (*Tamarindus indica*) add a mouthwatering tang to curries. Carob (*Ceratonia siliqua*) has sweetish, chewy seed pods which taste quite OK as long as you don't try to think of them as chocolate. The New Testament mentions God sending John the Baptist 'locusts' to eat in the desert. These 'locusts' were almost certainly not grasshoppers but carob pods, which are also known as locust beans and St John's bread. Carob seeds are very uniform in size and were once used as the counterweight against which gemstones were weighed. We derive the word 'carat' from the Greek name for a carob bean, *keration*, a unit still used for measuring gemstones today. The seeds of the Indian guar plant (*Cyamopsis tetragonoloba*) are the source of a gum used as a thickening agent in an enormous range of processed foods. And if that bungs you up too much, you can always take the pods of the legume senna (*Senna alexandrina*) as a laxative.

The legume family's usefulness doesn't end there. If you've ever put derris dust on your roses or used de-lousing powder on your chickens, you've used the pulverised root of a South East Asian legume, the *Derris* bush. For many years, derris was approved

Carob seeds were used as a counterweight for measuring gemstones.

for use by organic growers as a natural herbal insecticide. However, it was recently withdrawn from use in organic systems because it is so toxic. We can learn two things from this. One is that people who think anything 'natural', 'plant-based' or 'herbal' is gentle and safe are wrong. By the same token people who think that anything 'natural', 'plant-based' or 'herbal' is ineffective hocus-pocus are also wrong. Plants are living chemical factories. The active ingredient in the poison 1080, widely used in feral animal eradication programmes, is naturally present in several native members of the pea family, especially the so-called poison peas (*Gastrolobium* spp.). The chemicals that come out of plants are as real as the chemicals that are made in laboratories and they need to be treated with similar respect. Heroin, nicotine and strychnine are all plant extracts, yet they could hardly be described as either 'ineffective' or 'harmless'.

One legume, in particular, contains high levels of a toxin called phytohaemagglutinin or PHA. PHA causes red blood cells to clump together, interferes with the function of cell membranes and causes genetic material in the cell nucleus to start dividing when it shouldn't. Ingesting as few as five seeds of this legume causes severe vomiting and diarrhoea as the body tries to rid itself of the toxin. It's not pretty. The legume in question is a mainstay of many vegetarian diets, the red kidney bean. All dried beans contain PHA but the highest known source of it is the red kidney bean. PHA is easily broken down by boiling beans at 100°C for ten minutes. Poisoning only occurs when the kidney beans are not properly cooked. People have been poisoned when they cooked kidney beans in a slow cooker, which cooks at temperatures below 100°C. The beans come out of the slow cooker soft enough to eat but the toxin is still active. In fact, heating PHA to 80°C increases the action of the toxin. Vegetarians take note!

In a family as big as the legumes there are bound to be a few problem children, and indeed there are. Some of the world's nastiest woody weeds are legumes. Some species of broom (*Cytisus* and *Genista*) and gorse (*Ulex europaeus*) are thugs of the worst kind, taking over vast tracts of land to the exclusion of any other species, and resisting all but the most strenuous attempts to eradicate them. But that's just the beginning. The Giant Sensitive Plant (*Mimosa pigra*) is a screaming nightmare – and anything but sensitive. It forms impenetrable, six-metre-high thickets of grasping, hooked branches that tear human skin to ribbons. Native to the tropical Americas, Giant Sensitive Plant has already taken over colossal chunks of the Northern Territory. If left unchecked it will certainly consume most of tropical Australia. Unsurprisingly, the Giant Sensitive Plant is considered to be one of the worst weeds in the world.

The weeds of the family notwithstanding, legumes generally give back much more than they take. Let's take a look now at the heirloom vegetable members of the family.

CAPUCIJNER PEA

PEAS

You all know peas. They are the vegetables native to the freezer section of the supermarket, harvested by cutting the bag open and pouring them out. Not really, of course, but it is easy to think so because it is so rare to see peas sold in their pods these days. This isn't such a bad thing, however. Peas suffer little loss in quality from the snap-freezing process, whereas peas sold fresh in the pod lose their sweetness and tenderness quite quickly.

However, once you have eaten super-sweet home-grown peas I guarantee you will never want to go back to frozen peas. Sure, it takes time to pod the fiddly little blighters, but this is a great shared activity and it is a whole lot more fun than standing in a supermarket queue.

Peas (*Pisum sativum*) are native to southern Europe and the eastern Mediterranean, where they are found growing in waste ground and open scrub. They grow, flower and die in the brief rainy weeks of the Mediterranean spring. Wild peas look pretty much the same as cultivated peas: straggly plants that haul themselves up through surrounding vegetation, bearing pretty, butterfly-like flowers followed by finger-length pods of big, round, seeds.

Like potatoes and broad beans, the body of the pea plant is called a *haulm*. In nature, pea haulms straggle their way through and over shrubs and grasses using very fine tendrils at the tips of the leaves to secure themselves. The tendrils are actually thread-like modified leaves which wave around in circles until they come into contact with a support and then coil around it. This differs from the way in which beans climb, whereby the actual stem of the bean plant twines around its support. Beans do not have tendrils as peas do. For this reason beans and peas need different kinds of supporting structures in the garden. Beans do best with long, vertical

Pea plants climb by means of fine tendrils.

Bean vines twine around their support.

supports like bamboo canes or lengths of twine suspended from a wigwam. Beans can twine around poles of any diameter. Peas cannot. They need a close network of thin supports that their tendrils can grab on to, such as horizontal strings, chicken wire or plastic netting. The traditional supports for peas were called 'pea twigs' or 'pea brush'. These were twiggy branch prunings from hazelnuts or other fruit trees inserted into the ground amongst the pea seedlings, or mounted on vertical posts, for the peas to clamber their way through. Pea twigs look very rustic and lovely.

It's easy to think that peas all look the same. Look closer and you will realise that they don't. Some have white flowers, some have pink. Some have wrinkled seeds, some have smooth. Some have black seeds when they are dry; others grey, beige or greenish white. It was these subtle differences in the characteristics of pea plants that the Silesian monk Gregor Mendel used as the subject of his experiments into heredity in the 1850s, paving the way for the science of genetics.

Peas weren't always eaten fresh out of the pod as they are today. In their earliest incarnation, peas were a crop for drying and storing over winter, like wheat and barley, with which their history is closely intertwined. Peas were originally collected from the wild or gleaned as an edible bonus when they were found growing spontaneously in wheat fields. Pea remains have been found at Neolithic sites in Turkey dating back nearly 10 000 years. Archeological evidence from the the ancient agricultural town of Çatalhöyük in Turkey suggests that by 7500 BCE peas were undergoing domestication and selection. From the eastern Mediterranean domesticated peas spread west, arriving in Greece and other Mediterranean countries by the sixth millennium BCE and into Central Europe half a millennium later with Neolithic agriculture. Peas had travelled east to India and Afghanistan by 2000 BCE.

We know from Theophrastus and Pliny the Elder that the Greeks and Romans grew peas. By the time of the Roman empire peas were an important staple crop throughout Europe. Dried peas were ground and mixed with cereal flours to make what must have been a very nutritious bread. A common medieval staple dish was pease pudding, a thick porridge made from dried peas. It survived through the centuries, commemorated in the nursery rhyme 'Pease porridge hot, pease porridge cold, pease porridge in the pot nine days old'. Descendants of pease pudding survive in modern Europe in the form of hearty pea soups, such as the iconic Dutch pea and smoked sausage soup with the almost onomatopoeic name *snert*.

Considering how important peas were as a staple food for most of their history, it's perhaps not surprising that nobody dreamed of eating them fresh. It would have been foolhardy to harvest and eat your pea crop during summer's time of plenty when, if left to grow to full maturity, it could mean the difference between starvation or survival through the winter. For this reason the practice of eating fresh peas was at first the preserve of the rich. The Elizabethans dabbled in it. So did the Renaissance Italians. The practice of eating fresh peas really took off after it was taken up at the court of Louis XIV in the 1660s. It became something of a craze for the next four decades. In the 1690s, Louis XIV's secret second wife, Madame de Maintenon, wrote in a letter that eating fresh peas had become 'a fashion, a fury' amongst the court ladies, and later: 'The pea chapter continues. The impatience to eat them, the pleasure of eating them and the joy at having eaten them again are the three points which our princes have had to deal with for four days.'

As the custom of eating peas fresh grew in popularity, garden pea strains (for fresh eating) and field pea strains (for drying and stock feed) went their separate ways. It was in Victorian England that garden peas reached their zenith. The Victorians developed big, starchy 'marrowfat' peas especially for canning – the famous mushy peas. They also developed exquisitely tender, sugar-sweet peas for the table, which are the ones we are most familiar with today.

Shelling peas are not the only peas, however. In China, pea breeding took a different path from that in Europe. Peas were probably introduced to China during the Tang dynasty (618–907 CE); they were definitely not 'discovered' there 5000 years ago by the legendary Emperor Shennong, as Chinese history asserts and some authors have reported as fact. There, peas were selected for their crisp, edible pods, to be eaten before the seeds filled out: snow peas. Chinese snow peas were introduced to the west in the 1880s, whereupon which the French dubbed them *mangetout*, meaning 'eat-all'.

Sugarsnap peas, the ultimate fresh-eating peas, are mere babies by comparison. Snap peas or butter peas have been around since the seventeenth century but they never really took off as a separate class of peas. The first sugarsnap was bred serendipitously in the USA in the 1950s by plant breeder Calvin Lamborn, in conjunction with his colleague M.C. Parker. Lamborn was actually trying to breed a thick-podded, non-buckling snow pea. What he got was the sugarsnap pea, with very sweet, fleshy pods and very sweet full-size peas. Unlike snow peas, sugarsnaps are at their sweetest when the peas *have* filled out, at which point they have developed their maximum sugar levels. Lamborn's sugarsnap varieties began being released in the 1970s. Hopefully his breeding work will give rise to a whole new class of peas.

CASCADIA SUGAR SNAP PEA

PEAS AND THEIR PEOPLE
JIM BAGGETT, THE PODFATHER

•

Reading through seed catalogues, you might notice that many peas have names that point to the Pacific Northwest of the USA – Cascadia, Oregon Sugar Pod II, Oregon Giant. These open pollinated varieties are the result of the plant breeding programme at the Oregon State University (OSU) under the prolific plant breeder, Emeritus Professor Jim Baggett. Peas grow very well in the mild maritime climate of the Pacific Northwest so it is not surprising that they were a favourite subject of Baggett's, along with beans, squash and just about everything else. OSU vegetable varieties are still the mainstays of farmers in the Pacific Northwest, where vegetable processing is an important industry. To keep Baggett's good work going after he retired, the vegetable industry endowed a professorship in vegetable breeding at the OSU, named for Baggett and his mentor, William Frazier.

The current Baggett-Frazier professor is Jim Myers. Myers' emphasis is on traditional selective breeding techniques, in contrast to many institutions which are following up genetic modification as a means to improve vegetable varieties. Myers believes that 'Until the social and political aspects of genetically modified organisms are sorted out, we will see few GMO cultivars deployed in the vegetable world.' He says that stakeholders in his breeding programme want traditional, field-bred varieties because this mimics how they themselves work: in the field. They want vegetables bred for and tested in Oregon's conditions, not bred in vitro and tested in field trials half a world away.

VARIETIES

•

Peas and beans, like chickens, come in standard and bantam versions. The standard versions grow between 1.5 metres and 3 metres tall, while the dwarf varieties grow to 0.5–1 metre. Dwarf peas crop more quickly than the climbers but don't crop over as long a period, so it is a good idea to plant both kinds to extend your harvest.

Blue Pod Capucijner, Blauwschokkers/ Purple-podded Dutch

Capucijners are a type of drying pea thought to have originated with the Capuchin monks, the chaps after whom the cappuccino coffee is named, on account of their coffee-coloured robes. Capuchin peas came to be associated with the Netherlands, hence their Dutch name, capucijners or kapucijners (both pronounced ka-poo-say-ners). Incidentally the other Dutch name, Blauwschok-kers, means 'blue shockers'. Blue Pod Capucijner is a very old pea, mentioned in French and German sources dating as far back as 1580.

CAPUCIJNER PEA

Usually referred to as Purple-podded Dutch in Australia, it is quite a versatile pea. It is very pretty, bearing pink and burgundy flowers on tall haulms, followed by lovely dark purple pods. It is more robust and forgiving than many pea varieties, so it's good for less diligent gardeners. Its best culinary use is definitely as a dried pea but it can also be eaten fresh (the peas are green, not purple) when very young. Timing is everything, however, as the peas become hard and starchy very quickly.

Cascadia

An open-pollinated sugar snap pea bred at the Oregon State University by Jim Baggett. It combines the best features of climbing and dwarf varieties, being more compact than true climbers at 1.2 metres but bearing a good crop of super-sweet succulent pods over a longer season than true dwarf varieties. It is rather prone to powdery mildew but this problem does not seems to affect the pods as much as the plants themselves.

CASCADIA PEA

Golden Sweet or Golden Podded

An Indian heirloom snow pea whose seeds were collected in a marketplace in India. It is unique in having pretty pale lemon-yellow (not golden) pods following mauve and purple flowers on a tall plant. Unlike many snow peas, Golden Sweet improves in flavour as it ages, becoming sugar-sweet as the peas begin to fill out. However, this necessitates stringing the pods before eating them. Golden Sweet is sold as Golden Podded in Australia.

GOLDEN SWEET PEA

Mammoth Melting

An heirloom snow pea capable of giving heavy yields of sweet, 10-centimetre pods on compact plants 1.2 metres high. It prefers cooler conditions.

Melbourne Market or Massey Gem

An Australian shelling pea, once the mainstay of our frozen pea industry and still a good one for backyarders. The plants are 50 centimetres in height and bear well-filled pods of very sweet, smooth peas.

Oregon Giant

The industry-standard snow pea in Australia, this variety bears 13-centimetre pods on compact, powdery mildew-resistant plants.

Oregon Sugar Pod II

An excellent open pollinated snow pea which grows on a compact haulm to 90 centimetres tall with good resistance to powdery mildew. Oregon Sugar Pod II was first released in 1985 and is now a favourite amongst growers.

Sugar Ann

A dwarf sugarsnap pea with smaller pods at 6 centimetres, but they are by far the sweetest of all dwarf sugarsnap varieties. Together with Sugar Bon, Sugar Ann was bred by the originator of sugarsnap peas, Calvin Lamborn, and released in 1981 – a modern heirloom.

SUGAR BON PEA

Sugar Bon

A dwarf sugarsnap pea with good powdery mildew resistance and good-sized pods.

Sugarsnap

Sugarsnap is without a doubt the sweetest of all peas. Grown for its super-crisp, super-juicy, super-sweet pods following white flowers on tall plants. This variety is more tolerant of heat than some peas.

Tall Telephone or Alderman

An American podding pea from the 1880s. Still considered a worthwhile variety today, it bears long, fat pods with up to ten large, sweet peas on enormously strong haulms up to 2.5 metres in height. Tall Telephone is named after that newfangled contraption, the telephone, which was still in its infancy at the time this pea was bred. What a wonderful idea, to name a vegetable after a piece of technology. I suppose a comparable variety today might be called the iPea.

Alderman is the British name for the same variety.

Yakumo

Yakumo is a snow pea of dubious heritage. It is very new to the scene in Australia, having been offered in seed catalogues here for fewer than ten years. It is routinely advertised as a Japanese heirloom, however I can find no reference to it at all in Japanese literature or Japanese seed catalogues. It certainly fits the description of a Japanese red-flowered snow pea and it strongly resembles the French heirloom **Carouby de Maussane**. In

YAKUMO PEA

the absence of a pedigree, Yakumo can hardly be claimed to be an heirloom. Be that as it may, Yakumo distinguishes itself by bearing enormous pods, easily 15 centimetres in length, following two-tone pink flowers on a very strong, heat-resistant plant. It is an excellent variety for gardeners who are strapped for space, and anyone else for that matter.

BORLOTTO LINGUA DI FUOCO BEAN

COMMON OR FRENCH BEAN

You only have to look on a grocery shelf to grasp the astounding diversity of beans. You'll find glossy red kidney beans, burnished black turtle beans, satiny white haricot beans and spotty, dotty borlotti beans in the soup aisle; three-bean mix, navy beans and cannellini beans in the canned foods; green beans and yellow wax beans in the fruit and vegetable section. All these beans are derived from the same wild ancestor, *Phaseolus vulgaris*.

Despite the 'French' moniker, beans are not native to France, but to Central and South America, in a huge sweep from Mexico south to Argentina. Beans have had to adapt to a variety of habitats within this huge home range. They have adapted to a range of altitudes from the low foothills up to medium altitudes in the Andes.

They grow at a range of latitudes, from equatorial regions where the weather is the same all year around to more temperate latitudes where the seasonal variation is pronounced. There are two wild subspecies of bean, a small-seeded northern subspecies from Mexico south to Venezuela, and a large-seeded southern subspecies from Peru across to northern Argentina. Both wild subspecies have contributed their genes to the cultivated bean, resulting in a crop with a propensity for enormous genetic variability. Today, there are some 40 000 different cultivars of beans in existence.

Beans were domesticated on more than one occasion, probably first in Peru and then in Mexico some centuries later. Exactly how long ago it's hard to say. Some evidence suggests a date as early as 6000 BCE, while other evidence points to much later dates, perhaps the first century BCE. Bean starch has recently been recovered from human teeth recovered from an archaeological site in Peru, and dated as early as 7000 BCE, but whether this is from domesticated beans or wild beans is not known. Certainly people have been eating beans for an awfully long time.

Whatever the date of domestication, it's difficult to overstate the importance of beans to the nutrition of later South and Central American cultures. No plant food possesses the full suite of essential amino acids needed for human nutrition (with the exception of quinoa). However, when beans and corn are eaten together they complement each other's deficiencies to provide a more complete protein package. Together, beans and corn formed the basis of a diet which supported the great Mesoamerican civilisations of the Toltec, Olmec, Mayan and Aztec peoples. The Aztec empire was so dependent on beans as a source of mass nutrition that subjugated tribes were required to pay taxes to the Aztec in beans (collected, no doubt, by 'bean counters').

Beans found their way north via trade routes to North America, where they became as important to North American indigenous cultures as they were to their South American cousins. Along with pumpkins and corn, Native Americans considered beans one of the 'three sisters of agriculture'. The three crops were customarily planted together as a 'guild', with the beans twining up the tall cornstalks, and the pumpkins providing a living mulch on the ground below. The three sisters worked together perfectly in the garden, and in the diet as sources of complementary protein.

By the time the Spanish arrived in the Americas in the 1490s, beans were cultivated as far north as the northern USA and and as far south as Chile. The Spanish took beans back to Spain in their galleons where, unlike many new crops, they were accepted quite readily, perhaps because of their similarity to familiar broad beans.

BEANS AND THEIR PEOPLE
LOU'S PYRENEAN WHITE

•

'This is a bean with a *lotta* history,' Lou Larrieu, then seed trials manager at the Diggers Club, told me as she cracked open a pod of pearly white beans. She should know. Just like the beans in her hands, Lou's roots are in the French Pyrenees.

The variety in question originated around the town of Tarbes at the foot of the magnificent Pyrenees. The Tarbais bean was first developed during the eighteenth century. A century later it was responsible for keeping the region's economy afloat after its wine industry withered during the devastating *Phylloxera* outbreak, sometimes called the Great French Wine Blight. This bean did more than keep the region's farmers afloat; it made them rich and their town famous.

Tarbais beans were traditionally grown interplanted with corn, just as Native Americans had done for centuries. In this happy partnership the beans fix nitrogen and shade the soil for the corn, the corn supports the twining bean plants, and the farmer gets two crops from the same piece of land. By the 1930s, 10 000 hectares of the Hautes-Pyrénées region were under cultivation by this method. However, by the 1970s, two decades after the introduction of high-yielding F1 corn varieties, this figure had slumped to just 55 hectares. The Green Revolution had changed the face of agriculture, even in this far-flung corner of France, making it unviable for farmers to grow the crop for which their region had become famous. The Tarbais bean nearly died out.

The French are very proud of their culinary heritage, however, and today the Tarbais bean is undergoing a renaissance. True to Lou's Pyrenean roots, she reminded me that the region is home to one of France's most famous dishes, *cassoulet* – an incredibly rich stew of white beans, pork and confit duck. Naturally the large, white haricot Tarbais is *the* cassoulet bean *par excellence*.

Since 2000 the Tarbais bean has been placed under protected regional status (*Indication Géographique Protégée* or IGP) just as some French wines are. This protection means that when this bean is grown outside the officially controlled region, it cannot legally be labelled 'Tarbais', just as sparkling wine grown outside the approved region for producing champagne cannot be labelled 'Champagne', even if it is only grown a metre away.

This seems more than a little ludicrous. Surely the sacred oenological concept of *terroir* doesn't apply to dried beans, does it? The farmers of Tarbes argue that it does. They say that their bean, grown anywhere else, is just not the same.

Perhaps. However, the bean of Tarbes is a distinct cultivar, just as the chardonnay grape is. You might reasonably argue that chardonnay grapes taste different when grown in different climates and soils, but they are still the same genetic strain of grape, whether grown in the Côtes du Rhône or the Barossa Valley. You can still call them 'chardonnay grapes' no matter where they are grown. Similarly, the Tarbais bean might taste better when grown in Tarbes (to individuals with exquisitely refined palates), but it is still the same cultivar of bean whether it's grown in Australia or anywhere else in the world, and I don't see why it should not be labelled as such – the *haricot Tarbais*, or 'bean of Tarbes'. Still, I say if the farmers of Tarbes want the name that badly, let them have it. We can still grow and enjoy this bean under another name.

As I watched Lou working in the belting hot sun bringing in her crop of beans, it struck me as both happy and a little bit sad. Happy that someone with pride in her Pyrenean roots is growing and sharing this marvellous bean in the Antipodes. Sad that she is prevented from calling it by the name that would tie it to their shared heritage. I propose a new name for this splendid bean as grown on Australia terroir: 'Lou's Pyrenean White'.

LOU'S PYRENEAN WHITE BEAN

VARIETIES

•

Attempts to classify the 40 000 bean varieties are fraught. They are often grouped according to their growth habit (dwarf or bush beans vs. climbing or pole beans), the shape of the pod (round pod/flat pod/filet pod beans), the stage at which they are eaten (snap/shelling/dried beans) or some qualitative designation like 'wax', 'butter', 'string', 'greasy', or (weirdly) 'horticultural' or 'culinary' – as opposed to what other kind of bean, one might ask? These artificial classifications aren't actually very helpful since most beans will happily fit into more than one category. Cherokee Wax, for example, is a dwarf, round pod, butter or wax bean that can be eaten both as a snap bean and a dried bean.

The most useful distinction to gardeners is simply whether a variety is a climbing (or pole) bean or a bush (or dwarf) bean. This will tell you whether it needs a trellis or not. Bush beans are quicker to crop than climbing beans but climbing beans continue their harvest over a longer season. You might decide to sow a bush and a climbing variety at the same time in the spring, knowing that the bush variety will crop first and the climber will take over when the bush bean has finished cropping. The other distinction worth knowing is whether or not a variety is useful for fresh eating or for drying. Most beans are better at one than the other.

Australian Butter

This climbing variety was passed on to the Diggers Club by a home gardener who had been saving the seed herself. An excellent variety for the back-yard, it makes vigorous, healthy plants loaded with pale yellow, roundish wax beans. They become slightly stringy with age, so make sure you pick them young.

AUSTRALIAN BUTTER BEAN

Borlotto Lingua di Fuoco

'Tongue of Fire' in Italian, usually shortened simply to borlotti in Australia. It bears large crops of intensely colourful pods: palest green heavily flecked with hot pink. The pods are edible when very young but this variety is generally harvested after the pods have dried out completely. Each pod contains several small beige beans, spotted and

BORLOTTI BEAN

striped with wine-red. They are deliciously creamy in texture when cooked; essential in Italian and Portuguese cuisine. Borlotti beans exist in both bush and climbing forms. The climbing form is much more efficient unless you have a big garden and like bending over a lot.

Blue Lake Stringless

An old favourite climbing bean which produces sweet, roundish green pods with white seeds over a long season. It is a nice, 'normal' bean, if you like; a model towards which breeders have aspired.

Cherokee Wax

Cherokee Wax is a very old heirloom grown by east coast Native Americans. Its antiquity can be seen in its sprawling, semi-climbing nature. It bears mauve flowers, pale yellow wax pods and seeds which ripen from gunmetal blue to glossy black. Although Cherokee Wax's pods are coincidentally edible as a snap bean, they are quite stringy and frankly not as flavoursome as more recent varieties. It is best grown as a drying bean.

CHEROKEE WAX BEAN

Dragon's Tongue (aka Langue de Dragon, Merveille du Piemont)

Have you ever met a bean so succulent that juice dribbles down your chin as you crunch into it? Dragon's Tongue is such a bean. A French (or possibly Dutch or Italian) heirloom bush bean bearing long, plump, flat pods of ivory white flecked with violet purple that explode juice with every bite. When cooked the pods lose their violet flecks. Left to dry on the plant, they make very good dried beans, too. The down-side of this variety is that it

DRAGON'S TONGUE BEAN

is quite sickly. The plants are wont to turn their toes up if conditions are not exactly to their liking. Sow lots and expect a few losses, but do make sure you try it.

Flagrano

Flagrano is part of a group of beans called *flageo-lets*, beloved of the French. Flageolet beans are shelled and eaten boiled when the seeds are fully developed but before they are fully dry, much as we do with garden peas. Flagrano is a dwarf bean bearing very thin, straight pods with up to ten tiny, mint-green seeds.

FLAGRANO BEAN

Frost

Frost is nicknamed the yin-yang bean because of its patterning – half of the roundish seed is white and the other half is maroon. It is a semi-climbing dwarf bean good for drying. Another bean nick-named yin-yang is the Caribbean heirloom **Calypso**. Calypso is very similar to Frost, only it is a true dwarf and its beans are white and blue-black. They look just like little killer whales, hence its other name, **Orca**.

FROST BEAN

Giant of Stuttgart

An exceptionally tall climbing bean with vines up to 3 metres in height. White flowers are followed by 30-centimetre-long, chunky green pods which remain perfectly tender even when quite old. This is a very useful variety if you have lots of vertical space in your garden. You may need to invest in a ladder, however.

GIANT OF STUTTGART BEAN

Haricot Lou's Pyrenean White

A vigorous climbing bean whose flat green pods are no good at all for eating fresh. Leave them to dry completely on the vine, then crack open the parchment-coloured pods to harvest treasure inside. The beans are large, flat, smooth and pearly white. They are deliciously creamy when cooked. This is definitely NOT the famous French Haricot Tarbais. No, siree. It's much better than that.

Lazy Wife or Lazy Housewife

Lazy Wife – more frequently sold as Lazy Housewife in Australia – is a German heirloom climbing bean. Introduced to the USA around 1800, it was America's favourite green bean for the next hundred years. Seed merchant W. Atlee Burpee's 1888 seed catalogue famously raves about this variety, describing it as '. . . broad, thick, very fleshy and entirely stringless! Many persons have testified that they never ate a bean quite so good in distinct rich flavor.' They put the name 'Lazy Wife' down to its 'immense productiveness', noting that it 'seems rather discourteous to us'.

Unfortunately I feel duty-bound to report that I have always had trouble getting Lazy Wife bean to live up to its exalted reputation. It seems to loll around on the ground as a messy little bush for ages before making a late attempt at climbing, and its crops can be underwhelming in both quantity and quality. It is indeed lazy. Perhaps Lazy Wife needs the glasshouse-like summers of the eastern USA to give of its best. Try it and see what you think. If nothing else, it is worth growing for its name alone.

Incidentally, the bean we grow today as Lazy Wife is not the original version from Germany and Alsace, which had red seeds, not white. Ours seems to be an American namesake, known to the Amish as *Faule Fraa* (Lazy Wife) in their Pennsylvania Dutch language.

Merveille de Venise (Marvel of Venice)

A climbing bean with pale yellow-green, flat, stringless pods that remain tender for a long time. It is light cropping but of very high quality.

MARVEL OF VENICE BEAN

Purple King

Purple King is a very robust climbing bean with dark purple stems, purple-flushed leaves and violet-purple flowers. It bears generous crops of large, flat beans of darkest velvety purple. This is a great variety for cold areas as it keeps cropping well into cold weather and will even resist a light frost. It is also more tolerant of less-than-perfect soil conditions than most beans.

PURPLE KING BEAN

Rattlesnake

This robust climbing bean bears attractive violet flowers followed by roundish pods of matte green flecked with violet purple. They have a slightly crunchy-rubbery texture along the lines of Asian snake beans, making them a good substitute in cooler climates where snake beans struggle.

RATTLESNAKE BEAN

Red Kidney

Red Kidney is one of the best known of all dry beans. They grow on compact bushes in flat green pods that give no hint of their colourful contents. Splitting the dried pods to reveal the glossy red beans always feels like a surprise. Red kidney beans are a classic ingredient in the cooking of Mexico and Jamaica (where they are called red peas) but as mentioned earlier they are also the highest known source of the toxic lectin phytohaemagglutinin so they need to be carefully cooked before consumption.

RED KIDNEY BEAN

SCARLET RUNNER BEAN

RUNNER BEAN OR SEVEN-YEAR BEAN

Runner beans have been the preferred bean of British gardeners since they were introduced to Britain in around 1700. The Brits absolutely love runner beans. The French and Americans, on the other hand, are much more interested in French beans, and view the scarlet runner bean as no more than a pretty ornamental flower. Americans see the Brits' runner-bean-eating ways as another quaint example of their eccentricity, while the French see it as yet further proof of their culinary ineptitude.

Why are the British so in love with this bean? The scarlet runner bean (*Phaseolus coccineus*) is native to Central America, so technically speaking it is a tropical plant, like the banana or pineapple. Anyone familiar with Britain's notoriously drab climate will correctly deduce that Britain does not have the ideal conditions for growing bananas and pineapples. Indeed, British gardeners have a tradition of growing tropical vegetables like tomatoes, melons and cucumbers in glasshouses rather than in the open garden, so why are they in love with this tropical bean?

The answer is that although runner beans come from the tropics, they grow at very high altitudes where the weather is permanently mild and drizzly – just like a British summer. When temperatures go much above about 28°C, or nights remain uncomfortably warm, runner beans refuse to set pods. They don't crop well in France's continental climate or the oppressive summers of the eastern USA, which is of course why those cultures never got a taste for them. Runner beans' heat intolerance also means that they don't perform well in most areas of Australia during the summer months. However, they are very useful for growing in the spring and autumn during weather that slows the growth of French beans down to a crawl.

Runner beans may be harvested as a snap bean when they are young and tender, just as British gardeners do. They may also be harvested as a shelling bean when the seeds are fully developed but not yet hardened. When harvested at this stage the beans are the most amazing lurid pink-purple combo. Don't forget to cook them, however, because like a lot of members of the bean family they produce toxic compounds when the seeds mature, which need to be cooked out before they can be eaten.

Runner beans have enormous ornamental appeal, with showy flowers and luxuriant foliage that enthusiastically covers its trellis. If the young vines need some help from the gardener to find their support, bear in mind that runner beans twine clockwise as you look from above, while French beans twine anticlockwise. Just to be different.

Another nice difference between French and runner beans is that runner beans are perennial, hence their nickname 'seven-year beans'. Like any other herbaceous perennial, runner beans die back to a rootstock in winter, which can be left in the ground even in the coldest districts. They can stagger on for seven years if necessary but I find that the plants are best replaced after two or three years, as they get a bit woody and lose vigour after that time. The starchy rootstocks are said to be edible though I have never personally tested this.

The wild scarlet runner bean has flowers of bright orange-red, a flower colour frequently encountered in plants native to the Americas, from Canada right down to the Tierra del Fuego, and in species as diverse as cacti, orchids and bromeliads. The reason is that hummingbirds find this particular shade of red irresistible and any plant with flowers that colour is assured of pollination.

VARIETIES

•

The 'normal' scarlet runner bean, which might be the same as a variety called **Best of All**, is the variety most commonly grown. It has bright orange-red flowers and its dry seeds are chestnut-brown with black flecks. Named scarlet varieties like **Zenith** and **Scarlet Emperor** exist but these are rarely offered in this country. In any case the 'normal' type is pretty darn good. There is a handful of highly prized white-flowered, white-seeded cultivars such as **Czar** available in Europe. However, it is illegal to import bean seed from overseas. With luck they may already be lurking somewhere in Australia, so keep an eye out for them.

PAINTED LADY RUNNER BEAN

SUNSET RUNNER BEAN

Painted Lady

An American heirloom from 1855, Painted Lady has red and white bicolor flowers but is in other ways similar to the normal scarlet runner bean.

Sunset

Sunset has pale salmon-coloured flowers and pretty pink seeds flecked with black. It is very ornamental in the garden, combining well with other pastel-coloured flowers.

LIMA BEANS

LIMA BEAN OR BUTTER BEAN

Those of us who grew up watching Warner Bros. *Looney Tunes* cartoons will be familiar with Sylvester the Cat's immortal oath, 'Sufferin' succotash!'. Did you spend your childhood wondering what succotash meant? I did. I am pleased to be able to inform you now that succotash is an American stew made from corn kernels and Lima beans.

The Lima bean (*Phaseolus lunatus*) is another native of the Andes and mountainous regions of Central America. Its seeds are large, white, flat and half-moon-shaped, hence the epithet *lunatus*, Latin for 'crescent-shaped'. Lima beans are also called butter beans in some places. This is very confusing as wax beans, the yellow-coloured French beans, are also referred to as butter beans. When you see the giant butter beans sold dried or canned in groceries, they are in fact Lima beans.

Like common or French beans, it appears that Lima beans were domesticated from their wild ancestor on two separate occasions. The first was around 2000 BCE when the large-seeded varieties were developed in the Peruvian Andes. Then in 800 CE, much further north in Guatemala and Mexico, the small-seeded *sieva*-type Lima beans were selected.

Lima beans got their common name because they were once exported from Lima in Peru and therefore came to be associated with that city. The Spanish conquistadors were the first to take them back to Europe when they conquered the Inca civilisation in the sixteenth century. They took the beans to their other colonies, such as the Philippines, and to other subtropical destinations such as Madagascar, hence yet another misleading common name, 'Madagascar bean'.

Most varieties of Lima bean are large and white but there are also pale celadon-green varieties and ones with varying degrees of maroon-black flecking, from a few spots here and there right through to solid black.

Sadly, Lima beans are hardly grown at all in Australia although plenty are consumed, imported dried or canned from overseas. They are just as easy to grow as common beans and are probably even better than them in tropical parts of the country. In American culture Lima beans occupy a similar niche to Brussels sprouts in Anglo culture – universally hated by children and many adults besides – but this reputation is not at all justified. When properly cooked, Lima beans are tender and delicious, especially if the beans have been harvested early and dried before they are fully mature. Succotash is not a dish that necessarily needs to be suffered.

LIMA BEAN PODS

JAPANESE VIOLET-FLOWERED BROAD BEAN

BROAD BEANS

Broad beans, also called fava beans, are only distantly related to the New World French, runner and Lima beans. They are actually a kind of vetch (*Vicia*). Vetches are a genus of legumes grown as green manures, stock fodder and grain crops in some parts of the world. Vetches are mostly low, sprawling annuals which haul themselves up through neighbouring grasses and shrubs by means of twining tendrils, or simply slouch over the top of them. Broad beans (*Vicia faba*) are different. They grow into sturdy, upright plants up to two metres in height, and lack tendrils for climbing. Like other vetches, some broad bean varieties are grown as soil improvers and stock feed. These varieties are generally known as horse beans, field beans and tick beans to differentiate them from the varieties cultivated for human consumption.

The original ancestor of broad beans is lost in the mists of time. If it is descended from a single wild species, then that species is extinct. The broad bean has a couple of close living relatives but genetic assaying has revealed that they are not close enough to be its parents. The broad bean, like so many of our food plants, is an orphan. Wherever this foundling came from, it was already in cultivation in the eastern Mediterranean long before biblical times. The ancient Egyptians grew broad beans in abundance, as indeed their descendants do today. *Ful medames*, a broad bean mash flavoured with garlic, lemon and olive oil, is practically Egypt's national dish. Felafel, deep-fried balls of spiced broad bean meal, is a mainstay of Middle Eastern cuisine. Felafel is so popular around the eastern Mediterranean that everyone from the Greeks to the Turks, Lebanese, Egyptians and Israelis want to claim it as their own.

Vetches are grown for stock feed and green manure.

By 3000 BCE broad beans began to appear at Bronze Age sites as far north as Switzerland and as far west as Portugal. 'Beans' are mentioned several times in the Bible and the Talmud, which at that time can only have meant broad beans. By the Middle Ages broad beans had pushed even farther north into Europe, where they thrived despite the cold.

European attitudes to broad beans have always been mixed. On one hand they were viewed as peasant food unfit for civilised palates, yet they were wholeheartedly embraced at the same time. Broad beans often feature in the still life paintings of the Dutch masters. They are depicted almost as frequently as exotic symbols of wealth such as tulips, citrus fruits and fine tableware. Perhaps they were a symbol of plenty and a reminder that the common things in life also make us rich.

Broad beans certainly do that. They are fabulously productive and happy to grow in horrible soil. They provide an embarrassment of riches at a time of the year when it is most needed: the hungry gap. The hungry gap is that glorious season of mid-spring, when all the buds are bursting into blossom and the sun feels warm on your face and the world seems good again. But, counterintuitively, mid-spring is a very lean time in the vegetable garden. The winter crops have all finished but the summer crops haven't yet come on. Happily, this is just when those fleeting treats of spring – artichokes, asparagus, watercress and broad beans – come into their own.

People tend to either love or hate broad beans but for some unlucky souls things are quite a bit more serious. Sufferers of an inherited condition called favism, most prevalent in people from African and Mediterranean bloodlines, cannot produce an enzyme called G6PD. If individuals affected with favism eat broad beans it causes their red blood cells to suddenly break down, leading to weakness, muscle paralysis and, in the worst cases, death. However, G6PD deficiency can be tested for in babies with a family history of the condition and managed appropriately.

VARIETIES

•

Broad beans are sometimes divided into 'Windsor' and 'Longpod' categories. 'Windsor' varieties have short pods containing four to five large, flat seeds, while 'Longpod' varieties typically have six to eight smaller seeds. Don't pay too much attention to these classifications. They matter more to people who show vegetables competitively than to those who grow them to eat.

Aquadulce
An English heirloom loved for its early crops of fat pods containing 4–5 large, white seeds. Aquadulce is tough and reliable.

Broad Windsor
Another English heirloom, Broad Windsor crops over a long period and has deliciously flavoured beans. I have seen this variety sold in Australia as Windsor Long Pod,

AQUADULCE BROAD BEAN

which is, of course, pure oxymoron. There is also a French bean called Windsor which does indeed have long pods – perhaps Chinese whispers have been at work here.

Coles Dwarf

A shorter growing variety whose haulms are not as floppy as taller broad bean varieties, so it rarely requires staking. It bears full-sized pods of white seeds.

Crimson Flowered

Most broad beans have dirty white flowers with a black eye in the centre and some brown veins pencilled on the petals. This eighteenth-century heirloom variety is totally different. It has flowers which people who went to school in the 1970s will immediately recognise as the exact colour of the No. 4 Cuisenaire rod: crimson. (I note with crotchety-old-person-disdain that the No. 4 rod has been rebranded as 'purple' or, even less convincingly, 'lavender' in recent years).

The crimson-flowered broad bean came within a hair's breadth of extinction in the late twentieth century. Luckily for all of us an elderly Kentishwoman named Miss Cutbush gave her final crop of four seeds to the Henry Doubleday Research Association (HDRA) in the UK in 1978. Her father had grown Crimson Flowered as a market gardener nearly a century earlier. From this unique gift, the HDRA (now called Garden Organic) was able to revive the strain and today it is grown around the world.

Crimson Flowered is a truly wonderful cultivar for the flower garden. It bears copious quantities of flowers, prominently presented amongst the foliage. The beans are tasty enough, but unfortunately they are rather small. However, what this bean lacks in size it amply makes up for in quantity. This is the best variety for people who enjoy the zen of podding broad beans.

Exhibition Longpod

A very tall variety bearing long, fat pods of six to eight seeds. The name of this variety hints at the once-popular hobby of growing vegetables for competition. Only flawless pods with the maximum number of seeds, all of equal size and perfectly displayed, were chosen.

EXHIBITION LONGPOD
BROAD BEAN

SNAKE BEAN

The snake bean (*Vigna unguiculata subsp. sesquipedalis*) is a tropical Asian crop closely related to red azuki beans (*Vigna angularis*) and mung beans (*V. radiata*), but only distantly related to the New World French and runner beans. Snake beans are notable for their very long pods – *sesquipedalis* means 'foot-and-a-half' in Latin, referring to their extraordinary length. They are also called asparagus beans or yard-long beans, which is probably going over the top a bit. The beans have a slightly chewy, leathery texture which works perfectly in certain Asian dishes – in Thai *som tum*, for example. Snake beans are mostly bright green in colour but there are a few other cultivars around, too. There is a green cultivar with red beans, a purple-podded cultivar and one called **Red Noodle** that has spectacular dark red pods. A green, dwarf variety has recently become available.

SNAKE BEAN

CHAPTER TWO

THE

Gourd

FAMILY

ORNAMENTAL GOURD   (*Cucurbita pepo*)

The gourd family (Cucurbitaceae) has just under a thousand members, all native to tropical and subtropical parts of the world. Collectively called 'cucurbits', the members of the gourd family are notable for their very large fruits which are, botanically speaking, giant berries (i.e. fleshy, multi-seeded fruits formed from a single ovary).

The overwhelming majority of cucurbits are vines which scramble over the ground or drag themselves up into trees by means of their strong tendrils. However, one member of the family grows into a thick-trunked tree six metres in height. *Dendrosicyos socotranus*, the bizarre tree cucumber from the Yemeni island of Socotra, is unique amongst cucurbits. It is unimaginably odd. The closest analogy would be a baobab tree with a cucumber plant parked on top of it.

Most cucurbits have yellow flowers but a few are white. The beautiful Asian *Hodgsonia* has flowers like white morning glories with a fringe of golden curls streaming down from the edges of the petals. The Shirley Temple of the cucurbits, if you like. The Mediterranean squirting cucumber (*Ecballium elaterium*) is the jokester of the family. Its bizarre method of seed dispersal seems more like some kind of practical joke than a serious survival strategy. The squirting cucumber's fruits look like tiny hairy cucumbers. When you touch them they explode, shooting seeds and pulp out of a hole in their end. The little fruits literally blow themselves off their stems and squirt you with goop.

Cucurbits are amongst the oldest domesticated plants. *Lagenaria siceraria*, the bottle or calabash gourd, is thought to be the earliest domesticated plant. It was grown by humans as long as 12 000 years ago – the late Pleistocene epoch. Although immature calabash gourds are edible, the calabash was not domesticated for food, but as a 'container crop'. When dried, its fruits form a light, durable, hollow, woody shell. This shell is perfectly suited for carrying water. Native to tropical Africa with an outlying population in Asia, today the calabash is found throughout the tropics and subtropics in both the Old and New Worlds. How the calabash gourd came to be in the Americas 9000 years ago – long before Columbus' arrival – is a great mystery. Did it float across the ocean unaided? Unlikely. More likely it arrived with humans migrating across the land bridge that once existed between Asia and the Americas. This hypothesis is still being investigated. As more pieces of this puzzle are put together we will learn a lot about our own distant history.

The calabash gourd is still used today, just as it was all those thousands of years ago: for storage, holding liquids and making utensils of all kinds. Calabash gourds find their loftiest use in the construction of musical instruments. From the primitive *guiro* of Latin America, the *axatse* shaker, marimba-like *balafon* and graceful *kora* of

CALABASH GOURD

West Africa, to the sophisticated *sitar*, *veena* and *tanpura* of India, instruments from around the world use calabash gourds as resonators. This is a plant that has served humans well and will continue to do so in the future.

Another useful cucurbit is the luffa or loofah (*Luffa aegyptiaca*). Luffas look like big, stripy cucumbers. The fruits are edible when small but when fully mature they become stringy and fibrous. The fibres are tough and resist rotting. When dried and cleaned, what's left is a cylinder of stringy fibres that can be used as a natural scouring pad. For this reason luffas have earned the unappealing nickname 'dishrag gourds'.

Apart from the calabash gourd and luffa, most other cucurbits are grown for food. Cucurbits were probably originally domesticated for their seeds rather than

LUFFA

their flesh, which in nature contains bitter-tasting chemicals called *cucurbitins*, designed to discourage animals from eating them. Most domesticated cucurbits have had these bitter chemicals bred out of them. However, some are actually valued for their bitterness.

BITTER MELON

The bitter melon (*Mormodica charantia*) is an Asian delicacy. Bitter melons look like blistered, pale green cucumbers, which turn yellow with bright red seeds when left to ripen fully. As the name suggests they taste very bitter indeed, for which reason they are often paired with fatty meats like pork. Bitter melons are one of those plants that hover on the border between 'food' and 'medicine'. They are credited with a raft of health benefits and are eaten as much for their health value as their taste – perhaps more so.

Another bitter-tasting cucurbit is the Asian winter melon (*Benincasa hispida*). Winter melons are big, watermelon-like fruits with a waxy bloom on the skin, often seen stacked high in Asian groceries. Their flesh has a strange musty flavour and they get waxier the longer they are stored. Winter melons are used in South East Asia as a cooked vegetable and to make a cooling summer drink. In India, where they are called 'ash gourds', blocks of their flesh are candied and turned into tooth-achingly sweet treats called *petha*.

WINTER MELON

Choko or Chayote (*Sechium edule*) is a plant familiar to many older Australians. Too familiar, perhaps. Chokos have been a handy food source during tough economic times, especially in rural areas. For those lucky enough *not* to be familiar with the choko, the fruits look like green, wrinkled pears and grow on a rampant perennial vine. Older varieties are liberally sprinkled with a layer of prickles. The botanical name *edule* means 'edible'. Chokos are certainly that: edible. Prepared in the traditional Aussie way (boiled to death), they could hardly be called enjoyable. Bland and with a texture like a geriatric zucchini, eating choko can have a slightly punitive quality about it, like being forced to drink cod liver oil. To be fair to the choko, this might have something to do with our cooking technique. South

East Asian cultures seem to do a much better job of cooking chokos, pairing them with pungent, salty sauces and fragrant spices. Incidentally, chokos' shoot tips and tuberous roots can be eaten, too.

The colocynth or vine of Sodom (*Citrullus colocynthis*) is a close relative of the watermelon (*Citrullus lanatus*). Like the watermelon, it is a plant of semi-arid regions, growing and blooming when there is moisture available and dying off in times of drought, leaving its round, orange-sized fruits behind. Unlike the watermelon, which has undergone centuries of domestication to render it edible, the vine of Sodom's flesh is quite poisonous. Its seeds are edible and are eaten by north African nomads, but it is more commonly used in folk medicine. Wild watermelons called Afghan melons are weeds in semi-arid parts of Australia, as is another desert cucurbit, *Cucumis myriocarpus*, a kind of wild spiky cucumber known as the paddy melon, not to be confused with the cute marsupial pademelon.

On the subject of spiky cucumbers, *Cucumis metuliferus*, the African horned cucumber or 'kiwano' is an interesting thing. Horned cucumbers resemble stubby orange-yellow cucumbers covered in stout horns like a WWII naval mine. Inside, they have lots of seeds surrounded by pale green jelly. The flavour is like a slightly tangy cucumber with just a hint of melon. The horned cucumber enjoyed a certain amount of popularity in the 80s and 90s when Australians were first beginning to experiment with exotic fruits, but it never really developed a strong following. Perhaps this is because it is neither fish nor fowl: it is not as crisp and refreshing as a cucumber nor as sweet and tasty as a melon. The kindest thing you could say about a horned cucumber is that it is subtle. Incidentally, the name 'kiwano' is not a real common name but a trade mark registered by New Zealand fruit growers, hoping to repeat their success in rebranding the Chinese gooseberry the 'kiwifruit'.

TURK'S TURBAN PUMPKIN

SQUASH, INCLUDING PUMPKINS & ZUCCHINI

Squash are the Americas' answer to the Old World melons and gourds. Each variety of squash traces its ancestry to one of four species, *Cucurbita maxima*, *C. moschata*, *C. argyrosperma* (aka *C. mixta*) or *C. pepo*.

Cucurbita pepo is one of humankind's oldest food crops. It was already being cultivated in its native Mexico nearly 10 000 years ago. By 3000 BCE it was being grown in the eastern USA, thousands of kilometres from its Central American homeland. *C. moschata* shows up in Mexico around 8000–9000 years ago. It originated in the hot, humid lowlands of southern Central America and northern South America. *C. argyrosperma* seems to have been the next in cultivation some 8000 years ago in southern Mexico. *C. maxima*, native to Peru, is a relative Johnny-come-lately, domesticated a mere 4000 years ago.

It is likely that squash were originally domesticated for their large, edible

PUMPKIN JACK-O-LANTERNS

seeds. The sweet flesh that we grow them for today probably came much later. Some pumpkins are still grown primarily for their seeds. Styrian oil pumpkins, named for the Austrian state of Styria, have a thick, green oil pressed from their seeds. Pumpkin seed oil is a feature of cuisine in former Austro-Hungarian states, used raw as a flavouring rather than for cooking. The hull-less seeds, called pepitas, are an immensely popular addition to salads, cakes and breads. Seed pumpkins made their way to Israel with the Jewish diaspora from Eastern Europe, and not just hull-less varieties. An Israeli friend once proudly showed me a notch worn into his eye tooth by cracking open roasted pumpkin seeds for hours on end in front of the telly, noting that this was practically the national pastime in his country.

Squash is an odd sort of name, isn't it? It is derived from a Native American Massachusett language word, *askutasquash*. The word pumpkin is probably derived from Greek *pepon* via Latin *peponem*, meaning a melon. What is the difference between a pumpkin and a squash? Well, nothing, really. Squash is just an umbrella term that is used to refer to all four species of New World cucurbit. The term 'pumpkin' is applied to squash that have hard skins, are consumed at full maturity and store well. In their native USA, the word 'pumpkin' is used interchangeably with 'winter squash'. A winter squash is one that can be stored for winter consumption by virtue of its thick skin and dry flesh.

There are also varieties which the Americans refer to as summer squash. Summer squash are varieties that do not keep for long periods and are best eaten young. Summer squash are derived mostly from *C. pepo*. In Australia we don't use the term 'summer squash' much. If a particular squash is long and narrow in shape we tend to call it a 'zucchini' when it is young and a 'marrow' when it gets older. We reserve the term 'squash' for button squash, with circular, flattened fruits. Decorative gourds are descended from *C. pepo*, too, so they also come under the squash umbrella. It's all a bit confusing, but basically four species of squash share six common names between them. Perhaps we should adopt the American custom of calling them all 'squash' and be done with it.

Squash are deeply symbolic vegetables to Americans. They represent delivery from starvation, since it was pumpkins, along with corn, that Native Americans taught the English pilgrims to grow when they were facing famine, giving them the means to feed themselves in the new colony. For this reason pumpkin pie is a traditional food at Thanksgiving, along with other indigenous foods such as turkey and pecans. Pumpkins are also *de rigeur* for that other all-American holiday, Halloween. Halloween has its roots in the Christian Feast of All Hallows (or All Saints), although nowadays it's a mash-up of All Hallows Eve and older pagan festivals during which, in Ireland and Scotland, turnips were traditionally carved into faces. This Celtic custom was transplanted into America with its rich supply of pumpkins and, hey presto, the jack-o-lantern was born.

You might be surprised to hear that pumpkins are not universally liked around the world. A few years ago some vegetarian friends of mine were travelling in rural Romania, a part of the world not noted for its meat-free cuisine. Hungry, they flagged down a farmer driving a horse-drawn cart with a load of pumpkins on it, hoping to buy one from him to make themselves some pumpkin soup. The farmer was appalled by this idea, asking them incredulously, 'What for you want eat *pig* food?' This sums up how most of the world views pumpkin: fit only for livestock, not for human consumption. We Australians know better of course, as do the handful of other pumpkin-eating cultures: the Americans, Japanese and French.

The varieties that follow represent just a tiny fraction of all the pumpkin varieties in existence.

CUCURBITA MAXIMA

Pumpkins which are descended from *C. maxima* come in every imaginable shape and size. From pink torpedoes to orange orbs to blue teardrops, puffy or sleek, smooth-skinned or warty, pocket-sized or gargantuan. They are so diverse that you would hardly guess that they are related to one another. However, you can always pick *C. maxima* forms by their vigorous vines 3–5 metres long, with pale green, kidney-shaped, soft furry foliage.

Blue Hubbard

The bigger, but younger, brother to Golden Hubbard, introduced in 1909 by the Gregory seed company. It resembles Golden Hubbard in its spindle shape and warty texture, but its skin is pale blue in colour and the fruits are four times the size of Golden Hubbard, weighing up to 20 kilograms! Walking in a field of Blue Hubbards at harvest time is quite surreal. As the vines are dying back to reveal their giant fruits, it feels like walking through a herd of giant sea cucumbers grazing on kelp.

BLUE HUBBARD PUMPKIN

Bohemian

Bohemian is a medium-sized, pumpkin-shaped pumpkin. It has a smooth skin of the palest jade to white with salmon splotches. It is extremely attractive on the outside and its flesh is smooth, sweet and bright orange. This is a top-drawer pumpkin; highly recommended. There has been an inferior strain in circulation in recent years which bears smallish, football-shaped fruits.

BOHEMIAN PUMPKIN

Dill's Atlantic Giant

This is the biggest pumpkin in the world. The fruits regularly weigh in at 100 kilograms, with competition behemoths topping 700 kilograms! The humungous fruits are salmon-orange in colour with a bloated, Jabba the Hutt-like quality. I have probably turned you off eating one now, but don't be disappointed because they are not really fit for human consumption, the flesh being rather woolly and insipid. Atlantic Giant was introduced by Canadian Howard Dill as recently as 1978: a modern heirloom.

Galeux d'Eysines / Brodé Galeux d'Eysines

The French have a wonderful term which I'm sure they must have invented to describe this pumpkin: *jolie laide*. *Jolie laide* means something along the lines of 'pretty-ugly' or 'cute-ugly'. This variety has medium-large, pumpkin-shaped fruits with a smooth, pale apricot-salmon skin. Quite pretty, I hear you say. But here's where the ugly comes in. Out of that pretty, smooth skin erupt enormous beige, woody pimples. Hence the romantic-sounding French name, which translates as 'Scabby from Eysines' (Eysines being a town on the outskirts of Bordeaux). Don't be put off by the 'scabs'; the net result is a very beautiful pumpkin indeed. Not bad eating, with light orange, fine-textured flesh, but not one of the very best either. Grow it for looks.

Golden Hubbard

Introduced in 1898, this beloved American heirloom is stout and spindle-shaped. It has bright red-orange, warty skin with a dark green button on the blossom end; very decorative. The 5-kilogram fruits have flesh which is thick, sweet and substantial in texture. Both the Golden and Blue Hubbard are descended from a much older American heirloom called, simply, **Hubbard**. Hubbard had smaller, dark green fruits, but the classic spindle shape and warty skin it gave to its progeny are unmistakeable.

Jarrahdale

An Australian heirloom (I told you we were one of the world's great pumpkin cultures), from the West Australian town of the same name. The fruits are medium weight, round, flattened and lobed with ghostly blue-grey skin and bright green-orange, creamy flesh.

Marina di Chioggia

An Italian heirloom from the home town of many weird and wonderful vegetables, Chioggia, near Venice. Sometimes called the 'sea pumpkin of Chioggia', this variety has green-blue, bubbly skin which does make it looks like some kind of undersea creature. Inside, the 5-kilogram fruits have yellow-orange, dense, sweet flesh. See the Chioggia beetroot on page 237 for pronunciation advice.

Pink Banana

Pink Banana is a fitting name for this American heirloom, with fruits like long, salmon-pink bananas up to a metre in length and 20 kilograms in weight. The flesh is dry, smooth and sweet.

Queensland Blue

QUEENSLAND BLUE PUMPKIN

Thumping great blue-green, turban-shaped fruits with rich orange, creamy flesh and excellent keeping qualities make this iconic Australian heirloom great. So great that it has been embraced by the Americans – who already have dozens of good pumpkins of their own – since it was first introduced to the USA in 1932. Every older Australian knows the famous Queensland Blue pumpkin but many younger people have never heard of it because it has been comprehensively supplanted by small, Japanese-type F1 hybrid pumpkins (so-called 'Jap' pumpkins) in supermarkets over the past decade. You need an axe to cut into a 10-kilogram Queensland Blue, but its delicious contents make it worth the effort.

Rouge Vif d'Étampes

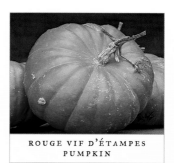

ROUGE VIF D'ÉTAMPES
PUMPKIN

Literally 'bright red from Étampes', a town just outside Paris. This French heirloom was first offered in the USA in 1883. Rouge Vif d'Étampes is as about as beautiful as a pumpkin can be. It bears large, flattened, bright orange-red fruits with satiny, lustrous skin. The fruits weigh in at 10 kilograms or more, and their orange-yellow flesh cooks to a sweet, smooth puree. Rouge Vif d'Étampes was originally grown as a soup variety, in the days when rather pale, thin pumpkin soup was the go. These days we think of it more as a roasting variety. Either way, the vines bear prolific, early crops so this is a good choice for areas with a short growing season. Rouge Vif d'Étampes often appears for sale under the nickname 'Cinderella'. It does have a certain fairytale quality about it.

Triamble

Another Australian heirloom from before the 1930s. The 5-kilogram fruits are distinctly three-lobed with pale greenish-blue skin and pale orange, fine-textured flesh.

TRIAMBLE PUMPKIN

Turk's Turban

Turk's Turban is named for its bizarre shape, like some kind of elaborately ruched Ottoman head-wear, or a giant acorn. The 'cap' of this 'acorn' is bright orange-red while the 'nut' part is cream, blotched and striped with dark green. It is an old French variety, first illustrated in Vilmorin's seed catalogue of 1871, although it was already being grown in the USA half a century earlier. The fruits are not especially large and, frankly, make pretty insipid eating. What this variety lacks in culinary value it more than makes up for in beauty, however. Worth growing for looks alone.

Utsugi Akagawa Amaguri / Red Kuri

A Japanese heirloom from Ishikawa prefecture. The name means 'Utsugi red-skinned sweet chestnut'. It is usually shortened to 'Red Kuri' (kuri meaning 'chestnut') or, incorrectly, 'Uchikuri' or 'Uchikikuri' (a misreading of its Japanese name).

POTIMARRON PUMPKIN

The Japanese like their pumpkins small. Red Kuri fits the bill perfectly, with fruits not much larger than softballs. They are very attractive: round to teardrop-shaped with smooth, soft, bright orange-red skin. The flesh is pale orange and tender. Red Kuri is a great variety for roasting skin and all.

Red Kuri is almost certainly one and the same with the French variety **Potimarron**, although they are sold as separate varieties in Australia. They are identical in every way and Potimarron is a combination of the French words *potiron*, 'pumpkin' and *marron*, 'chestnut'. Coincidence? I think not.

Victor, aka Red Warty Thing

This is a stunningly beautiful pumpkin. Stout, oblong fruits are brilliant orange-red covered with thousands of tiny warts. It's a pumpkin that begs to be stroked. First introduced in Massachusetts in 1897 by James Gregory under the name Victor, it has recently resurfaced as Red Warty Thing, a very apt name.

CUCURBITA MOSCHATA

The Japanese in particular love *C. moschata* and have bred several weird and wonderful varieties from it. The familiar butternut pumpkin also belongs to this species. You can spot *C. moschata* by its ruffled, dark green, silver-splashed leaves. The flesh of most varieties is very dark red-orange, although the butternuts tend to be much paler. *C. moschata* needs more consistent heat than either *C. maxima* and *C. pepo* varieties to thrive.

FUTTSU PUMPKIN

C. moschata pumpkins used to be known as gramma pumpkins, which may explain why pumpkins sold under the name 'Gramma' today can vary in shape from round and flattened to football-shaped or crooknecks. Every seed saver seems to have a different idea of what a 'gramma pumpkin' is.

MUSQUÉE DE PROVENCE
PUMPKIN

Futtsu Kurokawa

Futtsu for short, this is a very productive Japanese variety producing small, ribbed fruits with warty skin. They are green-black ageing to caramel-brown with a very well-flavoured, nutty, yellow-orange flesh.

Musquée de Provence

A handsome French heirloom first offered in the USA in 1899. It bears large fruits, 10 kilograms or so in weight. These are flattened and beautifully lobed with satiny, caramel-brown skin with a grey bloom. The flesh is very dark orange, dry and dense, and cooks up beautifully. A first-class pumpkin.

SHISHIGATANI PUMPKIN

Shishigatani

Shishigatani is a distinctive heirloom pumpkin from the Kyōto region in Japan. It is large for a Japanese pumpkin, similar in size to the common butternut. Shishigatani is hourglass-shaped with blistered skin, black when immature, ripening to a rich caramel-beige with a dove-grey bloom like a grape. You've never seen anything like it. It looks as if it would be more at home stuck to a coral reef than growing in a garden. Inside, the flesh is dark orange and creamy in texture.

Tromboncino

TROMBONCINO SQUASH

Tromboncino means 'little trombone' (or, less romantically, 'motorbike muffler') in Italian. This is a wonderful, whimsical name for a 1.5-metre-long, thin fruit which flares out into a bulbous end section like a little trombone bell. When the fruits of this strongly climbing variety grow hanging down they develop perfectly straight, but more often they develop all kinds of wacky twists, turns and folds, like some fantastical brass instrument from a Dr Seuss book. Tromboncino fruits are best eaten when still young, tender and pale green in colour, but can be picked larger and stored for winter use, upon which they turn beige. You might also see this variety listed as a zucchini, as it is almost always used as a summer squash but, unusually for a summer squash, it is descended from *C. moschata* (most are varieties of *C. pepo*).

Waltham Butternut

Waltham Butternut is a smallish, beige, hourglass-shaped pumpkin with pale orange flesh which makes either the best or worst pumpkin soup, depending on who you ask. This variety's origins are also contested. The credit for refining the strain and introducing it to commerce in around 1970 goes to Bob Young in Waltham, Massachusetts, but there is some evidence that the original work was done by hobby gardener Charles Leggett during the previous decades. Whoever is responsible, the idea was obviously to breed a smallish pumpkin which was more compact and evenly shaped than the old crookneck pumpkins, which can be stupidly long, curved affairs. This was certainly achieved and this modern heirloom variety remains a favourite today.

CUCURBITA ARGYROSPERMA

(aka *C. mixta*)

Varieties descended from *C. argyrosperma* are commonly called cushaw squash. Chances are you've never heard of them because cushaws are almost unknown in Australia. They do not display as much variation in their outward appearance as the other squash species, tending to be either bottle-shaped or crook-necked with a pale cream skin stippled or striped with light green.

GOLDEN STRIPE CUSHAW SQUASH

CUCURBITA PEPO

With such a long history of domestication it is perhaps no wonder that *C. pepo* has diversified into an enormous variety of forms from big orange beach balls and yellow discs to dark green sausages. Some cultivars of *C. pepo* have been selected for their sweet yellow flesh, hard skin and long-keeping qualities. These we call 'pumpkins', just like we do varieties of *C. maxima* and *C. moschata*. However, most of the soft-skinned, fresh-eating summer squash – which we call zucchini and button squash – belong under the *C. pepo* umbrella, too.

Some varieties of *C. pepo* grow into trailing vines, others remain as tight bushes. However, you can always spot *C. pepo* by its foliage. They all have dark green, triangular leaves, sometimes splashed with silver. Their leaves and stems are very scratchy and bristly, giving some people (me, for example) quite a nasty rash.

I have divided the *C. pepo* crops into pumpkin types, squash types and zucchini types. These categories are a bit artificial. They reflect how we use *C. pepo* varieties in the kitchen rather than any sort of botanical distinction.

PUMPKIN-TYPE *PEPOS*

•

The 'pumpkin' types of *Cucurbita pepo* are generally smaller and more compact than varieties descended from *C. maxima* and *C. moschata*. In general *C. pepo* pumpkins are better for smaller gardens, smaller households and, because they ripen several weeks earlier, cooler climates. Their flesh is paler coloured than that of true pumpkins, more a creamy gold colour than orange, so if you grow these varieties don't expect to get vibrant orange pumpkin soup. *C. pepo* pumpkins do not store as well as *maxima* and *moschata* varieties, so if you grow a mixture of the species, make sure you eat the *pepos* first.

Connecticut Field

Connecticut Field is the ultimate pumpkin for carving. It forms large, handsome fruits which are spherical, ribbed and bright orange with thin skin and pale orange flesh that is soft and easy to scoop out. The flesh is edible but perhaps not as dense and creamy as *maxima* and *moschata* pumpkin varieties, being somewhat more fibrous and watery. Nevertheless, this is a traditional variety for Thanksgiving pumpkin pie. It is a very old Native American variety which was passed on to the New England settlers by the local indigenous people. Connecticut Field's smaller, less fibrous offspring, **Jack-O-Lantern**, is more readily available in Australia and probably better eating, too.

Delicata

Thirty-centimetre-long, peanut-shaped fruits, a creamy yellow striped with green and orange, are produced on compact bushes, making this a good choice for small gardens. The flesh is pale, creamy orange and very sweet; delicious baked whole, skin and all. First introduced in 1894 by the Henderson seed company in the USA and still rightly popular.

DELICATA PUMPKIN

Jack Be Little

An adorable miniature pumpkin, small enough to fit in the palm of your hand but with classic orange-yellow colour and lobed pumpkin shape. Probably Asian in origin, this variety is now practically compulsory as a Halloween decoration in the USA. Not bad eating if you can bring yourself to cook the little cuties.

Kakai

Kakai is a Japanese pepita pumpkin descended from the Styrian oil pumpkins of Austria. Its flesh is thin, stringy and insipid but its dark olive-green, hulless seeds are abundant and excellent. Its mustard-orange fruits are the size and shape of soccer balls, beautifully striped and chequered with black-green, and grow on compact vines.

KAKAI PUMPKIN

Kumikumi/Kamokamo

This squash is a great mystery. It is a traditional Māori heirloom, grown long before the arrival of Europeans in New Zealand. Squash are all native to the Americas, so the question is, how did the kumikumi get to New Zealand? Were ancestral Māori trading with Native Americans? Did they pick up the kumikumi somewhere on their Pacific wanderings? If so, from whom? When we work out how the kumikumi got to New Zealand it will tell us something about our own history of trade and travel.

Kumikumi is a vining squash that bears round to oblong, distinctly ridged fruits, dark green, streaked with light green, ripening to yellow. They can be eaten when they are small and green or kept to overwinter. Their shoot tips are eaten steamed or boiled and their seeds can be eaten, too.

Table Queen

This is one of the 'acorn' type pumpkins, rarely seen in this country, which form small, neat fruits shaped like pawpaws. This is a very ancient cultivar, originally selected by Native Americans and introduced to horticulture in 1913. The fruits weigh under a kilogram, a perfect serving size for two. They are extremely handsome with a burnished,

TABLE QUEEN PUMPKIN

black-green skin. When ripe they develop bright yellow patches where they touch the ground, not the side exposed to the sun as you might expect. The flesh is pale orange-yellow and quite dry, good for cooking using methods that allow it to absorb some moisture.

SQUASH-TYPE *PEPOS*

•

Some squash varieties of *C. pepo* can be allowed to mature and used at a larger size – the maligned vegetable marrow types, for example. However, most squash are much more palatable when harvested at a very young age, just a day or two after the flowers drop. At this stage they are buttery and delicious.

Gem

Gem is a strongly vining South African heirloom squash that produces round, softball-sized fruits with dark green skin. They look like small, round, dark green zucchini on the outside but inside they have sweetish, yellowish flesh almost like a pumpkin-type pepo. South Africans have a great deal of affection for this unassuming little squash. In fact, they are nuts about it. In South Africa Gem squash

GEM SQUASH

are traditionally served boiled, slathered with butter and brown sugar and maybe a dusting of nutmeg. They are also perfect for roasting, one per person.

Patisson Panaché Jaune et Vert

Often simply called **Jaune et Vert** ('yellow and green') in Australia, I have grown this variety out from two different seed sources in two different climates and each time it has refused to thrive, while other squash varieties on either side of it have revelled in the growing conditions. Either I am going horribly wrong somewhere or the seed of this variety offered in Australia is a bit feeble. Bushy plants reportedly produce big crops of heavily scalloped, pale green pattypan squash, ageing to creamy yellow with dark green radial stripes.

Summer Crookneck

This is a very old heirloom, almost certainly a Native American cultivar from the eastern USA. It is probably identical to a squash taken to Europe by the Spanish in the seventeenth century, first documented in the USA in 1807. The plants are large but compact bushes which bear bottle-shaped fruits with a crooked neck. They have yellow, warty skin and translucent white flesh.

SUMMER CROOKNECK SQUASH

They are best harvested very young. Once they reach 15 centimetres across and the skin starts to harden they become a bit crunchy. Crookneck is prone to powdery mildew but this does not seem to inhibit its fruiting much. It is very robust and crops over a long season.

White Bush Scallop, Pattypan squash or Cymling squash

This is another very ancient heirloom from the north-eastern USA, the sister to Yellow Bush Scallop, first depicted by Mathias de l'Obel (after whom the genus *Lobelia* is named) in 1591. It bears heavy crops of very pale white-green, scalloped button fruits on a compact bushy plant. This variety just keeps on keeping on. Picking

EARLY WHITE
BUSH SCALLOP SQUASH

the fruits can become a full-time job. They are buttery and delicious when small but any fruits left on the bush turn into hard, white flying saucers, a handspan across, in a matter of days. The flying saucers are theoretically edible, but I can think of tastier vegetables. Their best use is as table decorations or biodegradable spacecraft for Lego men.

Vegetable Spaghetti

This unique squash looks like a big yellow zucchini on the outside but cut it open and it is full of translucent flesh that separates into spaghetti-like strands with the help of a fork. It sounds very Italian, but Vegetable Spaghetti was first offered by the Japanese seed house Sakata in 1934, possibly descended from Chinese germplasm. The immature fruits are succulent and tender and can be eaten whole, like zucchini.

Yellow Bush Scallop

YELLOW BUSH SCALLOP SQUASH

This is an ancient Native American heirloom from the north-eastern USA. The compact plants bear matte yellow fruits with a puffy upper hemisphere sitting atop a smaller lower hemisphere, like a muffin spilling over the top of its paper cup. Yellow Bush Scallop is not especially heavy cropping, but that can be a blessing with squash. It is quite prone to powdery mildew. Some of its more modern descendants are probably better choices for home gardeners, but it is good that we still have the genetic material from this original landrace on hand.

ZUCCHINI-TYPE *PEPO*S

•

Zucchini is the Italian word for 'little squash'. In Australia we have adopted this word for varieties of *C. pepo* which are soft-skinned and eaten young. The British call them by their French name, *courgettes*. Americans call them simply 'summer squash'.

Zucchini are great vegetables to grow at home. They are generally compact, easy-care plants. The main chore is keeping up with picking their heavy crops of fast-growing fruits. If you leave it for longer than a day or two between picking, the fruits can end up like giant baseball bats. Unloading buckets of surplus baseball bats on to your neighbours will not win you as many friends as you might hope. It's better to feed them to your chooks or compost them. One or two zucchini plants are all that are needed in most domestic gardens.

Zucchini plants are very prone to getting powdery mildew towards the end of their growing season. This is normal. Dry soil combined with humid air and cooler nights (classic autumn weather in much of Australia) encourages powdery mildew growth. Don't reach for the fungicide: there is nothing you can do. It simply means that your zucchini plant is getting old.

Black Beauty

If you have a family to feed, this is the zucchini for you. It is incredibly heavy cropping due to its habit of producing many growing points simultaneously (most zucchini produce just one or two at a time). Black Beauty is a bushy plant with scalloped, dark green leaves that can grow to enormous proportions. The fruits are the familiar zucchini type, sausage-like and glossy black-green. Black Beauty is so fecund that it often crops itself to an early death, so it's best to stagger your sowings over a few weeks to extend your harvest.

Golden

Chirpy, canary-yellow versions of Black Beauty, Golden zucchini grow on a compact bush with beautifully cut and silvered foliage. Unlike Black Beauty, Golden is mercifully light cropping. This makes it a good variety for balconies where the ludicrously abundant Black Beauty would be simply too much of a good thing.

Striata d'Italia

Striata d'Italia ('Italian Striped') is a compact bushy variety which fruits over a long season. Its handsome fruits are sausage-shaped and pale green striped with dark green. It is a member of the ancient and distinctive *cocozelle* group of zucchini.

Tondo di Nizza/Ronde de Nice

'Round of Nice' is a vining zucchini with pale green, round fruits. They are at their nicest when picked the size of a tennis ball but are still buttery and delicious even when quite large.

BLACK BEAUTY ZUCCHINI

GOLDEN ZUCCHINI

STRIATA D'ITALIA ZUCCHINI

TONDO DI NIZZA ZUCCHINI

LITTLE POTATO CUCUMBER

CUCUMBERS

Cucumbers are one of the few vegetables that get a mention in the Bible. They are found in Isaiah: 'And the daughter of Zion is left as a cottage in a vineyard, as a lodge in a garden of cucumbers, as a besieged citie', and again in Numbers, when the Israelites have grown tired of subsisting on manna in the desert: 'We remember the fish which wee did eate in Egypt freely: the cucumbers and the melons, and the leekes, and the onions, and the garlicke.'

From these passages you might wrongly deduce that cucumbers are native to the Middle East or North Africa. In fact, cucumbers didn't exist in the Levant in Old Testament times. What is being referred to in the original Hebrew texts is almost certainly the bland *chate* melon which the Egyptians cultivated. By the time the King James Bible was translated in the late sixteenth and early seventeenth centuries, *chate* melons had been forgotten. 'Cucumbers' was probably the nearest approximation.

Cucumbers (*Cucumis sativus*) are native to the foothills of the Himalayas, though their wild ancestor is unknown. There is evidence of their domestication in India 4000 years ago and in China a thousand years later. By the time of the Classical Greeks, cucumbers had found their way west to the Mediterranean. The Romans particularly loved them. Pliny the Elder tells us that Emperor Tiberius loved cucumbers so much that he had them grown out of season in special carts that were wheeled out into the sun during warm weather and wheeled back inside during inclement weather. A kind of early greenhouse was designed to protect the cucumbers in their mobile beds. Pre-dating the technology for making panes of glass, these early cucumber houses were made from small panes of *lapis specularis* – probably the translucent mineral mica. There is evidence that the Romans were growing cucumbers even in chilly London during their British occupation.

Archeological remains show that cucumbers were being grown in Poland in the seventh century CE. The Holy Roman Emperor Charlemagne directed that cucumbers should be grown in his gardens in the ninth century. In the eleventh century, the Spanish-Moorish botanist and gardener Ibn Bassal wrote detailed instructions on how to grow cucumbers, including instructions for making hot beds by composting donkey manure. Christopher Columbus took cucumber seeds with him from Spain to the Caribbean where they thrived in the hot, humid climate. From there they spread throughout the Spanish empire in the Americas.

By Henry VIII's time cucumbers were once again being grown in England, having been forgotten during the Dark Ages. The English became masters at growing this subtropical crop in their indifferent climate. Cucumbers were the preserve of the rich, who could afford the staff and infrastructure required to cosset them, along with other tropical crops like pineapples and melons. During Victorian times the technology became available to build glasshouses as we know them. It was at this point that cucumber cultivation really took off in England.

Victorian gardeners bred special parthenocarpic glasshouse varieties of cucumbers. Parthenocarpic means 'virgin fruiting'; in other words, they do not need to be pollinated by a male flower in the normal way in order to set fruit. If by chance parthenocarpic cucumbers *were* pollinated they became seedy and bitter in taste, so gardeners would painstakingly remove the male flowers as they appeared on the vines to prevent this from happening. The next step was breeding hybrid cucumbers which are both parthenocarpic and gynoecious. That is, all-female plants with no male flowers at all, capable of setting fruit without pollination. These highly specialised 'European glasshouse cucumbers' have been bred to live out their existence in hermetically sealed glasshouses so that bees cannot 'contaminate' them with pollen from the outside world. Interestingly, gynoecious hybrids were made possible by the discovery of an open-pollinated cucumber from Korea whose plants tended to be either all-male or all-female; yet another reminder that modern F1 hybrids are only possible because of the amazing diversity of the genetic material contained in heirlooms.

VARIETIES

•

Cucumbers fall into two broad categories: those with black spines and those with white spines. In both varieties the spines can be simply brushed off when they get to harvest size, if they haven't fallen off already. When picked very small as gherkins or cornichons the spines fall off during the pickling process. Wild cucumbers contain an unpleasant bitter toxin called *cucurbitacin* to deter animals. Domesticated cucumbers have been bred for low levels of cucurbitacin but occasionally you will get a throwback that produces bitter, acrid fruits. Black-spined cucumbers are quite prone to this bitterness problem, white-spined varieties much less so.

Crystal Apple
A white-spined Australian heirloom from before 1920, developed by Yates but which probably traces its lineage back to Chinese cucumbers. The fruits are round-oblong with cream skin and faint green stripes. The flesh is crisp and sweet and stores well. A very good home garden variety.

Hmong Red
This heirloom grown by the Hmong people from the mountains on the borders of Laos, Thailand, China and Vietnam was taken by Hmong migrants to the USA in the 1970s. The plants are strongly climbing and heavy cropping. The fruits are very stoutly built, 30 centimetres or more in length. They are said to remain edible even when very large. Like the Indian varieties Little Potato and Poona Kheera, Hmong Red's black-spined fruits ripen from pale creamy yellow to a rough brown-gold when

ripe. Unfortunately one scoundrel selling Hmong Red seed in the USA advertised it by using a picture of Lebanese cucumbers turned glossy lipstick-red using the magic of computers. This tawdry counterfeit is still bouncing around on the internet today. Don't be fooled. Hmong Red is brown in colour, not scarlet.

Japanese Climbing

A traditional Japanese cucumber first grown in the USA in the 1890s. It is a strongly climbing variety with big tendrils and generous crops. The slender, white-spined fruits are 20 centimetres in length, dark green, tender and very crunchy. The Japanese have a particular affection for cucumbers, which they find cooling to eat during their oppressive summers. This variety is only one of many Japanese heirlooms. Keep an eye out for **Sagami Hanjiro** ('Sagami half white') which has black-spined fruits that are green at the stem end, shading beautifully to white at the blossom end.

JAPANESE CLIMBING CUCUMBER

Lebanese

I remember Lebanese cucumbers seeming terribly exotic when they first hit supermarket shelves in the 1980s. Now they seem terribly mainstream. This is a great cucumber for small gardens. Compact vines produce 15-centimetre, dark, glossy green cucumbers with thin, edible skins and juicy, sweet flesh.

Lemon

This black-spined variety introduced in the 1890s forms rounded, cream-coloured fruits with a yellow overlay. They do look a bit like lemons. The flesh is crisp and the skin is thin. There are a lot of seeds but this is a good variety for home gardeners since it is very tolerant of cold and drought and the fruits store well without shrivelling.

LEBANESE CUCUMBER

LEMON CUCUMBER

Little Potato

An Indian heirloom with fruits that look exactly like . . . little potatoes. Knobbly, brown, russeted fruits with a white interior grow on compact plants. Their taste is quite tangy and refreshing and they keep much longer than green varieties. The plants are absolutely prolific.

Miniature White or Mini White

Ivory, black-spined, 10-centimetre fruits are produced in abundance on compact plants. It is primarily a pickling cucumber.

Paris Pickling/Cornichon Vert Petit de Paris

A French heirloom from the mid-nineteenth century, Paris Pickling is a black-spined variety bred to produce prodigious quantities of tiny, crisp fruits for pickling as cornichons.

MINIATURE WHITE CUCUMBER

Poona Kheera

'Poona Cucumber' in Hindi, this black-spined heirloom from the city of Pune in India has short, blunt fruits which start life white, then move through pale yellow to gold before maturing to caramel-brown with a skin like cracked leather. Inside, they remain crystalline white, sweet, crisp and juicy. Excellent quality fruits produced early on a healthy, robust vine.

PARIS PICKLING CUCUMBER

Telegraph Improved

This English heirloom from the 1890s performs just as well outside in Australia as it does in glasshouses in England. It is the model for the 45-centimetre-long, straight, dark green cucumber you see at the supermarket, which these days invariably come shrink-wrapped in plastic (how on earth did we ever manage in the days before shrink-wrapped cucumbers?). Telegraph Improved forms big, robust plants which produce good crops of sweet, smooth, almost seedless fruits that are never bitter. An excellent cucumber.

CANARY MELON

MELONS

When I was a boy I thought melons were horrible things. With their crunchy, juiceless flesh, not quite sweet enough to qualify as 'fruit', I couldn't understand why my dad claimed to like melons so much. I thought he was mad. Until the day I had my first *vine-ripened* melon. The first thing I noticed about it was the perfume, which hit me from several paces away. It was sweet, rich and almost artificially fruity, as if a high-school chemistry project on esters had got out of hand. To my complete surprise, when I picked up a slice of this melon, juice ran out of it and dripped off my elbow. When I bit into it the flavour was utterly, utterly sublime. I had never tasted anything so delicious in my entire life. Nor have I since. Melons are, without a word of hyperbole, the food of the gods.

The difference between the barely edible shop-bought melons of my boyhood and the sublime vine-grown melons of my adulthood is all to do with ripeness. Sweet melons ripen and subsequently go off very quickly. One day they are rock-hard, scentless and bland, the next they are sweet, perfumed and juicy; 48 hours later their smell becomes musty and they are beginning to rot from the inside out. This makes melons eminently unsuitable for long-distance transport and storage. They do not continue to ripen off the vine as many fruits do and they do not hold well in storage. Melons are fruits which, if they cannot be eaten at the peak of perfection, are not worth eating at all. If you want to taste melons at their best, you simply have to grow your own.

People have been growing their own melons for a long time. Such a long time, in fact, that it is not even certain where melons' wild ancestors originated. Afghanistan has been mooted because it is an important centre of melon diversification. Africa was the main contender until recently because it is home to some thirty species of wild *Cucumis*, the genus to which melons belong. Recent phylogenetic studies (by, amongst others, Australian botanist Ian Telford) point to India as the origin of the melon. Perhaps it was the Indus Valley Civilisation who first grew melons, distributing them along ancient trade routes to Afghanistan, Persia and Egypt.

By 2000 BCE the Egyptians were growing bland *chate* melons on the flood

Melons for sale in Japan: untouched by the hand of nature.

plains of the Nile. There are tomb paintings depicting melon-like fruits, and this evidence is corroborated by datable plant specimens. A millennium later they were being grown in Central Asia, although they may already have arrived there with earlier waves of humans. In the regions around Armenia, Persia, Afghanistan and the lands bordering the Black Sea melons flourished and diversified. The Romans and Greeks almost certainly grew *chate* melons if the Egyptians did, but it is difficult to tell from their writings because they used the same names interchangeably for gourds, cucumbers and watermelons. In the Middle Ages melons probably re-entered Europe via two routes. First through Italy (if they weren't there already), with its trade links to the near east and Central Asia, and then through Spain in the eleventh century courtesy of the Moors.

Melons began to appear in Italian, Spanish and French paintings during the sixteenth century. In northern Europe they did not appear until much later, well into the eighteenth century, when the technology and know-how became available to grow them in chillier climes. Growing plants that love heat in northern Europe is difficult, and to do so was considered a sign of discerning taste and ample means. Glass cloches, orangeries and newfangled glasshouses were given over to exotic crops like citrus, figs, grapes, pineapples and melons. Hotbeds were prepared for growing melons by making heaps of animal dung. When the dung began to compost and produce warmth, melons were either sown directly into it or grown in pots sunk into the dung to give them the high soil temperature they need. Melons were cosseted and given any amount of special care – trellising the vines, hand pollination, disbudding, pruning and fruit thinning. In the late nineteenth century, northern European aristocrats prided themselves on being able to grow melons out of season on their estates. In Edwardian England, melons became the ultimate culinary symbol of prestige. Presenting a melon to each of your guests at dinner was seen as the ultimate display of largesse because a single fruit was worth the equivalent of hundreds of dollars today. Yet the flamboyant Edwardians were mere amateurs compared with the overwrought practices surrounding melons in Japan today.

Musk melons are valued above all other fruit in Japan. Visit any upmarket department store in Japan and there will be a whole department within it devoted to immaculate, never-touched-by-human-hands musk melons, displayed in paper- or even silk-lined presentation boxes. These impeccable specimens are grown with forensic precision to ensure absolute uniformity. The F1 hybrid melon vines are grown in glasshouses which are heated in winter and cooled in summer to ensure optimum growing conditions 365 days of the year. Each developing melon fruit is individually suspended by a network of strings to ensure that it is never soiled by coming into contact with the earth. Hanging in midair, each melon grows perfectly spherical in shape and the T-shaped stem sets at just the angle pernickety Japanese consumers demand. Each vine is allowed to bear only a single fruit so that it gets all the nourishment from the vine. Each ripening fruit is provided with a little fabric sun hat to prevent sunburn. The sugar content of each melon is tested electronically to ensure that it is harvested at peak ripeness. Nothing is left to chance, or indeed to nature, which might besmirch the final product. The price of such a melon? Well, how much have you got? A couple of hundred bucks will buy you something respectable, but the very best melons can go for significantly more than that. And the taste? *Almost*, but not quite, as good as a melon grown in your own backyard (trust me: I've tried both).

Speaking of melons grown in your own backyard, if you're from NSW you probably call them 'rockmelons'. If you are Victorian you probably call them 'cantaloupes'. The thing is, the melons commonly seen on the market in Australia are categorically *not* cantaloupes. Sorry Melbourne; Sydney wins this round. If it's any consolation, the Americans routinely get it wrong, too, and in any case the name 'rockmelon' is not used much outside Australia so nobody knows what they are talking about anyway.

Melons (*Cucumis melo*), as they are properly called, are divided into several different groups. The 'normal' supermarket melons that look like they are wearing beige fishnet tights are members of the Reticulatus group. These are commonly called musk melons, netted melons or, in Australia, rockmelons. Musk melons are recognisable by their skins, which are to a greater or lesser degree covered in grey, corky tessellations although some, like **Vert Grimpant**, have virtually none. Musk melons are also easy to pick by their musky perfume. Their flesh may be orange or green.

True cantaloupes comprise the Cantalupensis group, probably named after the Italian town of Cantalupo (literally 'song of the wolf') near Rome, where they were once grown on the rich papal estates. Cantaloupes may be spherical or slightly flattened, smooth or bumpy-skinned. They are all, to a greater or lesser degree, lobed like pumpkins. The grooves which separate the lobes, called sutures, are clearly defined and they may be a different colour to the rest of the skin, giving many cantaloupe melons a striped appearance. Like musk melons, cantaloupes may have orange or green flesh, but they tend to have a more floral or fruity perfume and are generally considered to be the *crème de la crème* of melons, which is really saying something. Unfortunately true cantaloupes are almost unknown in Australia because they are the worst keepers of the lot.

The third important melon group is the Inodorus group. Inodorus melons are very variable but there is a 'gist' to them once you get your eye in. They can be very large in size and up to 3 kilograms in weight, or they can be as small as a softball. They can be blunt and oval in shape or elongated with pointed ends like a football. They all have hard, waxy skins. The skins can either be very smooth or wrinkled all over, as if they have spent too long soaking in the bath. Inodorus melons sometimes have a degree of netting, which can vary from none to quite a lot. Some of them could be mistaken for Reticulatus group musk melons. However, the Inodorus group's main distinguishing feature is their complete lack of perfume when fully ripe. Inodorus means 'odourless' in Latin. Like other melon groups their flesh may be orange or green, but it can also be white in colour. Round honeydew melons are the best known of the Inodorus group. Football-shaped casaba melons, sometimes seen at Mediterranean and Middle Eastern grocers, and the Chinese hami melon, also belong here. Inodorus melons are sometimes collectively called winter melons because their thick, waxy skins allow them to keep much better than other kinds of melons; up to a couple of months if stored correctly.

There are several other, smaller groups of melons. In many ways these resemble melons' close relative the cucumber more closely than the three main melon groups. One occasionally grown in this part of the world is the Flexuosus group, the snake melons. Flexuosus means 'bendy' and these melons do indeed have long, thin, sinuous fruits which resemble cucumbers in both appearance and flavour.

East Asian cultivars of melon are grown mostly as vegetables rather than as 'fruit'. They don't have the sublime perfume and sweetness of Eurasian melons. The Conomon group of Asian melons look more like cucumbers and their seedy, thin-fleshed fruits are crisp and mostly bland in flavour. Conomon melons are used across Asia, from the Indian subcontinent through China, Korea and Japan, and south into the South East Asian countries. The Japanese have a particular fondness for them. Called *uri* in Japanese, they are picked young and pickled in salt or picked mature for fermenting in sake lees to make Nara's famously big-flavoured *narazuke* pickles. There is a separate class of *uri* melons in Japan called *makuwa uri* that are very sweet, but these varieties are the minority exception to the 'crisp and bland' rule. **Sakata's Sweet** is a *makuwa uri* variety that is starting to make an appearance in Australian seed catalogues.

The first melons to arrive in the USA did so with the Spanish in the sixteenth century. Native Americans took to this new crop with gusto and made it their own, so much so that English settlers arriving there a century later could have mistaken the melon for a native plant. Later waves of settlers added their own melons to the mix – from Eastern Europe, Italy, Russia and the Middle East. It was in the cultural melting pot of the USA that the melon reached its apogee in the early twentieth century.

VARIETIES

•

There are hundreds of varieties of heirloom melons. A few of them are a bit unprepossessing but the overwhelming majority are FABULOUS. Grow as many as you are able.

Determining when a melon is perfectly ripe takes practice. Some varieties obligingly 'slip' from the vine when they are ripe, particularly cantaloupes and also some musk melons. The layer of cells where the fruit meets its stem are like perforations along a row of stamps. When the fruit is ripe the cells crack and the melon falls off the vine. As soon as you see these cracks appearing at the point where the melon attaches to its stalk, you can harvest it. Most cantaloupes and musk melons give off a strong perfume when they are ripe, so smelling them is a good indicator, too. Inodorus melons neither slip nor smell, but these varieties tend to change colour when they are ripe so you need to keep an eye out for that. This change could be as obvious as fruits changing from black to yellow, or as subtle as a few paler spots developing here and there. Once you discover how superlative vine-ripened melons are you'll soon get the hang of it!

Ananas

ANANAS MELON

Ananas means 'pineapple' in French, so this melon is probably named on account of its caramel-yellow, oblong exterior and pale yellow-white flesh, unusual for a musk melon. Like the pineapple, Ananas also has a fine, fruity flavour.

Armenian cucumber/
Snake melon

This bizarre member of the Flexuosus group bears grey-green, ribbed fruits up to 1 metre in length and 5 centimetres in width. Not only do they look like cucumbers, they also taste like them: crisp and refreshing, not sweet. Don't bother waiting for them to ripen as they become corky and inedible with age. They are best picked when still immature and used in any way you would use a cucumber. This is an ancient Armenian variety which found its way to Italy in the sixteenth century.

Banana

This American heirloom has long, cylindrical fruits with greyish-yellow skin. Its pale orange flesh is very highly perfumed but it can be disappointingly lacking in sweetness and juice if not grown well. Perhaps it is better suited to the tropical summers of the east coast of the USA. Strictly speaking a cantaloupe type, Banana seems to sit on the fence between cantaloupes and the very un-melony Flexuosus-type melons.

BANANA MELON

Canary/Yellow Canary

Canary is a brilliant yellow, almost fluorescent Inodorus melon. It is football-shaped with wrinkled skin and pale green-white flesh. The flesh is more melting than other members of its group and beautifully sweet and fruity. A lovely, lovely variety, well worth growing at home.

Charentais

The Rolls Royce of French cantaloupes, traditionally grown in the Poitou-Charente region of France. Its fruits are softball-sized, spherical and smooth-skinned with greenish stripes over an ecru base colour. The flesh is salmon-orange, juicy, dense and richly flavoured.

CHARENTAIS MELON

Collective Farm Woman

Who could resist a melon with a name like this? A Ukrainian heirloom saved from oblivion when it was passed on to the American Seed Savers' Exchange by Russian seedswoman Marina Danilenko, who had obtained it from a woman from a collective farm in Ukraine, once the food bowl of the USSR. It was reintroduced by Seed Savers in 1993.

COLLECTIVE FARM
WOMAN MELON

Collective Farm Woman has round, relatively small fruits for an Inodorus type, only the size of a softball. They are dark green with tiny orange-yellow flecks which gradually join up to make the whole fruit orange-yellow as it goes on ripening. The flesh is greenish white, has a bit of crunch to it, and is sweet and well flavoured. This variety stores quite well and is very forgiving of poor soil and inconsistent weather.

DELICE DE LA TABLE MELON

Délice de la Table

Literally 'delight of the table', this French heirloom cantaloupe is cut from the same cloth as Prescott Fond Blanc. It looks like a warty, ugly little pumpkin. Smaller in size, slightly more spherical in shape and blotchy orange in colour, Délice de la Table is also perhaps also slightly less intense in flavour than Prescott Fond Blanc.

Fordhook Gem

Virtually unknown in Australia, this large 'nutmeg' type musk melon was bred as a commercial variety by the venerable Burpee seed company in 1967. The fruits are large and nutmeg-shaped, with prominent sutures and fully netted. Inside the flesh is pea-green, juicy, sweet and complex, lacking the muskiness of the orange-fleshed musk melons. An excellent variety that had the rug pulled out from under it by the advent of F1 hybrid melons.

Hale's Best

This heirloom musk melon is the nearest thing to supermarket rockmelons. It is a biggish melon with characteristic beige-grey, fully netted skin lacking prominent sutures. The skin encloses pale orange, musky-scented, almost savoury flesh. Hale's Best was developed as a commercial variety in California in the 1920s and became the benchmark upon which modern F1 hybrids were modelled.

Ha'Ogen

If you think you don't like melons, try growing this cantaloupe variety. It couldn't be more different to your average supermarket melon. These fruits are spherical, somewhat bigger than a softball, and striped with dark green over a gold and green background. The emerald-green flesh matches the outer colour scheme perfectly. Ha'Ogen's flesh is gloriously

HAOGEN MELON

perfumed and dripping with juice, and the flavour is so fruity that it tastes almost artificial. It has none of the muskiness of the netted-skin rockmelons.

Ha'Ogen is probably Hungarian in origin, but has come to us via Israel. It gets its name from a kibbutz called Ha'Ogen, Hebrew for 'the anchor'. Ha'Ogen is a robust, vigorous cultivar that is much more forgiving of less-than-perfect conditions than other melons. It is a great one to grow at home.

Jenny Lind

An American heirloom named for a Swedish singing superstar of the nineteenth century, Jenny Lind is a small musk melon with very attractive turban-shaped fruits. These have a distinct 'button' on one end, just like the Turk's Turban pumpkin. The skin is yellow-green, netted all over, and the flesh is green and very sweet.

Minnesota Midget

This is an American musk melon bred at the University of Minnesota in 1948. It bears tennis ball-sized fruits on compact vines. The skin is pale orange and lightly netted with orange flesh. Possibly not the most excitingly flavoured of all melons, but a good choice for smaller gardens and areas where summers are short.

Noir des Carmes

'Black of the Carmelites' is a French heirloom cantaloupe, possibly identical to the 'Black Rock' cantaloupe mentioned in Abercrombie & Mawe's *Every Man His Own Gardener* of 1767. Noir des Carmes won't win any beauty contests. It has slightly flattened, medium-sized fruits, lobed like pumpkins. The skin is black-green turning to dull caramel-orange and splitting around the stalk as it ripens. The flesh is a rather dull, pale orange. However, the flavour is intense. This melon has only just become available in Australia. Try it.

Piel de Sapo

Piel de Sapo means 'toad skin' in Spanish. Not, perhaps, the best advertisement for this luscious melon, but apt just the same. It is a casaba-type melon, commonly encountered in Mediterranean countries and ideally suited to hot, dry climates. It has dark green, furrowed, warty skin and pale greenish white flesh, very refreshing and succulent.

PRESCOTT FOND BLANC MELON

Prescott Fond Blanc

A spectacularly ugly French heirloom cantaloupe derived from English germplasm, hence the English name 'Prescott'. At first glance it looks like a baby pumpkin. Its warty skin is a dirty cream colour. But within this ugly exterior lies treasure. The flesh is pale orange, perfumed and well-flavoured. It is prone to being rather thick-skinned and thin-fleshed but when well grown this melon is a real beauty.

Queen Anne's pocket melon

This rare and unique melon (a member of the obscure Dudaim group) has been in cultivation for a thousand years, long before any of the Queen Annes came along. It bears small, oval fruits the size and shape of a goose egg. Smooth and yellow, painted with cinnabar leopardskin stripes, the fruits are extremely beautiful, resembling works of lapidary more than vegetables. They have an unbelievably strong, bubblegum perfume. It makes your mouth water. But therein lies the rub, for they have no flavour whatsoever. Queen Anne's pocket melon is an not an eating melon but a *cosmetic* melon; one to be secreted in jacket pockets and handbags to scent the wearer's person. If you can get hold of the seeds this is a fun novelty to grow.

MOON AND STARS WATERMELON

WATERMELONS

The watermelon (*Citrullus lanatus*) is native to southwestern Africa, where its wild ancestors still grow today. Watermelons are adapted to arid climates, preferring to grow in hot desert sands under cloudless skies. They germinate, grow furiously and reproduce during the short windows of opportunity when the rains come. The vines die when the water runs out, but not before setting enormous quantities of seeds which hold tight, cocooned in their life support pod – the watermelon fruit – until the rains come again.

Like melons, watermelons were grown in Egypt by 2000 BCE. The Greeks and Romans knew them, too. The watermelon was traded around the Mediterranean during the Middle Ages. It was particularly esteemed by the Arabs and Ottoman Turks, finding its way to Spain courtesy of the Moors. The Spanish took watermelons to the Americas from Spain, and African landraces arrived with slaves from Africa. America thus became the rendezvous for a great diversity of genetic material. Watermelons thrived in the hot southern states of America and there they reached their zenith.

If the Japanese go to extraordinary lengths to grow perfect musk melons, their efforts with watermelons are even more ridiculous. Not satisfied with eating paltry *round* watermelons, the Japanese grow their watermelons inside plastic moulds to give them particular shapes. The first artificially shaped watermelon to hit the shelves was the cube. Cubic watermelons were ostensibly developed so that they could be packed and distributed more efficiently than round ones. In addition, it was said, square watermelons were the way of the future because they would fit better into tiny Japanese refrigerators. It was about efficiency. This flimsy argument fell over pretty comprehensively with the introduction of hourglass-shaped watermelons, pyramidal watermelons, love heart-shaped watermelons and watermelons moulded into bug-eyed faces, none of which are known for stacking particularly well. In more cynical moments one suspects that moulded watermelons are little more than a marketing gimmick. Consumers certainly pay a premium price for them. A cubic watermelon will set you back about $100, a love heart $400, a face-shaped watermelon $600, an hourglass (are you sitting down?) $800 and a pyramidal one (get the defibrillator) costs nearly $1000. To think we used to feed watermelons to the pigs on Aunty Gladys' farm.

The latest boondoggle in watermelon breeding is seedless varieties. Spitting out seeds has been part of the fun of eating watermelons for 4000 years. Now it seems that spitting out seeds has become just too time-consuming and inconvenient for busy, important people like us. Hence seedless hybrid varieties have become the norm. Unable to reproduce themselves like seedy old heirloom watermelons can, seedless watermelons are of course first-generation (F1) crosses that need to be remade over and over again. This in turn means that seed companies can patent them and extract a premium price from buyers. Honestly, people – is spitting out watermelon seeds such a terrible tribulation that we need to hand control of their breeding over to private corporations?

WATERMELONS AND THEIR PEOPLE
BLACKTAIL MOUNTAIN

•

Blacktail Mountain is a modern heirloom bred by Glenn Downs as recently as the 1970s. Taking Gregor Mendel's pioneering pea breeding experiments as his inspiration, Glenn used traditional selective breeding techniques to try to develop a watermelon with cold tolerance and a short growing season in mind, since these were the limitations which prevented him from growing ripe watermelons in the mountains of Idaho where he lived. What Glenn came up with was a stable, open-pollinated strain of watermelon which tolerates temperature fluctuation and ripens very early. All this by a teenage boy in just four years. No transgenic modification, no secretive hybridisation with intellectual property rights attached, no massive R&D budget to be recouped, no plant variety patenting. Just a boy wanting to grow a decent watermelon and happy to share. Horticulture is richer for his work.

BLACKTAIL MOUNTAIN WATERMELON

VARIETIES

•

There are two kinds of watermelon. The ones with which we are most familiar are those grown for the sweet, soft flesh surrounding the seeds (called a 'placenta' in botanical parlance). Other varieties are grown for their thick, juicy rinds. These are called the 'citron' watermelons. The flesh of citron watermelons is bland and crunchy; you wouldn't look at it twice. However, when the rind is candied, or made into jam or pickles, it is transformed into something quite delicious. Citron watermelons keep for months and you need a hefty cleaver or axe to cut them open.

Blacktail Mountain

Blacktail Mountain's fruits look like beautiful black soccer balls when ripe, and have a thin rind and plenty of good red flesh. An excellent variety for areas with shorter or cooler summers.

Carolina Cross/Weeks North Carolina Giant

Competition fruits of Carolina Cross have weighed in at a whopping 118 kilograms. This leviathan is definitely the one to grow if you have a football team to feed. Carolina Cross was selected by North Carolina seedsman Edward Weeks in the 1960s. The fruits are very long, apple-green with dark green tiger stripes and pink flesh. In non-competition situations fruits average somewhere in the region of 60 centimetres in length and 20 kilograms in weight, which is still quite big enough, thank you.

Cream of Saskatchewan

CREAM OF SASKATCHEWAN
WATERMELON

A small, round watermelon with pale green skin striped with dark green. Its flesh is very pale yellow-white with a very sweet, refined flavour. You will never see this watermelon at market because the fruits split as soon as they are ripe. Despite its Canadian-sounding name Cream of Saskatchewan's origins are obscure. It was first listed by the Seed Savers Exchange in 1984.

Golden Midget

It is notoriously difficult to judge when a watermelon is ripe. Nothing is more irritating than picking a watermelon only to find white, sugarless flesh inside.

Plant breeders Elwyn Meader and Albert Yeager of the University of New Hampshire wanted to breed a watermelon that showed you when it was ripe. Golden Midget was the result in 1958. When Golden Midget's fruits are ripe, not only they but also the nearby leaves turn golden yellow. This small, salmon-fleshed variety needs plenty of heat to develop good flavour.

GOLDEN MIDGET
WATERMELON

Moon and Stars

This iconic American heirloom watermelon helped to kick off the whole heritage seed revival. First introduced as Sun, Moon and Stars by Peter Henderson in 1926, it is unique in that both the fruits and the foliage are spatter-painted with bright yellow dots. Often each fruit has one or two spots much bigger than the rest – the sun and moon – surrounded by a galaxy of tiny stars. The round or pear-shaped fruits have a background colour of midnight-green. Inside the flesh can be pink, apricot or yellow depending on the strain. This gorgeous watermelon nearly fell into oblivion just sixty years after its introduction. Luckily it was tracked down by Kent Whealy, co-founder of the fledgling Seed Savers Exchange in Iowa, still being grown and preserved by a single individual, Merle Van Doren of Missouri. Seed Savers reintroduced it in 1982.

Orangeglo

A big, oblong watermelon with 'normal' apple-green, tiger-striped skin. Inside, however, the flesh is bright mango-orange with excellent flavour right to the pith. An outstanding, robust and productive variety.

Red Seeded Citron

This variety has beautiful round fruits with blotchy skins and white flesh. Like all citron types its flesh is white and unpalatable but it makes beautiful jams and preserves. There is a green seeded citron variety, too, but the one with red and fawn seeds is more common.

Sugar Baby

This is what the Americans call an 'icebox' watermelon – one that is small enough to fit in the fridge. It looks for all the world like a cannonball, black and spherical. The flesh is pale pink and sweet. It was introduced in 1955 and is still a good variety for home gardens as it is productive, quick-cropping and compact.

CHAPTER THREE

THE

Grass

FAMILY

BAMBOO

(Phyllostachys edulis)

The influential German plant breeder Karl Foerster called grasses 'the hair of the world'. He was right. Vast tracts of our planet are carpeted with grass of one sort or another. From the wide savannahs of southern Africa to the wind-blasted islands of the subantarctic, grasses are everywhere. There is even one species of grass that hunkers down in rocky crags on Antarctica itself; one of only two flowering plants found on that frozen continent.

The grass family (Poaceae) is undoubtedly the most economically important of all plant families. The bulk of calories consumed by humankind comes from grain crops – wheat, rice, barley, oats, maize and millet. Indeed, grasses have shaped our species' history. Due to their phenomenally abundant seeds, which can be stored for long periods, and their willingness to grow where we want them to, grasses catalysed the most important turning point in human history: the Neolithic agricultural revolution. Ten thousand years later, humankind still relies on the same handful of grass species to support our burgeoning population. Put quite starkly, without grasses we would starve. Ironically, the grass family also gives people in rich nations the means to grow fat and unhealthy thanks to the ubiquity of cane sugar and high-fructose corn syrup.

The grass family has not only fed us but also sheltered us for millennia. Thatching made from grasses and structures made from bamboos – the giants of the grass family – have long been used to keep out the weather. In Asia's booming mega-cities you can still see bamboo scaffolding being used in the construction of steel and glass skyscrapers. In Japan, traditional bamboo and rice straw structures are still highly valued for their rustic beauty and impermanence. Bamboos provide an important source of food in Asia, in the form of their tender young shoots. However, there is really only one grass that qualifies as an heirloom vegetable: corn.

BAMBOO SHOOTS

PERUVIAN HEIRLOOM CORN

CORN — SWEET, POPPING & MAIZE

Imagine a field of glossy cornstalks, creaking in the summer breeze, drenched in a golden afternoon light. A scene of perfect wholesomeness...or is it? In fact, corn is one of the most manipulative of all plants. For 9000 years, corn has used humankind as a pawn in its quest for world domination. It has used us to expand its empire from a tiny area of southern Mexico to cover vast swathes of agricultural land around the globe.

Domesticated corn (*Zea mays*) is descended from one or more related Central American grasses called *teosinte* in the Nahuatl language of the Aztec. You would never recognise the teosintes as the progenitors of corn. They produce small ears of up to a dozen kernels, each enclosed in a very hard seed coat. Like other wild grasses, when teosintes' seeds are ripe the head shatters and the seeds fall to the ground. Teosintes' seed cases are tooth-breakingly hard and the seeds are difficult to collect because they scatter so easily. None of these attributes makes the teosintes ideal candidates for a human food source. However, they must also have possessed a degree of genetic variability and a propensity to mutate, making them ripe for domestication.

Through selective breeding and natural hybridisation, maize, or corn, was domesticated, probably mostly from *Zea mays* subsp. *parviglumis*. At some point teosinte's tiny heads of heavily armoured seeds morphed into corn's huge cobs, studded with hundreds of naked seeds. But now corn had a problem. Unlike its wild ancestors, it was unable to disperse its seeds. The seeds of domesticated corns stay embedded in their heavy, woody cobs, which eventually slump to the ground at the foot of the mother plant. It's not a recipe for survival, let alone world domination. Yet by giving up the ability for its seed heads to shatter and disperse, corn made itself more attractive to humans. Seeds which stayed on the cob were easy for us to collect, store and transport. Corn became reliant on humans to distribute its genes. And spread them far and wide we did.

From about 2500 BCE corn began its expansion from its Mexican heartland to as far north as Canada and as far south as Chile. In Peru it flourished and diversified. Cold-tolerant strains were selected in the Peruvian Andes and tropical strains in the steamy Peruvian lowlands. Drought-tolerant strains were selected by the Pueblo peoples of the US desert states. Corn was the basis of the great pre-Colombian cultures. It was a staple for the Moche, Inca and Maya. The magnificent empire of the Aztec was dependent on it, together with beans. The Aztec slashed vast tracts of forest to make way for the cultivation of corn. The Aztec maize god Centeotl was one of the most revered in their pantheon and much of their religious year revolved around the cultivation and harvest of corn. It seems that the tables had turned; humans were now dependent on corn for their survival.

Corn's next conquest was the Old World. The Spanish took corn back to Europe from the Caribbean around 1500, calling it by its Taíno name, *mahiz*, whence 'maize'. It spread as far into northern Europe as it could. From Spain and Portugal, corn travelled to the colonies in Africa and Asia, where it was eagerly adopted for both human consumption and stockfeed.

Today, it is estimated that corn provides about 20 per cent of the calories consumed by the human species. In poorer countries corn is consumed as . . . corn. As a grain, in other words. However, in richer nations corn is consumed indirectly, in the form of meat from corn-fed livestock, and as high-fructose corn syrup used as a sweetener in processed foods. Ironically, corn is simultaneously keeping the poor from starvation and killing the rich with lifestyle diseases.

For most of its history, corn has been used as a cereal crop. Sweetcorn – the 'vegetable' form of corn – is a relative newcomer on the scene. Even newer are the varieties being bred not for eating but for converting into biofuel, a phenomenon that raises all kinds of interesting questions about our relationship with food and our environment. Is growing a crop to put into cars better or worse for the environment than using petroleum-based oil? Is using arable land for growing car 'food' a good use of that increasingly scarce resource? Is using oil to grow an oil substitute defeating the purpose of the exercise? The answers to these questions are not straightforward.

Corn is not only a raw material for fuelling people, livestock and cars, but industry as well. It finds its way into products as diverse as plastics, explosives and pharmaceuticals. Corn is so important as an industrial raw product that it is vital that it remains cheap. The USA government, normally so keen on 'letting the market decide', heavily subsidies American farmers to grow corn in order to keep its price artificially low. Corn clearly has the American economy by the short-and-curlies.

In recent years it has been estimated that 85 per cent of the USA's corn crop was composed of a handful of genetically modified strains. GM corns have been altered to produce the insecticidal *Bacillus thuringiensis* (Bt) toxin (which is, incidentally, used in its natural form in organic farming systems), and to resist the herbicide glyphosate. The USA's vast GM monocultures may be resistant to insect attack and herbicide use, but what aren't they resistant to? Given its utter reliance on corn, perhaps it is unwise for the USA to put all its eggs in the one corn basket, even if it suits biotech companies for them to do so. Let us not forget the Irish potato famine.

Corn's mother country, Mexico, has recently begun growing genetically modified corn. Corn is wind pollinated, so one wonders what will happen when GM pollen finds its way to ancient Mexican landraces of corn and ancestral teosintes. Will we see a race of insect- and herbicide-resistant super weeds? Will the companies that are now so anxious to protect their 'intellectual property' rights be equally anxious to take responsibility for such an eventuality? We shall see.

What is clear is that corn's quest for world domination continues. From its homeland in Mexico, corn has come to cover vast tracts of the earth's surface. It has inveigled itself into so many human activities and made itself so indispensable to us that we are enslaved by it. Checkmate.

CORN AND ITS PEOPLE:
THE STORY OF PAINTED MOUNTAIN

•

Dave Christensen comes from the cold, dry northern plains of Montana, USA. Modern hybrid corns, selected for the midwestern corn belt of the USA, won't grow where Dave lives so thirty years ago he set himself the task of breeding the most cold- and drought-hardy variety of open-pollinated corn in the world.

Dave discovered that there had once been many cultivars of corn in the harsh northern Rockies and great plains. These tough varieties had sustained Native Americans and frontier colonists for generations but they were now teetering on the edge of extinction, some of them maintained only by single families. If these corns were lost, their genes would be lost forever. Dave realised that those genes might be useful to people living in harsh climates around the world. He decided to rescue as many of these heirlooms as he could and incorporate them into his breeding work before they became extinct. The corn which Dave bred used over 70 traditional Native American heirlooms in its pedigree. He named it Painted Mountain. Painted Mountain has since proved itself in harsh climates in other parts

PAINTED MOUNTAIN CORN

of the world, including rugged Ryanggang province in North Korea, where childhood malnutrition is rife. Painted Mountain is a corn that is helping to feed the world's poor, on the ground right now. It was bred the old-fashioned way by a single concerned individual with no patents and no genetic modification.

Painted Mountain is one of the most beautiful varieties of corn in existence. Its big cobs grow on compact plants just 1.5 metres tall, showing lots of purple in the foliage and stems. Each cob has a different, unique colour scheme. Some have solid colours, others are spotted with two, three or four different colours, others striped with rows of contrasting colour. Each individual kernel looks like a different-coloured jewel: garnets, rubies, topaz, Ceylon sapphires, and champagne and pink diamonds. Those colours come from anthocyanins, plant pigments that benefit human health due to their antioxidant qualities. Painted Mountain also contains unusually high levels of vitamin A and the amino acid lysine.

The Quechua people of Peru derive a rich purple dye from black corn.

VARIETIES

•

Corn can be divided into several different categories according to its use. Sweetcorn is the most familiar, eaten straight off the cob when young and tender. There are also dent corns and flint corns for grinding into corn meal, hominy or grits; soft corn for grinding into flour; and special popping corns for making popcorn. Everyone thinks corn is yellow. Actually it comes in an enormous range of colours including black, red, orange, blue and white. One ancient Mexican variety, **Oaxaca Green Dent**, is an amazing shade of moss green. There are hundreds of varieties of open-pollinated corn, of which only a measly few are available in this country.

There are three kinds of sweetcorn: open-pollinated heirloom sweetcorns, Sugar Enhanced F1 hybrids and Supersweet F1 hybrids. F1 hybrid sweetcorns are much sweeter than traditional open-pollinated corns, although the flavour of the Supersweet hybrids is frankly a bit one-dimensional – sugary with not a lot of corn flavour. Sugar Enhanced F1 hybrids are less sweet than Supersweets but at least taste like corn. Supersweet F1 hybrids are highly bred beasts that have been developed with commercial production, not home gardeners, in mind. They require hothouse conditions to perform well: consistent high temperatures and irrigation. If they are pollinated by an heirloom or a Sugar Enhanced hybrid corn their kernels become starchy and the crop is ruined. Sugar Enhanced F1 hybrids are better choice for home gardeners as they are not so fussy about who pollinates them. Heirlooms are the easiest to grow, being much more tolerant of fluctuating conditions (like what happens in the real world). Have the water boiling before you pick them, though: the sugars of heirlooms are quickly converted to starch.

Bloody Butcher

An American dent corn from the 1840s. Impressive 30-centimetre cobs carry hundreds of blood-red and bull's blood-coloured kernels used for making cornmeal, definitely not for eating straight from the cob. The cobs grow on spectacular cornstalks up to 4 metres tall.

Golden Bantam

Golden Bantam was first released by Vilmorin in 1902. It bears 15-centimetre cobs with eight rows

GOLDEN BANTAM CORN

of seed on compact plants that can reach 1.5 metres. However, the variety grown in Australia is an improved version released twenty years later. The plant is larger in all its parts, with twelve rows of tender, pale yellow kernels on cobs that can grow to 20 centimetres long. Golden Bantam is the most reliable heirloom sweetcorn for home gardeners.

Hopi Blue

A flint corn traditionally grown by the Hopi people of Arizona and New Mexico, used as a staple food and in ceremonies. Hopi Blue ears are covered with dark blue-black kernels which make amazing blue tortillas and corn chips and can be eaten as sweetcorn when very young.

Stowell's Evergreen

I have never seen this white sweetcorn variety offered in Australia but its story needs to be told. This variety was bred and refined over several years by farmer Nathaniel Newman Stowell in New Jersey by crossing two Native American heirloom corns. By 1848 he had perfected his new strain. In 1855 he sold two ears of it to a friend for $4 on the understanding that the seed was for personal use only. Stowell's duplicitous 'friend' immediately sold the ears to Thoburn & Co seed company for US$20 000. They released it commercially the following year. Stowell's 'friend' obviously made a huge profit but it can't have done much for his karma.

True Gold

True Gold has pale yellow kernels on a 20-centimetre cob that hold their sweetness well although they do become chewy the yellower the kernels get. Later cropping than Golden Bantam.

TRUE GOLD CORN

CHAPTER FOUR

THE

Carrot

FAMILY

(Anethum graveolens)

The carrot family, or Apiaceae, contains over 3500 species. Apiaceae comes from *apium*, the Latin name for celery. The old family name Umbelliferae is still in regular use, too. It refers to the fact that this family's flowers are borne in compound *umbels*. An umbel is a type of inflorescence that develops much as a firework does: a single stem shoots up to a certain point and then explodes into a starburst of smaller branches, each of which divides still further into a shower of tiny flowers. The word umbel is distantly related to the word umbrella (both eventually trace their origin to the Latin word for a sun shade). The flower heads of this family do indeed resemble little umbrellas. Members of the Apiaceae family are still routinely referred to as *umbellifers* by gardeners, a lovely word befitting plants with a lovely flowering habit.

The umbellifers are very familiar to us. Most of us have a selection of umbellifers in our kitchen cupboards. Coriander, parsley, chervil, cumin, caraway, anise, dill and fennel are all umbellifers. There are also some less well-known herbs such as lovage, angelica, alexanders and myrrh, or sweet cicely. Umbellifers contain aromatic oils in their seeds and foliage, hence their use as culinary and medicinal plants. Traditional Chinese medicine (TCM) makes use of literally dozens of umbellifers. Two of the most commonly used herbs in TCM are umbellifers: *dang gui*, often romanised as *dong quai* (*Angelica sinensis*), and *chai hu* (*Bupleurum chinense*).

Eryngium foetidum is a kind of sea holly native to Central and South America, widely used as a herb in Latin American and South East Asian cooking. In Australia you are most likely to encounter its hollow-stemmed, sawtooth leaves floating in a bowl of tom yum. The leaves are subtly tangy and aromatic and add something really special to a dish. I have always simply called this herb 'secret ingredient' since I am yet to hear a user-friendly common name. A friend with a Lao background once told me laconically, 'Yeah, we just call that one French mint' but that is just plain confusing because it is neither French nor particularly minty. Vietnamese-speakers call it *ngo gai* and Thai speakers call it *pak chee farang*, meaning 'foreigners' coriander'. This is probably as good as anything given its coriander-like flavour and New World provenance. In its native Latin America it is known as *culantro* – not to be confused with *cilantro*, the Latin American name for coriander (*Coriandrum sativum*).

The spice asafoetida (*Ferula assa-foetida*), called *hing* in Hindi, rejoices in the common name of 'devil's dung' in English owing to its very strong, rather nasty smell. Unlike most spices it is not the seeds or leaves of asafoetida that are utilised. Rather, a thick resin is harvested from the stems and roots of this giant, fennel-like plant. Despite its rank smell, asafoetida resin is an essential spice in Indian cuisine, used in tiny quantities. When cooked its flavour mellows to a warm oniony flavour.

Pappadums owe their unique taste to asafoetida. Asafoetida is also suspected of being one of the secret spices in Worcestershire sauce. Next time you drink a Bloody Mary as a hangover cure, you can cheer yourself up wondering whether or not there is devil's dung in it.

Another species of *Ferula*, galbanum (*F. gummosa*) also has its scented resin harvested. Native to Iran, galbanum has been traded since ancient times. It is mentioned in the Old Testament as a burned incense. Galbanum is still used in perfumery as a 'green' note. Its piney, resinous fragrance has found its way into such iconic perfumes as Chanel No. 19.

Asafoetida and galbanum once had a mysterious ancient cousin called silphium. Silphium was also a resin collected from an umbellifer, almost certainly another species of *Ferula*. Some scholars have pointed to *Ferula tingitana* as a possible identity for silphium but this is far from certain. Silphium was used as a richly flavoured spice and also in medicine. Its most famous application was in birth control. It seems to have been the world's first morning-after pill, preventing fertilised eggs from implanting in the womb of women who took it. It has been mooted that the ubiquitous 'love heart' symbol, first seen in ancient times and still in use today, began life as a stylised representation of a silphium seed: a symbol of carefree, erotic love. Maybe, maybe not. In any case, silphium was in hot demand throughout antiquity. The Minoans and Egyptians knew of it and later the Greeks and Romans. Herodotus tells us that the only known source of silphium was a narrow coastal strip of land near the ancient city of Cyrene, now in Libya. Silphium was the pillar of the Cyrenian economy. It was so important to them that their coins were stamped with its image. The Romans in particular couldn't get enough of it. High demand led to soaring prices as silphium became increasingly scarce. By the first century CE it was worth more than its weight in silver. No doubt some shrewd Cyrenian businesspeople were rubbing their hands together and making a motza out of this increasingly scarce commodity. Then, in the second century, silphium disappeared forever, driven to extinction by over-harvesting. The city of Cyrene never recovered. It struggled on for another century or so before it too became extinct, a victim of its own suicidal greed. All those wealthy Cyrenians are worm food now and their city is a ruin. But their pathetic legacy remains: a handful of metal coins embossed with the image of the plant they annihilated.

On the subject of antiquity and suicide, no exploration of the carrot family would be complete without mention of hemlock (*Conium maculatum*). Hemlock is the poison that Socrates used to kill himself after he was sentenced to death by the Athenian state for thinking too much. Hemlock looks alarmingly like the herb sweet cicely, only it is much more common. A widespread agricultural weed in Australia, hemlock's lacy white flowers are often to be seen in damp places on farms and roadsides in late spring and early summer. Hemlock is easily distinguished from other umbellifers by its purple-spotted stems (*maculatum* means 'spotted') and by its mousey smell.

HEMLOCK (*Conium maculatum*)

The carrot family contains some beautiful ornamental plants. First among these are the Queen Anne's Laces. Queen Anne's Lace is a common name that gets applied to more than one species of umbellifer on account of their white, lacy flower heads. The wild carrot *Daucus carota*, tall annuals *Ammi majus* and *A. visnaga*, short annual *Orlaya grandiflora* and perennial *Anthriscus sylvestris* all share this common name. Even deadly hemlock gets called Queen Anne's Lace. This potential for confusion is the exact reason why botanists and gardeners use scientific names rather than common names.

Flowering umbellifers come in other colours besides white. *Astrantia* flowers can fall anywhere on a spectrum from pale green through dusty pinks to dark plum. *Smyrnium perfoliatum* is acid yellow. Eryngiums, the sea hollies, come in unbelievable metallic blues, usually with a ruff of thistle-like spines. *Angelica gigas* has vampish burgundy flowers atop black-purple stems: very moody.

SEA HOLLY (*Eryngium*)   MASTERWORT (*Astrantia*)

Umbellifers almost always have foliage that is divided into smaller leaflets, sometimes these are very fine indeed. Bronze fennel is an ornamental variety of the well-known herb with gauzy bronze-purple foliage instead of the usual dark green, making it very useful as a foil for flowers and bold foliage plants. *Ferula communis*, an ornamental relative of asafoetida, makes impressive rosettes of feathery leaves followed by 3-metre-tall spires of golden yellow floral spheres. Its sturdy, ribbed stems are said to have inspired the fluted columns of classical Greek architecture.

You could be forgiven for thinking that *Melanoselinum decipiens* from the island of Madeira is a palm tree. With a 2-metre-tall, ringed trunk and huge, hanging palm-like leaves, it looks for all the world like a palm. Only its classic carroty flowers give lie to its disguise. It's a very easy plant to grow; jungly and lots of fun.

Most members of the carrot family are annuals, biennials or short-lived perennials but a few are woody shrubs. *Bupleurum fruticosum*, the 'shrubby hare's ear', is a beautiful evergreen shrub from the Mediterranean with neat, waxy leaves and the family's trademark umbellate flowers. It is a first-class drought-tolerant shrub for southern Australian gardens, always neat and handsome. I can't understand why it's not more widely grown. Perhaps because, like all umbellifers, its seed has short viability and is prone to erratic germination, neither of which the horticultural industry has much stomach for.

Some of the most interesting umbellifers in the world come from that ark of bizarre flora, New Zealand. Spaniards or spear grass (*Aciphylla* spp.) are perennials with stiletto-sharp foliage growing in porcupine-like defensive clumps, presumably as protection against New Zealand's extinct race of giant flightless birds, the moa. Although viciously armed, spaniards are extremely beautiful, with metallic foliage in shades of burnished copper, pewter and gold, and stunning flower spikes up to 3 metres tall in the biggest species.

SHRUBBY HARE'S EAR (*Bupleurum fruticosum*)

On New Zealand's frigid, wind-blasted subantarctic islands, a giant über-carrot has evolved: the Campbell Island Carrot (*Anisotome latifolia*). The Campbell Island Carrot is one of the largest species in the community of surreal, supersize perennials that dominate the island, the awesomely titled *megaherbs*. Campbell Island Carrots form metre-wide rosettes of leathery, dark green leaves like parsley on steroids. Every so often the rosettes send up an inflorescence as tall as a person. Hundreds of pale pink flowers are arranged in heads like billowing bunches of marshmallows. It must be quite a sight to see giant carrots flowering alongside giant yellow lilies

GIANT SPANIARD (*Aciphylla scott-thomsonii*)

and giant purple daisies in their vast megaherb meadows, punctuated here and there with the occasional crazy-eyed albatross. Like being on a different planet.

Before moving on to the heirloom vegetable members of the family, there are some minor Apiaceae crops that deserve explanation. Skirret (*Sium sisarum*) is a tall perennial wetland plant from Asia with bunches of long, thin, white roots. It was much appreciated in Europe for its sweet, parsnip-like flavour from the Middle Ages, especially by people farming on marginal land, but it never really took off in the way parsnips and carrots did, so no breeding work has been done with it. Arracacha (*Arracacia xanthorrhiza*) is a similar type of crop from the Andes. From a celery-like plant grows a big rootstock of white, yellow or purple, carrot-like tubers. Arracacha is quite popular in parts of South America, particularly Brazil, but so far it has not enjoyed the international popularity of its compatriot, the potato. Rock samphire (*Crithmum maritimum*, not to be confused with true marsh samphire (*Salicornia europaea*)) is a coastal European native once harvested wild and sold at market, still occasionally seen today in European fishmongers. A succulent plant, its leaves are juicy with a resinous, salty flavour that marries well with fatty fish. Rock samphire is very easy to grow in a pot or in the garden (true samphire is impossible to grow unless you are unlucky enough to live in a tidal salt marsh).

PURPLE, LOBBERICHER AND BELGIAN WHITE CARROTS

CARROTS

When I was a lad I was told to eat my carrots because they would help me see in the dark. In the past, carrots have been prescribed for a litany of ailments from dog bites to syphilis and, predictably, as an aphrodisiac. (One can only imagine family meals in ancient Greece: 'Eat your carrots, son. They're aphrodisiac.')

When and where the carrot was transformed from a woody medicinal root into a succulent culinary vegetable is difficult to say. It might have happened more than once in more than one place as the wild carrot (*Daucus carota*) is native to a good swathe of Europe and western Asia. The Egyptians may have already known the cultivated carrot. Frescoes on tomb walls depict a conical root vegetable though frankly these are hardly conclusive. The Greeks collected wild carrots for medicine and possibly grew a cultivated carrot for food. In the first century CE the Greek physician Dioscorides described two root crops that could have been wild and cultivated carrots, calling them *staphylinos keras* and *staphylinos agrios*. By the late antique period the Romans clearly thought this is what he meant, too, because a sixth-century Byzantine edition of Dioscorides' pharmacopoeia *De Materia Medica*, still in its original Greek language (annotated here and there in Arabic) contains clear and beautifully illuminated depictions of a whitish wild carrot (*staphylinos agrios*) and, interestingly, what appears to be an orange cultivated carrot (*staphylinos keras*).

The early Romans had an irritating habit of referring to root vegetables interchangeably as *pastinaca* (from the verb *pastinare*, to dig up), perhaps in the way that some of us use the word 'spinach' to refer to both silverbeet and true spinach and 'shallot' to refer to both spring onions and true shallots. This makes it difficult to know which root vegetable Roman commentators were talking about. Probably in most cases they were referring to the parsnip but perhaps sometimes they meant carrots. By the second century the Romans were using the words *daucus* and *carota* for carrots.

Meanwhile in Afghanistan yellow and purple carrots with greyer, fuzzier foliage than their European cousins were in cultivation by the tenth century. Over the next two centuries Afghan carrots were introduced into Europe. The Moors took them to Spain in the eleventh century. By 1300 purple carrots were mentioned in Italian recipes. Yellow carrots were being cultivated in Flanders in the sixteenth century, possibly taken there by the region's Spanish overlords. The Europeans now had all the genetic material necessary to create modern, orange carrots. In spite of the sixth-century illustration of an orange carrot in the Byzantine *de Materia Medica* and reports of orange carrots from Syria, it seems that 'modern' orange carrots were bred in the Netherlands in the seventeenth century, probably by crossing yellow and purple carrots with European white carrots. Legend has it that orange carrots were bred by the Dutch as a novelty in honour of the House of Orange, the Dutch stadtholder (later, royal) family. It's a nice story, but there is nothing to suggest there is any truth in it. Be that as it may, the Dutch masters' paintings are riddled with depictions of orange carrots, so they must have been quite proud of them.

Once orange carrots got a foothold, they left all the other colours for dead. Maybe it had to do with taste. The old Afghan purple carrots are noticeably resinous in flavour and not too sweet. Yellow and white carrots are sweeter but very mild in flavour; some might go as far as to say insipid. Perhaps like Goldilocks' porridge, orange carrots were just right – sweet and well-flavoured without being either harsh or insipid.

Orange carrots, with their rich genetic heritage, made themselves more attractive to gardeners as well as gourmands. By the eighteenth century, different shapes and sizes of carrot were beginning to appear: stout ones, wedge-shaped ones, little round ones. They were being selected for different soil types and different climates. Some were proving themselves good for overwintering and some for eating young. Perhaps their bolt resistance improved, too. Wild carrots are annuals, flowering quickly in their first season without forming a big root. Cultivated carrots with ancient bloodlines tend to bolt fairly quickly too, but orange carrots are functionally biennials. That is, they grow for a whole season before flowering in their second. This means, of course, that they have a longer growing period in which to form a bigger root.

Whatever the reason for the popularity of orange carrots, in the nineteenth century they really diversified. Some of the carrots developed in France and the Netherlands in the nineteenth century are still grown commercially today.

CARROTS AND THEIR PEOPLE:
THE DRAGON'S TALE

•

The Dragon carrot is almost invariably sold as Purple Dragon in Australia. It is *not*, as the seed catalogues would have us believe, 'the original Afghan carrot' nor 'a 1000-year-old heirloom'. Dragon was, in point of fact, bred by Dr John Navazio, an American plant breeder from the Organic Seed Alliance, in 1995, using USDA germplasm collected in China. No doubt these factual errors will echo around the internet for decades to come and rob Dr Navazio of the kudos he deserves for breeding a modern heirloom. John continues the work of generations of plant breeders by applying traditional breeding techniques to develop the 'heirlooms of the future'. That is, he develops open-pollinated vegetable strains which are suited to modern, scaled-up organic farming. In his own words:

> Some companies thought the heirlooms were going to answer all the questions; I don't share that belief. Good heirlooms can certainly be used in the modern world but there's always room for improvement.

The Dragon carrot is certainly one of those improvements. Its sparse foliage allows for closer planting and much greater yields.

Ironically, several F1 purple carrot hybrids have been bred in recent years, trying to capture some of the cachet of their heirloom forebears. Purple Haze and Deep Purple are two such hybrids. Clearly, rock-related names are compulsory for purple carrots. Look forward to one called 'Smoke on the Water' any minute now.

DRAGON CARROT

VARIETIES

•

Carrots fall into several categories according to their cropping habits. Amsterdam and Nantes types crop early and are tender, sweet and crisp. They are the best varieties for eating raw. Chantenay types are robust and crop best over summer. Autumn King types are good for late sowings to hold in the ground over winter. They can be very large in size: horse carrots.

BELGIAN WHITE CARROT

Belgian White/Blanche à Collet Vert

A white, green-topped carrot with roots that can grow very large indeed – up to 50 centimetres long in loose soil. Belgian White was developed by the French seedsman Henry Vilmorin in the 1830s, as an experiment, from a wild carrot he found growing in Belgium. The English immediately pronounced this carrot fit only for horses and I'm inclined to agree with them. It is edible, of course, but its flavour is subtle (read 'insipid') and its texture is not exactly what you'd call 'crisp'. Like all carrots with primitive bloodlines it is prone to bolting in its first year.

Chantenay

The Chantenay group of carrots are rather butch-looking, square-shouldered carrots first introduced around 1820. Pale orange in colour and growing to around 15 centimetres in length, they are good carrots for heavy soils as they can punch their way through clay better than the delicate Nantes types. Chantenays are exceptionally sweet and crunchy but more heavy-duty than Nantes types, so they stand up better to long storage. In fact, they seem to improve with storage, becoming sweeter. There are several strains of Chantenay available such as Red Cored Chantenay and Royal Chantenay, all of them variations on a very good theme.

RED-CORED CHANTENAY
CARROT

Dragon

Robust and reliable, Dragon has a purple skin, pale orange flesh, a yellow core and a slightly spicy flavour. Its flesh is denser than that of crisp salad carrots like the Nantes types, making it a good carrot for cooking.

Kintoki

A Japanese heirloom carrot with very large, bright red roots.

KINTOKI CARROT

Lobbericher

This could be the root which Pliny the Elder mentions being grown in the Lower Rhine region. Named for the German (not Austrian, as some seed catalogues say) town of Lobberich, this carrot is notable for its beautiful canary-yellow colour. Lobbericher carrot has been considered primarily a stock feed carrot (or so-called 'field carrot') in the past. However, being quite sweet and not overly 'carrotty', it should not be discounted for human food. It certainly looks very pretty on the plate.

Parisian Market

This nineteenth-century French heirloom forms cute little orange roots the size and shape of squash balls. These are a boon to gardeners with heavy or stony soil, or no soil at all, because unlike most carrots they don't need deep, loose soil in order to form a long root. They perform very well in pots and indeed in potting mix, which is good news for balcony gardeners. The only minor drawback is that they are quite prone to splitting with age, so it is best to sow small runs of seed frequently rather than sowing lots all at once. They are delicious raw or lightly steamed, but they won't put up with extended cooking. An excellent carrot for beginner gardeners.

LOBBERICHER CARROT

Scarlet Nantes

A blunt-tipped, cylindrical, 15-centimetre-long orange carrot developed by the French seed company Vilmorin around 1850. Named for the French town of Nantes on the Loire river, this carrot is tender, sweet and as good as coreless; perfect for eating raw. There are several strains of Nantes-type carrots, such as Early Nantes and Nantes Half Long.

SCARLET NANTES CARROT

St Valery

St Valery was already considered an old variety when it was listed by the French seedsmen Vilmorin in 1885. It is a very high-quality carrot, producing orange, conical roots up to 25 centimetres long in good soils.

Western Red

A dinky-di Australian heirloom carrot, Western Red was our most important commercial variety before the introduction of hybrid varieties in the 1980s. Western Red is an Autumn King type carrot, bright orange, up to 30 centimetres in length with sturdy wide shoulders and a long taper. It's a real carrot's carrot. High yielding and disease resistant, this is a great variety for a late sowing to overwinter in the ground.

COBHAM PARSNIP

PARSNIP

The parsnip (*Pastinaca sativa*) is native to Eurasia. Wild parsnips, like wild carrots, have thin, branched, stringy-textured white roots. They are not much chop for eating. Perhaps parsnips were originally grown for their fragrant seeds, as a spice or medicine. Their hairy, resinous foliage gives many people a contact rash so it's unlikely that they were originally grown as a leaf crop. Exactly who is responsible for developing the plump sweet roots we know today is a mystery. White, wedge-shaped roots pop up in Roman art occasionally so perhaps it was them, or one of the cultures they colonised. The Romans used the same terms for carrots and parsnips interchangeably so it's difficult to know exactly what they were referring to.

By late medieval times parsnips were being grown as a staple crop in northern Europe. It's difficult to imagine a Europe without potatoes, but before potatoes arrived in Europe, parsnips and turnips were the root vegetables of choice. Parsnip roots convert their starch into sugar during frosty weather, so they were appreciated for their sweetness. Before sugar was common or affordable, parsnips were used as a sweetening agent in cakes and desserts, unthinkable as it is today. After potatoes were introduced from the New World and sugar became more available, the popularity of parsnips waned. In many parts of Europe they came to be thought of more as stock fodder than human food. However, parsnips retained a certain degree of popularity in northern Europe and in the nineteenth century enjoyed something of a resurgence there.

VARIETIES

•

The very long, tapering roots we know today emerged in the Netherlands and England during their heyday in the nineteenth century. Varieties with short, wedge-shaped roots and rounded, turnip-like roots developed across northern and central Europe, where they are still encountered today in varieties like **Kral** and **Halblange Weisse**. Unfortunately only a handful of parsnip varieties are available in Australia.

Cobham Improved Marrow
Usually shortened to simply Cobham, this reliable variety produces fine-textured, sweet, 20-centimetre roots.

Harris Model
This old favourite produces high-quality, fine-textured, sharply tapered roots 30 centimetres in length with a sweet, nutty flavour.

Hollow Crown
This English heirloom from the 1920s is the only variety routinely seen for sale in Australia. Its roots are slightly sunken at the top, hence its name. The roots are very wide at the top but quickly taper into a very thin point. They can be very long on well-dug soils, up to 60 centimetres in length.

HARRIS MODEL PARSNIP

Melbourne Whiteskin
A heavy-cropping late variety with wedge-shaped roots.

TALL UTAH CELERY

CELERY & CELERIAC

Celery (*Apium graveolens*) once enjoyed enormous popularity. Indeed the entire Apiaceae family is named for it. These days it plays second fiddle to the carrot.

Celery is native to the Mediterranean basin, where it grows in boggy places. It has been used in medicine and ritual since ancient times. Celery has turned up in several ancient grave sites, most notably in the tomb of the pharaoh Tutankhamun from 1325 BCE. The sixth-century BCE Greek colony of Selinunte in Sicily took its name from *selinon*, the Greek word for celery and parsley. Selinunte's coinage depicted a celery leaf.

For most of the time it has been associated with humans, celery was not recognisable as the juicy-stemmed vegetable we grow today. It resembled a super-sized parsley, grown for its pungent leaves and seeds. This wild form of celery (*A. graveolens* var. *secalinum*) still exists today as the herb smallage. It wasn't until the sixteenth century that celeries with fleshy leaf petioles began to be selected in Italy and France. These varieties are known as *A. graveolens* var. *dulce*: sweet celeries.

Celery is quite difficult to grow well. It needs a lot of water and a soil that is extremely rich in organic matter, reflecting its marshy origins. It is very sensitive to checks in its growth, meaning that if it dries out or suffers heat stress for even a day or two, it will bolt to seed, depriving you of your juicy crop. To get the sweetest, most tender stalks, celery plants need to be 'blanched' by excluding light from the developing stems. Traditionally this was done by drawing earth up over them or by tying paper cylinders around the stems. If you want to grow older celery varieties at home, be prepared to undertake this palaver. Newer varieties respond well to being closely planted, allowing them to blanch one another as they grow together. These so-called 'self-blanching' celeries are probably the best for home gardeners.

VARIETIES

•

Golden Self Blanching
A French heirloom from the 1880s that has stood the test of time. Vigorous, compact plants produce tender, delicately flavoured stems that blanch to a golden-green colour.

Red Stalk
An eighteenth-century heirloom with red-tinged stalks that blanch to pale pink. It has thin, stringy stalks with a very pungent flavour and it is prone to bolting. All things considered, it's not the best variety for modern backyards but it is very interesting from a historical point of view, giving gardeners an idea of how far celery breeding has come.

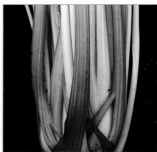

RED CELERY

Stringless American
A tall, stringless variety with very chunky stems and good flavour. This variety is sweet enough to be eaten unblanched.

Tall Utah
A tall, tightly bunched variety with stringless green stems that can be eaten without blanching.

STRINGLESS CELERY

CELERIAC

•

Celeriac is derived from the same wild species as celery, *Apium graveolens*. Celeriac was selected for its large, blocky root rather than its fleshy stems as celery was. Hence its botanical designation, var. *rapaceum*, literally the 'turnip bearing' celery.

Despite its lumpen appearance, celeriac is quite difficult to grow in our part of the world. It hates hot weather and is very prone to bolting to seed before it has had sufficient time to form its substantial root. Celeriac remains fairly uncommon in the marketplace in Australia. Perhaps because of its scarcity, celeriac has become something of a connoisseur's item in this country, appearing as a novelty on the menus of our fine dining establishments. This is more than a little ironic, since in its native Europe celeriac is so common that it is possible to buy it in vending machines! It can be had in little plastic trays from fast food joints across northern European and the former eastern bloc countries, engulfed in a thick mayonnaise dressing and euphemistically described as 'salad'. In Australia it is prepared in exactly the same way, only under the rather more grand title of 'remoulade'. This bizarre social disjunction aside, celeriac is a lovely and useful vegetable. It tastes much milder than its pungent cousin, celery, and has a texture which is both tender and crunchy at the same time.

If you want to challenge yourself, try growing celeriac. The only variety routinely seen in Australia is **Giant Prague**, widely considered to be the best variety. You might also find **White Alabaster**.

BRONZE FENNEL

FLORENCE FENNEL

Fennel (*Foeniculum vulgare*) is a well-known herb with finely cut, anise-scented leaves and yellow flowers. Its foliage is traditionally used with fish and its fragrant seeds find their way into all kinds of curries, sweets and herbal medicines.

Don't think that fennel is cute because it's a 'herb', however. Fennel can be a terrible environmental thug. It is actually listed as a noxious weed in certain parts of Australia, where it self-seeds rampantly along train lines and makes itself unwelcome on the edges of bushland.

Florence fennel is a special variety of fennel grown for its very swollen leaf bases, which form a fleshy 'bulb' rather than growing tall in the way that the herb fennel does. Florence fennel is harvested before it goes to seed, so it rarely has the chance to become weedy. Florence fennel is technically known as the Azoricum group of fennel, which suggests it is from the Azores. However, the scant evidence surrounding its history all points to medieval Italy as its place of origin.

Florence fennel is rarely sold by cultivar in Australia, although you might occasionally come across **Bianco Perfezione** or **Montebianco**.

BIANCO PERFEZIONE FENNEL

CHAPTER FIVE

THE

Cabbage

FAMILY

MANTOVANO CABBAGE

(Brassica oleracea)

The cabbage family, or Brassicaceae, contains nearly 4000 species distributed across well over 300 genera. The vegetable members of this family are a fascinating exercise in variation on a theme. A startling diversity of forms has been selected over a couple of thousand years – from the chunky cabbage to the elegant bok choy, leafy kale and knobbly swede – from just three wild ancestors. Apart from some very familiar vegetables, the brassica family also contains many other interesting culinary and ornamental plants.

Mustard (*Sinapis alba*), horseradish (*Armoracia rusticana*) and wasabi (*Wasabia japonica*) are members of the brassica family that many of us have a permanent lunch date with. Each of them produces a unique, eye-watering condiment, essential

WASABI

to certain culinary traditions. Horseradish lifts roast beef to a new level. Hot dogs *sans* mustard is just not the same and sushi without wasabi is unthinkable.

Watercress (*Nasturtium officinale*) is unique amongst the brassica crops in that it is essentially a wild wetland plant. It is not easy to cultivate. It is happiest in cold, alkaline, running water, but it can be grown in the garden with a bit of extra care. There are several edible land cresses but none is as good as watercress, with its unique nutty-pungent flavour and crunchy texture.

As well as vegetables, the brassica family contains some charming cottage flowers. They were popular in our grandparents' day but are now sadly neglected. It is apt, then, that one of the nicest ornamental brassicas is called the wallflower. Wallflowers (*Erysimum cheiri*) are overlooked beauties that bloom obligingly in the middle of winter, in warming tones of yellow, brick-red, tan and ochre. Their cousins the stocks (*Matthiola incana*) have pink and purple flowers and are grown as much for their heavy perfume as for their colour. Honesty (*Lunaria annua*) has pretty purple flowers in early spring but its real prizes are its satiny, translucent seed pods, or 'moon pennies'. Honesty is practically compulsory in dried flower arrangements. The dyers' herb woad (*Isatis tinctoria*) is also a brassica. It was once the most important source of blue dye before indigo, a member of the pea family, usurped

WALLFLOWER

that position during the sixteenth century. Sweet alyssum (*Lobularia maritima*) is probably the best-known ornamental brassica. It is as popular as it ever was for prettying up concrete driveways and tyre swans in suburbs around the nation. Its beautiful perfume wafts up to meet you on hot days.

SWEET ALYSSUM

You might never guess that sweet alyssum is a relative of the lumpy old cabbage, or that ethereal honesty has the slightest thing in common with a cauliflower. Yet all the members of the brassica family share an unmistakeable floral structure. Despite coming in a variety of colours and sizes, brassica flowers all have the same four-petalled cross shape. This feature gives the family its other name: the Cruciferae, or 'cross-bearers'.

In 1935 the Korean-Japanese plant breeder U Jangchun published a theory on the interrelationship between the cultivated brassicas, based on his breeding observations. He posited that three wild species of brassica – *Brassica oleracea*, *B. nigra* and *B. rapa* – gave rise to three hybrids: *B. napus*, *B. juncea* and *B. carinata*. His theory was that these six plants gave rise to all of the astounding variety of brassica crops we know today. Recent genetic testing has shown that U's theory was indeed correct.

Together, these six brassicas are now referred to as the rather arcane-sounding 'triangle of U'. The three wild brassicas (*Brassica oleracea*, *B. nigra* and *B. rapa*) sit in the corners of the triangle of U. Along its sides lie their three hybrids (*B. napus*, *B. juncea* and *B. carinata*). The genetics of these hybrids is fascinating because, whereas humans inherit half of our chromosomes from our mothers and half from our fathers, the hybrid brassicas inherited *both sets* of chromosomes from their mothers and *both sets* from their fathers. That makes them *amphidiploids*: they contain twice the usual amount of genetic material. This gives them the potential for an enormous amount of variability.

Let's have a look around the triangle of U to see who is related to whom. You might be surprised.

Old-fashioned honesty is a brassica.

BRUSSELS SPROUT FOLIAGE

BRASSICA OLERACEA

On the seaside cliffs of Europe grows a tough plant called
Brassica oleracea. It clings to the thin, chalky soils on
the cliff tops, braving salt spray and incessant wind. It's
a gawky and unprepossessing plant with a branching, woody
trunk and scalloped, almost succulent foliage. In summer
it bears a spray of yellow, cross-shaped flowers. This plant
is wild cabbage, the ancestor of all the cole crops.

The domestication of wild cabbage is shrouded in the mists of time. The ancient
Celts may have had a hand in it, because it is from their words *bresic* that we derive
'brassica', and *kol* that we get 'cole' and 'kale'.

The Greeks mentioned a vegetable which sounds suspiciously like a cultivated
brassica in their writings. The Romans definitely grew them. In the second century
BCE, Cato the Elder extolled the virtues of brassicas in his book *De Agri Cultura*.
In fact, Cato thought brassicas were so good for the constitution that he devoted

two whole chapters to them; a welcome relief, it has to be said, from the rest of his book, which is full of stern injunctions to discipline slaves adequately and to ensure that one's womenfolk are kept on a sufficiently tight leash.

Cato recommends that vinegared brassica leaves be eaten before and after a banquet to relieve that inconvenient feeling of satiety that can just ruin a good binge. He also recommends saving the urine of people who eat brassicas regularly for bathing babies and the infirm. I can't think why that idea never caught on. Cato tantalisingly mentions three kinds of brassica: 'Pythagorean brassica', 'curly' or 'celery-leaved' brassica, and 'mild brassica', which, two centuries later, Pliny the Elder elucidates is cabbage. Pliny mentions radishes, turnips and rape too.

The Romans took brassicas to the far-flung corners of their dominion. In the intervening two thousand years the wild cabbage has morphed into the half-dozen cole crops we know today. Through breeding and selection, some ancestral cole crops developed enlarged, tender leaves. These became the cabbages and kales. Others developed massive heads of flower buds. These became broccoli and cauliflowers. One variety was selected for its juicy, thick stems – kohlrabi – and another for its proliferous side shoots – Brussels sprouts.

Despite centuries of breeding and selection, it seems that all of the cole crops are just a generation away from going native. When crossed with one another, the different cole crops revert back to the wild seaside cabbage alarmingly easily. Keeping the different strains pure is no easy task. Plants used for seed collection must be isolated from other flowering cole crops by a distance of several kilometres to avoid cross-pollination. They can be grown inside insect-proof cages to exclude bees carrying pollen from a different brassica variety but then, of course, uncontaminated bees have to be artificially introduced into the cages in order to pollinate the seed plants. Frankly, it's a bit of a palaver and best left to the experts. It's easier to buy brassica seeds afresh each year than to save your own.

CABBAGE

•

Cabbages comprise the Capitata group of the *Brassica oleracea* complex. Capitata means 'headed' in Latin, referring to the rosette of overlapping leaves which forms a dense, self-blanching head. Cabbages are the most stolidly European of crops. They were originally developed with pickling and winter storage in mind, in the days when winter famine was a real possibility. Nowadays, with food abundant and refrigeration ubiquitous, cabbages have lost a lot of their popularity.

Cabbages come in a couple of distinct forms. Drumhead cabbages are the most familiar in Australia, with round or slightly flattened soccer ball-like heads. Oxheart cabbages have pointed, conical heads and are very popular in Northern Europe. Both kinds of cabbages can have foliage that is either flat or *savoyed*. Savoy foliage is puckered like seersucker. It is thinner and less fleshy in texture than 'normal' flat cabbage foliage.

VARIETIES

•

Couve Tronchuda

A Portuguese heirloom with more than a touch of kale about it. In fact, some authors give it its own group, *B. oleracea*, Tronchuda group. Tronchuda forms loose heads of bluish, scalloped leaves with delicious, chunky white midribs. Tronchuda will never be seen in the marketplace as it doesn't form a 'normal' tight, dense head. It is, however, an excellent variety for backyarders on account of its heat tolerance, ease of cultivation and superb flavour.

Golden Acre

The problem with most cabbage varieties for home gardeners is that they take up a lot of bed space for a long time and then give you one huge cabbage which ends up going mouldy in the fridge. Golden Acre is different. It is a mini-cabbage. It has fast-cropping plants half the size of standard varieties, so they can be planted twice as close and cleared out to make way for the next crop sooner. The green round heads are just 15 centimetres across; a useful size for most households.

January King

A gorgeous nineteenth-century English heirloom with semi-savoy, blue foliage tipped with turquoise and rosy purple. It bears 2-kilogram heads late in the season, which hold well over winter. A compact cabbage well suited to backyards.

JANUARY KING CABBAGE

Mantovano

An Italian variety from Mantua. It is a savoy drumhead cabbage of the type favoured in northern Italian cuisine. It stands up well to hotter weather.

Premium Late Flat Dutch or Drumhead

Introduced to the USA from Europe in the mid-nineteenth century, this is the classic white cabbage, with flattened heads the shape of squashed soccer balls. The heads weigh up to 7 kilograms. They are white with very thick, succulent leaves that hold well on the plant over winter. This is the cabbage to grow if you are making sauerkraut or have an enormous extended family. Otherwise it can be a bit overwhelming.

Red Drumhead

Red Drumhead is incredibly ornamental, with tight, spherical heads of glossy, deep red-purple, nestled in steel-blue, bloomy foliage with purple veins. The heads weigh in at a useful 3 kilograms and cook to a beautiful dark purple colour. This variety was introduced to the USA in the 1860s from the German seedsman Wendel.

RED DRUMHEAD CABBAGE

Winnigstedt or Winnigstädt

Often misspelled Winningstadt, this cabbage comes from the Saxon town of Winnigstedt, near Braunschweig. It was taken to the USA by German migrants after the American Revolution and first introduced to horticulture in 1866. It forms huge plants, easily a metre across, containing a relatively small, conical green head. The heads are very densely packed; good for making sauerkraut.

KALE

•

Kales make up the Acephala group of the *Brassica oleracea* complex, acephala meaning 'headless' in Greek. This is a good description of what kales are: basically just non-heading cabbages.

Kales are a favourite of northern European cultures as they are very tolerant of cold. Kales have made a huge comeback in recent years. It is easy to see why. They are simple to grow compared with other brassicas, productive over a long season, versatile in the kitchen and highly ornamental garden plants into the bargain. Kales are perhaps less sweet in flavour and less succulent in texture than their cabbage cousins but they are good subjects for small gardens because they can be harvested leaf by leaf as needed, in contrast to cabbages, which make you wait months for a head to form and then oblige you to use it fairly quickly. Like all cole crops, kales taste sweeter in cold weather, especially after a good frost.

VARIETIES

•

Like cabbages, the foliage of kales may be either flat or savoyed. It may also be tightly curled like parsley, or lacy and dissected like a fern, making kales very ornamental garden subjects.

Dwarf Blue Curled

Similar in overall design to standard Scotch Kale, Dwarf Blue Curled is, as the name suggests, shorter at 40 centimetres and bluer in colour.

Red Russian / Ragged Jack

I have included this ersatz kale here because it functions like a true kale both in the garden and in the kitchen. Strictly speaking, however, Red Russian is a variety of *Brassica napus*, so it is more closely related to canola and swede than to true kales. Red Russian has ruffled, lacy leaves that are blue-green with purple veining and thinner in texture than true kales. Red Russian was taken to Canada by Siberian traders in the nineteenth century. Needless to say, it laughs at cold weather.

Scotch Kale/Curly Kale

Scotch Kale looks like a bit like a giant curly parsley. Its leaves are pinked and frilly, a duller shade of green than parsley, but at one metre tall it's a much bolder plant.

Tuscan Black/Nero di Toscano/ Cavolo Nero/Lacinato

This eighteenth-century Italian variety has narrow, fluted foliage of dark, leaden green. The foliage texture is heavily savoyed and looks like nothing so much as elephant hide, though it is much easier to chew and suitable for vegetarians. The leaves fountain upwards from the metre-tall trunk like a miniature palm tree, lending a nice prehistoric feel to the garden.

Walking Stick Kale/ Walking Stick Cabbage

This astounding heirloom is native to the Channel Islands, in the heart of the wild cabbage's native range. In the islands' mild climate, Walking Stick Kales are not cut back by winter frosts so they just keep growing and growing. Upwards. Eventually the rosette of big, oval leaves is stranded atop a towering trunk 2–5 metres in height. The trunks were traditionally cut and lacquered to make walking sticks and the foliage was used to feed cows, although it is perfectly edible for humans, too. Walking Stick Kale is a wonderful curiosity to grow if you can get the seeds and don't mind getting on a ladder to harvest your dinner.

RED RUSSIAN KALE

GREEN CURLY KALE

TUSCAN BLACK KALE

WALKING STICK KALE

BROCCOLI

•

Known universally by its Italian name today, broccoli was once known as 'Italian asparagus' in English. Broccolis form the Italicus group of the *B. oleracea* complex.

Modern F1 hybrid broccolis are one-trick ponies. They are designed to crop *en masse*, each plant bearing a single, gigantic head, so that farmers can harvest them in one fell swoop and remove the spent plants in readiness for the next crop. This is not at all what home gardeners need from broccoli. Home gardeners need broccoli plants to give little and often over an extended season. Heirloom broccolis do just that. Ten plants from the same seed batch will begin cropping at ten different times, each plant beginning with a medium-sized main head and, after that has been harvested, continuing to produce dozens of side shoots over several weeks,

Sprouting broccolis produce copious side shoots after the main head has been harvested.

or even months. Heirloom broccolis give bigger harvests over a longer period than commercial hybrid broccolis.

A fairly new vegetable seen in supermarkets is something called broccolini. Broccolini is not an heirloom but an F1 hybrid between a true broccoli and Chinese broccoli or gai lan. The word 'broccolini' is the Italian diminutive of the word broccoli, just as zucchini is the diminutive of 'zuccho', pumpkin. In a triumph of commerce over language, the word 'broccolini' has actually been registered as a trademark. It's a bit like trademarking the words 'tinny', 'chocky bikky' or 'brekky'.

VARIETIES

•

Broccoli comes in green, purple and, more rarely, white varieties. They all cook to a darker or lighter shade of green. Some varieties of broccoli are strongly heading, others are strongly branching. Choose one that suits your needs best.

Calabrese/Green Sprouting

An ancient Italian heirloom strain first taken to the USA in the 1880s, these typically bear a 10–12-centimetre, dark green central head followed by a good crop of smaller side shoots. Each plant can bear a couple of kilos of sprouts over the course of its life.

De Cicco

An Italian heirloom, very similar to Calabrese, though perhaps more compact, bluer in colour and earlier to crop.

GREEN SPROUTING BROCCOLI

Purple Sprouting

Purple sprouting broccoli resembles green sprouting Calabrese in its habit of bearing a small-medium central head followed by a generous crop of smaller side shoots. However, the sprouts are, as the name suggests, a beautiful violet-purple. The colour cooks out to a dark green. The flavour is more mustardy than that of green Calabrese and

PURPLE SPROUTING BROCCOLI

the plants are bigger, more robust, and very tolerant of adverse conditions. When sown in late summer the plants continue growing through the depths of winter and crop during the hungry gap of spring when not much else is available in the vegetable garden. This makes it an excellent vegetable for gardens in cold climates.

Several distinct strains of purple sprouting broccoli are available, and there are even a few new F1 hybrid purple sprouting broccoli, reflecting its growing popularity with gardeners and cooks. There is a similar but rarely seen white sprouting broccoli, too.

Waltham 29

An American open-pollinated variety first introduced in 1954. This is perhaps the closest thing to a 'normal' hybrid broccoli (reflected in its rather prosaic name). It produces large-ish 10–20-centimetre green heads and not much in the way of side shoots.

CAULIFLOWER

•

Cauliflowers comprise the Botrytis group of the *B. oleracea* complex. Those of you familiar with wine will immediately recognise the word *botrytis* as the 'noble rot' that affects grapes. The word botrytis is derived from Greek 'botrys' meaning a bunch of grapes, with the '-itis' suffix used for diseases (as in 'tonsillitis'). Someone obviously thought cauliflowers resemble a big bunch of mildewy grapes.

On the subject of disease, it has to be said that cauliflower is not an easy crop to grow well. Caulis require very rich soil and perfect nutrition, and they resent any check in their growth from heat waves, drought, and so on. Cauliflowers are prone to several mineral deficiencies, pests and diseases. These are not reasons *not* to grow them, but gardeners need to be aware that this is a crop that requires a certain amount of skill to grow well.

VARIETIES

•

Nowadays cauliflowers come in one colour: white. This was not always so. Heirloom cauliflowers can be fluoro green, violet purple or egg-yolk orange in addition to white. Hybridisers have showed not a skerrick of interest in non-white cauliflowers since the advent of F1 hybrids more than fifty years ago. All F1 cauliflowers simply had to be white. However, since the coloured heirloom cauliflowers have gained popularity in the past few years, a rash of coloured F1 hybrids has broken out in imitation of them, including Graffiti (purple) and Sunset (orange). Copycats.

The 'curds', or heads, of white cauliflowers are easily damaged by sun and frost. The coloured varieties of cauliflower are much more forgiving and are therefore much better subjects for home gardeners.

Early Snowball
An old American standard variety producing modestly sized, ivory-white curds.

Macerata
An Italian heirloom with bright fluoro green heads. The plants are huge – a metre or more across – and vigorous and dependable.

MACERATA CAULIFLOWER

Purple Cape
An eighteenth-century heirloom, probably South African but possibly Italian, with pretty, light purple curds. It became popular in Europe and the USA in the early nineteenth century. It has stood the test of time where many cauliflower varieties have fallen by the wayside. It is still a good home variety. Its curds keep their colour quite well when cooked. The flavour is mustardy – more like broccoli than white cauliflower.

PURPLE CAPE CAULIFLOWER

Sicilian Purple/di Sicilia Violetto
A broccoli-like cauliflower which forms white heads with a dark purple cast. The purple turns to green when cooked.

Romanesco

Mother Nature clearly dropped one LSD too many the day she designed romanesco. Imagine a psychedelic cauliflower and you pretty much have romanesco. Romanesco's curds are the most fluorescent Day-Glo green imaginable, arranged into ever-diminishing fractal minarets, twisting in and out of one another. If you stare at it for long enough your retinas start to ache.

Romanesco is a plant apart, a unique outlier of the cauliflower group.

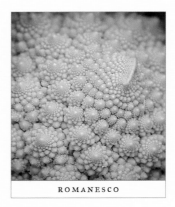

ROMANESCO

BRUSSELS SPROUTS

•

Brussels sprouts are the Gemmifera group of *Brassica oleracea*. Gemmifera, meaning 'bearing jewels', is a rather glorious denomination for a vegetable that is notoriously disliked by children and many adults besides. The 'jewels' are of course the little cabbagey nuggets which grow along the length of Brussels sprouts' tall trunk. Brussels sprouts are unique among cole crops in that they have been selected for their tasty axillary buds.

Not everyone finds sprouts tasty. Leaving aside those individuals who don't do them justice in the kitchen (boiled to death, anyone?), recent studies have shown that certain people perceive the bitter chemicals in Brussels sprouts more keenly than the rest of us. To them, sprouts really *do* taste acrid and nasty. These people are called 'supertasters'. So it seems that human genetics is to blame for some of Brussels sprouts' bad press. Sorry, Brussels sprouts: it's not you, it's us.

The history of Brussels sprouts is even more hazy and indistinct than that of other vegetables. Run a search on the internet and you will come away with the distinct impression that Brussels sprouts first appeared in ancient Rome in the fifth century. Or the Low Countries in the thirteenth century . . . or possibly Burgundy in the fifteenth century . . . or was it Brussels in 1587 . . . or 1750? There are many historical threads to pick up, and none of them leads anywhere in particular. Perhaps each story contains a kernel of truth. On balance I'm inclined to think that Brussels sprouts probably appeared later rather than earlier, somewhere in northern Europe, Belgium being as good as anywhere else. We do know that the Englishman Charles Marshall mentions Brussels sprouts by name in his 1796 *A Plain and Easy Introduction to the Knowledge and Practice of Gardening*. Not long thereafter Benjamin Franklin imported seed to the USA and began growing them there.

Brussels sprouts are not easy to grow in our part of the world. Even more than other cole crops, Brussels sprouts won't tolerate a check in their growth. They need a constant, even supply of moisture and a climate that is mild and damp in summer with a proper, cold, frosty winter. In other words, they need Belgian weather. In Australia, the chances are that if your area gets a proper frosty winter then it also experiences a belting-hot summer, which Brussels sprouts resent. Sprouts like to do all their growing during the shortening days of late summer and autumn, attaining their full size by the onset of winter. Late summer and autumn can be punishingly hot and dry in Australia, and sprout plants rarely make it through this period in good shape. Sprouts also need a deep, well-structured soil to give of their best and are very sensitive to imperfect levels of trace elements. As you can imagine all of these factors severely limit the localities where Brussels sprouts can be commercially grown in Australia. When you see Brussels sprouts for sale in shops, spare a thought for the considerable prowess that has gone into growing them.

VARIETIES

•

It has to be said that heirloom varieties of Brussels sprouts leave a fair bit to be desired. Most strains display a very high degree of variability, with many individuals in a seedling swarm refusing point-blank to form nice, tight sprouts. If you are looking for uniformity and reliability in your backyard sprout crop then, it pains me to say it, F1 hybrids are going to do the job better. If, however, you don't mind harvesting loose, so-called 'blown' sprouts of all shapes and sizes, then one of the heirloom varieties might suit you. In any case, the large, round leaves of Brussels sprout plants are perfectly edible and, far from being a starvation food, are one of the most tender and delicious of all cole crops.

Long Island Improved

A compact, green variety which rarely needs staking, Long Island Improved was an important commercial variety in the days before F1 hybrids. The young sprouts are prone to blowing before they have formed a proper button, but when grown well it is serviceable enough for backyarders.

LONG ISLAND
BRUSSELS SPROUT

RUBINE BRUSSELS SPROUT

Rubine/Ruby

At its best, Rubine is a supremely beautiful ornamental vegetable. As the autumn comes to a close the plant becomes a gorgeous red-purple, powdered with dove-grey bloom like a plum. Viewed on a dewy autumn morning, Rubine is beautiful enough to make your heart stop. Unfortunately, Rubine is rarely seen at its best in Australian gardens. It hates our oppressive summers, so it tends to look tired and moth-eaten by autumn, when it should actually be looking its best. Perhaps the greatest tragedy of this variety is that its stunning purple sprouts – which really do deserve the title of 'jewels' in their raw state, cook up to an alarming shade of blue-grey and beige (definitely not 'caviar-black' as I have seen them described elsewhere). If you live in a cool-summer climate with perfect soil, by all means give Rubine a go. Otherwise, leave it to the Europeans.

There is also a superior red Brussels sprout called **Red Bull**, which I am yet to see in this country.

KOHLRABI

•

If the Brussels sprout's 'jewel-bearing' moniker seems a little highfalutin for such a prosaic vegetable, then kohlrabi's botanical title suits it perfectly. Kohlrabi belongs to the Gongylodes group of *Brassica oleracea,* gongylodes meaning 'knobbly' or 'lump-forming'. This refers to the massively swollen stem of the kohlrabi, selected by humans over many hundreds of years to be sweet and crunchy rather than bitter and coarse. The name 'kohlrabi' is probably originally derived from Latin *caulo-rapa*; meaning 'trunk turnip', but has come to us via the Teutonic languages. In German *Kohl* has come to mean cabbage and *Rübe* is a collective term for root crops such as turnips and beet. The German term *Kohlrübe* nowadays refers uniquely to the swede, but probably gave us the word kohlrabi on its way there. Linguistics gives us almost as many clues to the origins and interrelationships of vegetables as genetics do, although it throws in the occasional red herring, too.

VIENNA WHITE KOHLRABI

Speaking of red herrings, we usually think of kohlrabi as a root vegetable, and in many ways it does resemble true root vegetables like parsnips or carrots. But botanically speaking it is the trunk of the kohlrabi plant that we eat. It's easy to understand this when you see a kohlrabi plant growing in the ground, with the edible trunk portion held well above the soil surface. Eating a 'trunk' doesn't sound that appetising, yet kohlrabi is extremely popular in certain parts of the world so it can't be that bad. The nations of the former Austro-Hungarian empire can't get enough of kohlrabi. This is reflected in the names of the most commonly grown cultivars, Purple and White Vienna. In Budapest's central market it is possible to see great ziggurats of kohlrabi stacked almost to the ceiling, waiting for enthusiastic buyers. Kohlrabi is a great favourite in the Indian subcontinent, too, where it turns up in all manner of dishes.

VARIETIES

•

Very few different varieties of kohlrabi are seen in Australia. **Purple Vienna** and **White Vienna** are the most commonly encountered. They are essentially the same as one another but for their skin colours: purple and white. In all other ways they are classic kohlrabi.

RAPE FLOWERS

BRASSICA RAPA

The next stop on our tour of the triangle of U brings us to *Brassica rapa*. *B. rapa* is native to quite a large chunk of Eurasia. There are examples of its seeds at Swiss archaeological sites dating back to Neolithic times, indicating that humans have gathered it from the wild, probably for its oily seeds, for a very long time. *B. rapa* was probably domesticated separately in the East and the West, which would account for the strongly divergent forms grown in Asia and Europe. We will revisit the Asian varieties later. First we will examine the main western form of *B. rapa*: the turnip.

TURNIP

•

The turnip is a variety of *B. rapa* grown for its fleshy root. Technically speaking, it is not the turnip's root that we eat but its swollen hypocotyl. A hypocotyl is the fleshy section of stem between the root and the first set of seed leaves in a baby seedling – the long white stem of a mung bean sprout is a good example. The hypocotyl's job is to elongate quickly in order to push the seedling's leaves out of the ground and into the sunlight. In most plants the hypocotyl disappears once it has done this job but in some vegetables such as swedes, radishes and beetroots, it keeps growing into a fleshy storage organ.

I suspect the words 'hypocotyl' and 'fleshy storage organ' probably aren't making your mouth water. Yet a well-grown turnip is a wonderful, wonderful thing. No vegetable is more unfairly underrated. Sweet, aromatic and crisp when eaten raw, melting and succulent when cooked, the turnip has been given a bad name by its idiot cousin, the swede. Turnips and swedes are so similar in appearance that they are routinely confused with one another. But they couldn't be more different to eat.

Turnips were grown in Babylon in the seventh century BCE. Theophrastus mentions them in the fourth century BCE. Both Pliny the Elder and Columnella refer to turnips in their writings in the first century CE. The turnip was an important European staple for hundreds of years until it was supplanted by the newfangled potato. The turnip made its way east to Asia, possibly along the silk routes, and by the eighth century it had reached Japan, where it remains one of that country's favourite vegetables.

As mentioned earlier, the turnip is incredibly versatile in the kitchen. This is reflected in how many different cuisines it pops up in. In French cuisine we find turnips steamed, braised or pureed. In Japan they are pickled or simmered in stock. The turnip behaves like three different vegetables depending on how it is served. Eaten raw, turnip roots are crisp and sweet with a mustardy perfume that is mouth-watering and refreshing. Cooked, the roots become very tender, sponging up the flavour of the liquid they are cooked in. The foliage and flowering stems of turnips are also delicious as cooked greens. In my opinion turnip greens are one of the most delicious of all green vegetables.

VARIETIES

•

There are two very different kinds of turnip: those grown for their roots and those developed especially for their tender leaves and flower heads.

Bianca Lodigiana

An Italian turnip from Lombardy. It has flattened white roots with a mild, sweet taste and lots of tasty greens. It is tender and good for eating raw, and holds very well over winter.

BIANCA LODIGIANA TURNIP

Broccoli Raab/Rabe

Not really a broccoli at all but a rootless turnip grown for its big leaves and flower heads, which resemble broccoli.

Cima di Rapa

Cima di rapa ('turnip tops') is an Italian leaf turnip, selected for its juicy leaves and broccoli-like flowering tops rather than its roots, which are tiny. Cima di rapa is a very quick leafy green to grow during the cooler months, ready to harvest just 3–4 weeks after sowing.

Golden Ball/Orange Jelly/Boule d'Or

A well-flavoured French heirloom from the 1850s with autumnal, straw-yellow flesh which is sweet, mild and perfumed.

Hinona

A Japanese heirloom from Shiga prefecture with long, snaky roots to 25 centimetres in length and 2.5 centimetres in width. They are white with bright purple on top. The edible leaves are very attractive, with purple stems and veins and a purple cast.

Purple Top Milan

A nineteenth-century Italian heirloom via France with very flat, disc-shaped roots. They are mostly purple, with some white on the very bottom. This variety can be a bit hot and mustardy if growing conditions are not perfect.

HINONA TURNIP

Purple Top White Globe

A round turnip that is white with a purple top.
An American heirloom from the 1880s.

White Egg

A nineteenth-century heirloom with white, globe-
to egg-shaped roots which are very tender and
sweet. Good for eating raw.

PURPLE TOP GLOBE TURNIP

CANOLA FLOWERS

BRASSICA NAPUS

Brassica napus is where the triangle of U starts to get really interesting. *B. napus* is not a naturally occurring species but a hybrid between *B. rapa,* the wild turnip, and *B. oleracea,* the wild cabbage. *Brassica napus* is amphidiploid, meaning it has four sets of chromosomes instead of the usual two. With such a lot of genetic material to draw on, *B. napus* has the potential to show enormous variation in its outward appearance. And indeed it does. Perhaps the most familiar form of *B. napus* in this country is canola; a specially developed Canadian strain of the oilseed crop, rape. It is a familiar sight in early summer, colouring fields brilliant yellow with its flowers. The most common vegetable form of *B. napus* in western nations is the dumpy swede.

SWEDE

•

Perhaps I was a bit harsh on the swede earlier. The swede does have quite a few things going for it. It is incredibly cold-tolerant for one thing, and very quick to grow. But compared with the turnip, the swede is coarser in texture, more pungent in flavour and lends itself to fewer applications in the kitchen. The swede was very popular with older generations for putting into stews and hearty soups, where its sweet-pungent flavour stood up well to fattier cuts of meat. My Nan used to put swede in her legendary mince. The swede would soak up the meat juices as it bubbled away in her pressure cooker, ending up as tender little cubes of meaty sweetness. For my entire childhood I didn't have a clue what those little cubes were, I just knew that I liked them.

Knowing that swede is the love child of cabbage and turnip makes more sense of it. Swede looks like an oversize, coarse turnip but tastes decidedly cabbagey. Swede couldn't be more different from its willowy sibling canola, which is all wiry flower heads and no root to speak of. It's hard to imagine that they are related at all.

VARIETIES

•

Swede varieties are rarely sold by name in this country. You might find **Laurentian**, a classic variety with heart-shaped, dirty white roots topped with purple skin. The flesh cooks to a pale creamy yellow.

Another *B. napus* variety is the Ragged Jack or Red Russian 'kale'. It's not really a kale at all but a very good impostor with its large, tender leaves (see entry under Kale on page 152).

LAURENTIAN SWEDE

American Purple Top has dark purple shoulders and orange-yellow flesh. **Gilfeather** is another American variety. It is the most turnip-like of all the swedes. Its roots are white, topped with green rather than the usual purple, and sweeter in flavour. Incidentally, in the USA swedes are known as 'rutabaga'.

RED GIANT MUSTARD

ASIAN GREENS

To the uninitiated, Asian greens all look pretty similar. In comparison with, say, a red cabbage and a white cauliflower, which are so obviously different, it can be difficult to tell the different Asian greens apart. There is a tendency amongst garden and food writers to be a bit dismissive of Asian vegetables, brushing them aside as an undifferentiated bloc of green, stemmy-lookin' things. In actuality they are much more interesting than that.

That Asian brassicas look so similar to one another, yet so different from western brassicas, belies the fact that both western and Asian brassicas emerged from the same bloodlines. The only difference is that they have developed in isolation from one another, at opposite ends of the Eurasian continent. It is a fascinating lesson in selective breeding to see how the six triangle of U brassicas have become so strikingly divergent in their outward forms in the west, while in Asian cultures they seem to be converging on a single point of uniformity.

As an example, let's look at three fairly well-known Asian greens: gai lan, choy sum and gai choy. Each of these crops could best be described as a bunch of bright green, fleshy stems, topped with large paddle-shaped leaves. They look almost identical at first glance. Yet gai lan is descended from *Brassica oleracea*, like cabbage and Brussels sprouts. Choy sum is descended from *B. rapa*, just like the turnip. Gai choy is a variety of *B. juncea*, so it is actually a kind of mustard.

In a blind taste test you'd probably work this out immediately. Gai lan has the sweet chunkiness of broccoli stems, choy sum has the trademark nutty perfume of turnips and gai choy has the distinctive biting pungency of mustard.

Asian brassicas belong to the triangle of U just as western brassica crops do. However, they are distributed on the triangle quite differently, reflecting their more easterly geographical origins. While most of the western brassicas are descended from *Brassica oleracea* – which grows wild in Europe – the only uniquely Asian crop descended from that species is gai lan, or Chinese broccoli. The majority of the Asian brassicas fall under the umbrella of *Brassica rapa*, which seems to have had a more easterly distribution than *B. oleracea*. In the West, *B. rapa* is represented only by turnips and field rape, an oilseed crop. However, in Asia it has diversified into a plethora of different green vegetables including bok choy, choy sum and, astonishingly, Chinese cabbage.

Brassica juncea is a hybrid of *B. rapa* (turnip) and *B. nigra* (black mustard). It is barely represented at all amongst western brassicas, but many Asian greens trace their history back to it.

B. napus is more commonly represented in northern Asia – Japan, Korea and northern China – mirroring its more northerly distribution in Europe (Scandinavia and Russia for example).

VARIETIES

•

Because they are relatively unfamiliar to many readers I have lumped the Asian brassicas together here, noting their different backgrounds and affiliations under each heading. This is a gross oversimplification, but at least it gives you an idea of the genetic diversity contained in these outwardly very similar crops.

Bok choy/Pak choy/ Pak tsoi/Baak choy

The many names of this vegetable are merely different ways of transliterating its Cantonese name, which means literally 'white vegetable'. This refers to the thick, fleshy white stems that most varieties of bok choy have. There are several cultivars of bok choy, some of them forming tall, hefty rosettes with dark green leaves and classic white stems. Others, such as the miniature Shanghai choy, are pale green in both leaf and stem. Bok choy is descended from *B. rapa* so it is genetically identical to western turnips.

BOK CHOY

Chinese cabbage

Variously known as **wombok**, **wong bok** or **wong nga baak** in Australia, **napa cabbage** in the USA and **hakusai** in Japan, it's hard to believe that the Chinese cabbage is actually a kind of turnip (*Brassica rapa*) and not at all related to the European cabbage (*B. oleracea*). Lacking the succulent root of 'normal' turnips, this variety of *B. rapa* is instead grown for the huge, tender midribs of its leaves, which are as white and light as polystyrene. The

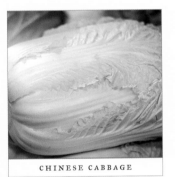

CHINESE CABBAGE

leaves grow clasping one around the other to form a giant, boxy head very much like a true cabbage, although they are noticeably oblong rather than round in shape.

Eaten raw, Chinese cabbage is as crisp and light as bean sprouts. When cooked it is as silky as chiffon. However I suspect most of the world's Chinese cabbage is consumed neither raw nor cooked, but finds its way into pickling crocks with salt, chilli and garlic to be fermented into Korea's favourite food, kimchi. To say that Koreans 'love' kimchi is a lamentable understatement. They are, in point of fact, absolutely bonkers about the stuff. They eat it for breakfast, lunch and dinner, and they discuss its finer points in between times. I think it would be a nice gesture if we all started calling this vegetable by its Korean name, **bae chu**.

Choy sum

Choy sum is Asia's answer to Italian cima di rapa. It is a turnip relative grown for its leaves, juicy stems, flower buds and fresh young yellow flowers. Choy sum is a transliteration of the Cantonese name, which literally translates as 'vegetable heart'.

CHOY SUM

Gai choy

Also known as mustard greens, this is indeed a kind of mustard (*Brassica juncea*), selected for its fleshy leaf bases and large tender leaves. The interesting thing about gai choy is how similar this mustard looks to bok choy and Chinese cabbage, to which it is only distantly related. Gai choy is the Cantonese pronunciation for its Chinese name, 'mustard vegetable'. Gai choy is frequently encountered pickled in Asian groceries, often labelled rather ambiguously along the lines of 'salted vegetable'.

Gai lan / Kai laan

Just as European broccoli represents the Italicus group of *Brassica oleracea*, gai lan has its own group, too: the Alboglabrus group, named for its white (rather than yellow) flowers. Gai lan has chunky, tender, sweet stems and thick, oval leaves, which cook to a spectacularly rich shade of dark green. The classic way of serving gai lan is blanched, drizzled with oyster sauce. Gai lan or kai laan is derived from the Cantonese pronunciation for its Chinese name, which literally means 'mustard orchid', making this delicious vegetable sound even more exotic than it is already.

GAI LAN

KOMATSUNA

Komatsuna

Literally 'little pine vegetable' in Japanese, this is another leafing variety of the turnip, *B. rapa*. Komatsuna plants are extremely fast-growing to 40 centimetres, with mid-green, oar-shaped leaves. It is a very useful green to have in the garden over winter.

Mizuna/mibuna

These pretty Japanese leafy greens are both descended from *B. rapa*. In other words, they are turnips. However, mizuna has light green ferny foliage and mibuna has dark green foliage the shape of paddle pop sticks. They are very quick growing crops and grow well in cold soil over winter. Mizuna, mibuna and komatsuna are generally eaten lightly pickled in salt and kombu kelp in Japan, but they are great for salads, too.

MIZUNA

Nanohana

Nanohana is a Japanese strain of the hybrid *Brassica napus*. Nanohana has been selected not for its chunky roots, like its cousin the swede, but for its delicate flower buds, similar to broccoli. Fields of nanohana flower spectacularly yellow early in the Japanese spring, just as its relative canola does here. The Japanese look forward to pickled nanohana buds on their dinner plates, as this crop coincides with their beloved cherry blossom season and the first sunny days of spring.

OTHER BRASSICA CROPS

At this point we say goodbye to the triangle of U and look at two other brassica crops, rocket and radish.

ROCKET

•

Rocket is not one vegetable, but two. Common rocket, arugula or roquette (*Eruca sativa*) used to be the more common of the two, but it has had its popularity usurped by wild or sand rocket (*Diplotaxis tenuifolia*), sometimes known by its Italian name, *rucola selvatica*, in recent years. Wild rocket is the one you dish out with a set of self-serve tongs in the supermarket. It is actually listed as a noxious weed in Victoria and South Australia due to its prodigious self-seeding. Technically speaking, noxious weeds cannot be legally grown or traded. I always find it paradoxical that a plant can be simultaneously considered a noxious weed that needs to be eradicated, and a commercial crop from which somebody makes their livelihood. Blackberries and fennel are two other examples of plants that are simultaneously listed as noxious weeds and cultivated as food crops.

Sand rocket is a perennial plant with yellow flowers, while common rocket is an annual with beige, brown-veined flowers. Its leaves are bigger and paddle shaped with less deeply scalloped margins than wild rocket. Both kinds have their place in the garden. Common rocket grows better during the colder months, and sand rocket is better during the warmer months. They taste remarkably similar – like peppery peanuts.

COMMON ROCKET

CHINA ROSE RADISH

RADISH

•

Radishes (*Raphanus sativa*) are one of the fastest crops known to horticulture. At only three weeks from germination to harvest, they are often recommended for children, with their notoriously short attention spans, to grow. This sounds like a good idea on paper. But I think that radishes' throat-gripping, acrid taste makes them the *least* appropriate crop for kids. If one taste is guaranteed to turn kids off vegetable gardening, then 'acrid' is it. If you really want to encourage kids to grow vegies, let them sow sweetcorn, watermelons or pumpkins. Resign yourself to doing the hard gardening yards for a few months while the kids lose interest, then let them come back and do the glory jobs of harvesting and eating, not forgetting to heap praise on them for their amazing prowess. Exactly like you do with your boss.

Radishes are native to Asia. Like turnips, radishes developed in different directions in East and West. In Europe, radishes were bred small and brightly coloured for immediate fresh consumption. In Asia they became big cooking vegetables designed for longer storage. The Japanese daikon radishes are the best known examples of this, but large *mooli*-type radishes are found all over Asia. Many Asian radishes have high-quality edible greens as well as roots. Daikon greens are a favourite in Japan. **Saisai** radishes are grown especially for their tender, hairless leaves and broccoli-like flower buds.

VARIETIES

•

Radishes fall into two different categories: summer and winter radishes. Summer radishes are grown through the spring and summer for immediate consumption. They are ready to harvest a few weeks after sowing and don't hold well in the ground, becoming woolly and coarse very quickly. Winter radishes are sown in late summer for harvest in autumn and winter. They take longer to reach full size but they hold very well in the ground during the colder months without losing quality. They are very versatile: good for eating raw in salads, and also pickled, steamed, simmered in stews and soups, and stir fried.

China Rose

A venerable winter radish with pretty, bright pink roots 15 centimetres long.

Chinese Green/Luobo

Another old Chinese winter cooking radish. This has stout roots 25 centimetres long, dark jade-green on the outside and pale green inside. It doesn't perform well in hot weather.

CHINESE GREEN RADISH

Chinese Red Meat/Watermelon

This old variety forms pale green-white, blocky radishes. Quite boring to look at until you slice them, revealing their hot pink interiors – hence the 'watermelon' nickname. The flesh is quite sweet, lacking some of the normal radishy pungency. This variety bolts very quickly in hot weather so it is best planted in early spring or autumn.

WATERMELON RADISH

French Breakfast

An heirloom summer radish with 5-centimetre, finger-shaped roots of bright red tipped with white. Personally speaking, radishes aren't even close to the top of my list of breakfast foods, but to each his/her own, I suppose.

Helios

A rare yellow ball-shaped radish named for the Greek god of the sun.

Long Black Spanish

Similar to Round Black Spanish (see next page), but the roots are drawn out to 20 centimetres in length.

Minowase

A Japanese heirloom daikon so good that it has spawned a race of Minowase F1 hybrids (Minowase Summer Cross No. 3 F1, Minowase Long White F1, etc). This is the classic daikon radish with pearly white roots up to 50 centimetres in length topped with copious, delicious greens. The white root has flesh as crisp and juicy as a bean shoot; sweet when grown in the winter but more peppery when grown in the summer. The heirloom variety of Minowase shows more variation in shape, size, harvest date and tendency to bolt than its F1 children, but this doesn't represent any sort of deal-breaker for home gardeners. In fact, staggered harvest dates and variation in size could be considered a bonus for a home gardener.

FRENCH BREAKFAST RADISH

BLACK SPANISH LONG RADISH

MINOWASE RADISH

Philadelphia White Box

An American variety first listed in the 1930s but probably much older, Philadelphia White Box has plump, white, slightly flattened roots with a bitey flavour.

Rat's Tail

This South Asian variety doesn't form any root to speak of. However, its long, cylindrical seed pods are delicious. Picked young (before they reach 20 centimetres in length), they are crisp and bean-like, and can be eaten raw, stir-fried or pickled. Fortunately they taste a lot better than their name suggests.

Round Black Spanish

A sixteenth-century European winter radish with deeply unattractive-looking black, rough roots which are very similar in appearance to black Perigord truffles, although they are much cheaper to buy. Inside, the flesh is crisp, brilliant white and quite pungent. It is good for raw winter salads.

BLACK SPANISH ROUND RADISH

Round Red

Nobody could accuse this summer radish of false advertising. It is, just as the name says, round and red. A classic-looking radish.

White Icicle

As the name suggests, this is a skinny, white, carrot-like radish.

CHAPTER SIX

THE

Nightshade

FAMILY

The nightshade family, or Solanaceae, contains around 4000 species in ninety genera, present on every continent except Antarctica. Nightshades have a long history of association with humans as food and medicine, for ritual and pleasure. Nightshades are among the most familiar of all food crops: tomatoes, potatoes, capsicums and eggplants are all nightshades. Indeed, the edible nightshades have come to epitomise certain national cuisines. Try to imagine Italian food without tomatoes, Thai food without chillies or German food without potatoes. It's impossible.

In addition to some of the most sumptuous of all garden vegetables, the nightshade family contains some of the most reviled of all toxic plants. First among the killers is the deadly nightshade, *Atropa belladonna*. Deadly nightshade's botanical name is one of the most telling of all scientific names. *Atropa* comes from the name of Atropos, one of the three Fates of Greek mythology. It was she who cut the thread of human life with her dreadful scissors, deciding the moment and manner of death. *Belladonna* comes from the Latin for 'beautiful lady'. This refers to a Renaissance-era beauty technique in which women dropped the juice of deadly nightshade plants into their eyes. The juice caused their pupils to dilate, making them look more alluring.

This alarming practice hints at the medical uses of the deadly nightshade. The drug obtained from it, *atropine*, is useful in cardiology and opthalmology, amongst other things. Atropine is so useful that the World Health Organisation (WHO) has included it in its list of essential drugs. Deaths from deadly nightshade are rare but non-lethal poisonings are fairly common after people accidentally ingest the glistening black berries, which look very appetising and taste quite pleasant. Symptoms lasting for several days include raging thirst, difficulty speaking and swallowing, hallucinations, delirium, vomiting, palpitations and coma. You have to eat an awful lot of berries to kill yourself, however, as the deadly nightshade's toxins are concentrated in its roots.

True deadly nightshade is a native of Europe. It is exceedingly rare in Australia. The plant from which parents snatch back their children in horror here is almost invariably a member of the black nightshade complex (*Solanum nigrum* and related species). Far from being deadly, most of the black nightshade complex are actually quite edible. The flavour of their fully ripe berries resembles a slightly unripe tomato with a saccharin aftertaste. They are not the best for eating fresh but they do make a reasonable, though runny, jam. Cultivated strains of black nightshade are readily available, such as the much-improved garden huckleberry, a firm favourite in the USA. Some members of the black nightshade complex are important as cooked

DEADLY NIGHTSHADE (*Atropa belladonna*)

BLACK NIGHTSHADE (*Solanum nigrum*)

greens in Africa and Asia. The worst that could be said about the black nightshades is that they are mildly toxic, but you could say the same thing about potatoes and tomatoes. I don't see anybody freaking out about them.

Deadly and black nightshades are easy to tell apart so there is really no cause for anxiety. Deadly nightshade is a robust, hip-high perennial with fuzzy leaves and puce, bell-shaped flowers. Its lustrous, marble-sized berries are borne singly, each surrounded by a large, green, star-shaped calyx. The black nightshades are smaller in all their proportions, annual, sprawling, more smooth-leaved, with tiny white, star-shaped flowers and matte-textured, pea-sized black berries borne in generous bunches.

While the unfairly maligned black nightshade is the target of many a backyard search-and-destroy mission, an infinitely more sinister member of the nightshade family lurks unmolested behind supermarket checkouts across the country: tobacco. It is no secret that tobacco (*Nicotiana tabacum*) is responsible for thousands of deaths each year. Yet our society continues to tolerate it, such are this plant's powers of persuasion. The genus *Nicotiana* contains some lovely ornamental plants, such as the elegant night-scented tobacco *N. sylvestris*, which is almost certainly the ancestor of cultivated tobacco. *N. alata* bears masses of hot pink or lime-green flowers and *N. langsdorffii* produces airy clouds of dainty, apple-green bells, each with a dab of bright blue pollen inside.

TOBACCO

NICOTIANA LANGSDORFFII

Angels' trumpets (*Brugmansia* spp.) are spectacular ornamental shrubs which no subtropical garden should be without. Famous for their enormous, pendulous, trumpet-shaped flowers which are heavily perfumed at night, angels' trumpets are another member of the nightshade family that you don't want to mess with. Many people know that angels' trumpets contain hallucinogenic compounds. What they don't know is that people who take angels' trumpet experience horrible, horrible side effects which last for several days. This is definitely not something to try at home.

Angels' trumpets also contain atropine, the toxic alkaloid found in deadly night-shade. So does the mystical herb mandrake (*Mandragora officinarum*). Mandrake was both coveted and feared in medieval times for its supposed magical qualities. Its roots were considered indispensable in both love potions and the black arts. Harvesting a mandrake root was not believed to be a straightforward affair. The roots are shaped like tiny naked humans, complete with fleshy little arms and legs, and they were reputed to scream when pulled from the ground, causing the person doing the pulling to fall dead on the spot. That is pure superstition of course, but in medieval times nobody was taking any chances. All kinds of elaborate schemes were devised to harvest mandrake, including tying it to a dog's collar, calling the dog from a safe distance and letting it do the suicide mission for you.

Thankfully, not all members of the nightshade family are out to get us. It is hard to imagine anything less threatening than the humble petunia, probably the best-known ornamental plant in the nightshade family. Since petunias were introduced from South America in the 1840s they have been condemned to some of horticulture's most ignominious tasks; namely, injecting lurid colour into hanging baskets and bedding schemes. British pubs would be drab places indeed in the absence of petunias, and municipal flower clocks could scarcely exist without them. Enough said.

PETUNIA

Wolfberries (*Lycium barbarum* and *L. chinense*) are touted as the latest must-have super-food, although the jury is still out on the myriad health benefits claimed for them. Wolfberries are invariably sold under the exotic moniker 'Tibetan goji berry' (from their Mandarin name *gou qi*). This is ironic when you consider that the harsh alpine deserts of the Tibetan plateau are about the only place in Eurasia where wolfberries *won't* grow. On the other hand they are a fairly common weed of waste ground across many parts of Europe and Asia. One suspects that the marketing people have had a hand in this. 'Tibetan goji berry' has a more saleable ring to it than 'Common Eurasian roadside weed', even though the latter is a more accurate representation of the wolfberry's habitat.

GOJI BERRY

Tomatoes, potatoes, capsicums and eggplants are the best-known edible night-shades but there are several more besides. The tamarillo or tree tomato (*Solanum betaceum*) is a short-lived subtropical tree from the Andes. It is an adaptable plant; one of the few fruits which grows well in shade. It is very ornamental, too, with big, heart-shaped leaves and colourful fruits which hang like baubles beneath the leaves during autumn and winter. The egg-sized fruits have a satiny skin that comes in two colours: rich blood-red and warm orange. The flesh has an unusual texture, consisting of a firm yellow outer layer surrounding a seedy, passionfruit-like pulp. The taste of tamarillos is an acquired one, reminiscent of a savoury passionfruit. Maybe it is this savouriness that has stopped the tamarillo from achieving wider acceptance. The trick is to think of it more as a vegetable than a fruit, just as we do with its cousin the tomato.

The Golden Fruit of the Andes (*Solanum quitoense*) is also known as *naran-jilla* ('little orange' in Spanish) in its native South America. It is a luxuriant shrub

NARANJILLA

bearing zucchini-like leaves half a metre in length, covered with purple fuzz and with a row of purple spines down the middle. The fruits are round, orange and covered in golden stubble. They taste utterly sublime. Unfortunately they are extremely shy-fruiting in Australia. Many South American nightshades, tomatoes included, are adapted to be pollinated by a special kind of bee which vibrates the flowers in order to make them release pollen. This is called 'buzz pollination'. Buzz pollinators are few and far between in Australia, which might account for the naranjilla's unwillingness to fruit here. Or perhaps naranjillas miss their home high in the tropical cloud forest where temperatures are a mild 18°C every single day of the seasonless year. Either way, the naranjilla is worth growing for its gorgeous foliage alone, even if it never sets fruit.

The pepino (*Solanum muricatum*) never has trouble setting fruit. In fact it never stops. The pepino also comes from the Andes. It is a small, evergreen shrub with classic purple potato flowers. The egg-like fruits are the size of a small mango, with a satiny, ivory skin striped here and there with violet. The flesh is firm and a very pale orange colour, with a taste like a very insipid melon. Actually, 'taste' is probably too strong a word. It's more as if somebody simply waved a melon over it. Personally, I find it difficult to get excited about pepinos. They are just a bit too bland for my palate. They could have a big future if some breeding and selection work was done to enhance their sweetness and flavour. Some breeding work has been done on them in New Zealand; however, considering the thousands of years of breeding and selection that has already gone into other Andean crops like potatoes and tomatoes, the pepino has quite a lot of catching up to do.

TOMATILLO

Despite their name, Cape gooseberries are neither South African nor gooseberries. They are nightshades and, as their scientific name *Physalis peruviana* suggests, they come from Peru. Cape gooseberries are sprawling annual plants which produce yellow berries like tiny spherical tomatoes, enclosed in a hollow, papery calyx. The fruits have an odd flavour reminiscent of tomato and pineapple. They are produced in huge numbers and are said to make an excellent jam due to their high pectin content. Closely related to the Cape gooseberry is the tomatillo, *Physalis philadelphica*, from Mexico (not Philadelphia). Tomatillos look like big green cherry tomatoes wrapped in the *Physalis'* trademark papery calyx. They are an important ingredient in Mexican cuisine, best known as the main ingredient in salsa verde.

There are two ornamental nightshades which make regular appearances in floristry. Closely related to the Cape gooseberry is the gorgeous Chinese lantern (*Physalis alkekengi*). It bears neat vermilion fruit husks like little paper lanterns. The nipple fruit (*Solanum mammosum*) gets its naughty name from its pumpkin-orange fruits which look for all the world like little plastic cow udders. Nipple fruits have a distinctly artificial quality about them. If you didn't know better, you would say they were manufactured in a factory, not grown in a garden.

Australia has its share of native nightshades in the form of bush tomatoes. The kutjera or desert raisin (*Solanum centrale*) is a thorny desert shrub which bears small, highly flavoured fruits. Called *kampurarpa* in Pitjantjatjara, desert raisins are a traditional food for people from the Central Desert. The Tanami apple (*Solanum chippendalei*) is a desert bush tomato from further north. Its larger but milder fruits grow on a beautiful sage-grey felted bush with big mauve flowers. They look stunning set against the red desert sand. Bush tomatoes have caught the attention of city cooks and are being grown commercially now by Aboriginal people on the Anangu Pitjantjatjara Yankunytjatjara (APY) lands in South Australia.

Three bush tomatoes from south-eastern Australia, *Solanum laciniatum, S. aviculare* and *S. linearifolium*, are commonly called kangaroo apples. Kangaroo apples are large, short-lived shrubs with very attractive cut foliage hanging on dark purple stems. European gardeners grow kangaroo apples for their jungly foliage, bedding them out with other frost-tender plants during the summer months and digging them up and bringing them indoors in winter. In Australia they are enthusiastically planted as bush tucker plants by permaculturists. The small, thin-fleshed fruits are indeed edible . . . in the same way that birch bark and lichen are edible. That is to say, they are totally unpalatable, but they won't kill you. Only they might. Like most nightshades the fruits are borderline toxic unless they are fully ripe, by which time the birds have eaten them all anyway. As a food source kangaroo apples are as good as useless. What they *are* good for is as a rootstock for grafting eggplants on to and, surprisingly, for extracting a precursor chemical used in making human steroids, including the contraceptive pill (don't try this at home).

COSTOLUTO GENOVESE TOMATO

TOMATOES

Like the maligned black nightshades, tomatoes were once thought to be toxic. When they were first introduced to Europe from Mexico by the Spanish in the early 1500s, tomatoes were regarded with considerable suspicion. In 1597 John Gerard wrote his famous *Herball* (or rather, plagiarised most of it from the Flemish botanist Rembert Dodoens). Of tomatoes, Gerard wrote 'In Spaine and those hot regions they used to eat [tomatoes] prepared and boil'd with pepper salt and oil; but they yeeld very little nourishment to the body and the same naught and corrupt.' He added for good measure that 'the whole plant is of ranke and stinking savour'.

Clearly, John Gerard needed to lighten up a bit. Most of us consider the tomato to be the Queen of Vegetables, enjoying a cult status which cabbage and celery can only dream of. Even people who rarely lift a finger in the garden are religious about planting tomato seedlings every spring, staking and tending the vines with a devotion not accorded to other, lowlier, vegetables. Why? Perhaps because the smell of a tomato plant, far from being rank and stinking, has the power to transport us back to the endless summer days of childhood. Or perhaps because eating a perfectly ripe, home-grown tomato is an experience that money can't buy.

Why do tomatoes taste so wonderful? Like many other fruits, tomatoes have a high sugar content. However, the same could be said of peas or corn. You don't see anyone treating peas and corn with the kind of reverence reserved for tomatoes, so it must be something else that makes tomatoes so special. Perhaps it is the elusive fifth taste, *umami*, that holds the key. Umami does not have a recognisable flavour in the way that the other basic tastes – sweet, sour, salty and bitter – do. Rather, umami lends foods a mouth-filling richness. Think of parmesan cheese, anchovies, cooked mushrooms and even Vegemite. They all have a particular *savoury* quality: that's umami. The ultimate umami ingredient is the flavour enhancer monosodium glutamate (MSG). MSG is made by adding sodium to glutamates derived by bacterial fermentation of sugars. It turns out that tomatoes are particularly rich in glutamates. When you sprinkle salt (sodium) on to a slice of tomato (glutamates), you are essentially making your own MSG: delicious. Before you reach for your asthma puffer I should tell you that the overwhelming weight of scientific literature shows that MSG is perfectly harmless. You can feel quite free to enjoy a tomato sandwich, or Chinese takeaway, with impunity.

There are ten or so species of wild tomato, all native to South America from Chile through Peru, Ecuador, Bolivia and the Galapagos Islands. The cultivated tomato is *Solanum lycopersicum* (formerly *Lycopersicon esculentum*). *Lycopersicum* derives from the Greek for 'wolf's peach'. The cultivated tomato grows wild throughout Central and South America. Like many crops, it is probably not a naturally occurring plant species but a *cultigen* – a plant that has evolved by human selection rather than by natural selection. The cultivated tomato may have descended from the wild species *Solanum pimpinellifolium*, with which it interbreeds readily. Tomatoes also interbreed happily with *S. cheesmaniae* from the Galapagos Islands. *S. cheesmaniae* is a yellow-fruited species that grows on the rocky sea shore, right down to the high tide mark. It is extremely salt-tolerant. In fact it can be irrigated with seawater, a very promising trait for future tomato breeding.

If the South Americans domesticated tomatoes, they left no clues behind. Even the Moche civilisation of Peru, who manufactured countless ceramic vessels depicting potatoes, sweet potatoes, cassava, gourds, squash, beans and corn, left none at all depicting tomatoes, suggesting that they weren't a major food source during the Moche empire which lasted from the first to the eighth centuries CE. In spite of wild tomatoes' South American origins, all available evidence points to the cultivated tomato being domesticated much further north, in Mexico, in around the fifth century. It is not certain how ancestral tomatoes got to Mexico in the first place. Perhaps they tagged along as weeds of another crop, popping up unbidden but welcomed for their tiny red or yellow fruits.

By the time the Spaniard Hernán Cortés conquered Mexico in 1519, the Aztec were growing a large, yellow-ridged tomato cultivar. The Aztec called this plant *tomatl*. *Tomatl* were taken back to Spain amongst the spoils of conquest. From there they were transported to Spain's many territories. In the sixteenth century this included the Italian city of Naples. Thus the Spanish and Italians became the first foreigners to try this new fruit. The Spanish named it *tomate* after its Nahuatl name but the Italians dubbed it *pomodoro* – the golden apple. Tomatoes have come to be associated with Italian cuisine more than any other vegetable. Naples has an especially strong association with the tomato – think Napoli sauce – but the earliest mention of the *pomodoro* comes from Venice in 1544, by Pier Andrea Mattioli (after whom the old-fashioned flowers called stocks, or *Matthiola*, are named). Mattioli described the *pomodoro* as being like a new kind of mandrake, and he went on to offer a serving suggestion: fried in oil with salt and pepper.

Not everyone in Europe was convinced that the tomato was OK for eating. The Elizabethans grew it strictly as an ornamental curiosity, for its large, attractive berries. It took the tomato several hundred years to achieve wide acceptance. When it finally did, during the late eighteenth and early nineteenth centuries, it naturally enough became enormously popular. People all over Europe bred their own local strains suited to their local conditions and culinary preferences. In Italy, big beefsteak and paste tomatoes were favoured. In the Crimea, black tomatoes were quite the thing. The French liked neat, round salad tomatoes. During the late nineteenth and early twentieth centuries, these hundreds of European cultivars found their way to the USA with waves of migrants. There they thrived in the rich growing conditions and tropical-like summers. There was an explosion of new varieties. Seed catalogues from the USA around the year 1900 list dozens and dozens of distinct varieties. Perhaps it was fatigue from this bewildering choice of varieties that allowed the new F1 hybrid tomatoes of the 1950s to comprehensively push the heirlooms aside. Whatever the reason, the new hybrids were touted as the way of the future. The old heirlooms very nearly died out but for a few old-timers and the steadfast Amish saving seed. We owe them a debt of thanks for the amazing variety of shapes, colours and flavours that is once more available to us today.

TOMATOES AND THEIR PEOPLE:
TOMMY TOMATOSEED AND DANCING WITH SMURFS

•

Tom 'Tommy Tomatoseed' Wagner has been breeding tomatoes since he was a boy. He is the genius who gave us the Green Zebra tomato. Tom began developing Green Zebra at the age of ten, finally introducing it to horticulture thirty years later in 1983 through his company Tater Mater (get it?). Green Zebra is now one of the top-selling 'heirloom' varieties even though it is just thirty years old. Now, if a ten-year-old boy can breed vegetables, surely anyone can. Why should all the plant breeding be left to giant gene tech companies, who want to patent any gene that looks useful and lock it away for their private use, when anyone can do it in their own backyard?

Tom thinks we need more tomato breeders, not fewer. He welcomes gardeners tinkering with his varieties and developing their own new varieties from them. To this end he releases his new experimental strains to the public on the express understanding that they are works in progress which need to be finished off and properly stabilised. Tom keeps meticulous pedigrees for all his tomatoes and makes this information available to all and sundry. His work, in the tradition of tomato breeders of the past 2500 years, is completely open source.

Tom is currently working on, amongst many other projects, blue tomatoes. He's breeding several small cherry tomatoes and large salad types with blue skin, and which grow on blue vines. He has bred some amazing colours – **Blue Pitts** is bright purple, **Stripes of Yore** is yellow with green and dark blue stripes, **Blue Streak** and the wonderfully named **Dances With Smurfs** are both darkest indigo. Tom's blue tomatoes are still works in progress. Their flavour is still being improved

BLUE PITTS TOMATO

STRIPES OF YORE TOMATO

BLUE STREAK TOMATO

DANCES WITH SMURFS TOMATO

Tom Wagner wants to create tomatoes with blue vines,
not just blue fruit.

and as they all ripen to red or orange the blue flush of their skin fades to a greater
or lesser degree. With Tom's skill and experience there is no doubt that he and his
merry band of followers will come up with something wonderful. Keep an eye out
for blue tomatoes very soon.

VARIETIES

•

There are somewhere between 4000 and 75000 tomato cultivars in existence, depending on who you ask. Anyway, lots of them. Some tomatoes are round, some sausage-shaped, some ribbed, some boxy. There are tomatoes as small as currants and as large as grapefruit. There are tomatoes adapted to short summers, cool summers, dry summers, and wet summers. There are varieties for eating whole, for slicing, bottling, drying or stuffing. Some are meaty, some are juicy, some are hollow like capsicums. There is almost every combination of morphological, horticultural and culinary attributes you can imagine, which is why heirloom tomatoes are the superior choice for home gardeners and gourmets. Space permits only a tantalising glimpse of known varieties here. Hopefully it's enough to whet your appetite for seeking out more.

Tomato plants are defined as having either determinate or indeterminate growth. They can be compact bushes (determinate) or rangy vines (indeterminate), in other words. Commercial tomato varieties are always determinate as they are easier to harvest mechanically, but this is of no consequence to home gardeners. Most heirloom tomatoes have indeterminate growth, so they continue to grow and fruit over a very long season. They just keep on keeping on.

Amish Paste

This variety was acquired from Amish farmers in Pennsylvania, who are the stewards of an amazing treasure trove of heirloom vegetables. Amish Paste is orange–red, lumpy and around the size of a tennis ball. Decidedly unattractive to look at, it is actually incredibly useful and tastes great. While it is ostensibly a paste variety (i.e. fleshy and light on seeds), Amish Paste is good for just about

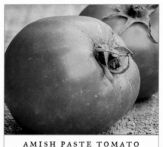

AMISH PASTE TOMATO

anything. It makes fantastic tomato sauce, dries well and, in contrast to most paste tomatoes, which taste mealy and bland when eaten fresh, Amish Paste is delicious straight off the vine. A great all-round tomato.

Aunt Ruby's German Green

A family heirloom tomato named after Ruby Arnold whose German grandfather took seed with him when he migrated from Germany to the United States. It's lucky for us that he did: this is a first-class beefsteak tomato. It is not unusual for Aunt Ruby's German Green to weigh around 500g, often more. The skin and flesh are olive–yellow, striped with dark lime-green. The flesh is meaty and succulent with a refreshing tang absent in most beefsteak varieties. Like all green tomato varieties, pick this one when the base colour begins to yellow and the flesh becomes soft to the touch.

AUNT RUBY'S GERMAN GREEN TOMATO

Big Rainbow

A whacking big beefsteak tomato that is yellow, marbled inside and out with red. Like all beefsteak varieties it is prone to catfacing (a condition where the bottom of the tomato becomes scarred and malformed), and to corkiness around the stem, but these sins are easily forgiven. Big Rainbow's flesh is meaty, quite light and bright-flavoured for

BIG RAINBOW TOMATO

a beefsteak. Big Rainbow was passed on to the American Seed Savers' Exchange by Dorothy Beiswenger in the 1980s.

Black Cherry

Most cherry tomatoes can be relied upon for good flavour, even when slightly under-ripe. Black Cherry is no exception. As a bonus, it has some of the smokiness and depth of flavour associated with black beefsteak tomatoes like Black Krim. Black Cherry bears heavy crops of chocolate-brown spheres loaded on to long trusses. They ripen well even when nights are cool.

Black Cherry is not to be confused with a similar cherry tomato variety called **Brown Berry** which never seems to ripen in my experience, remaining bland and uninteresting regardless of the weather.

Black Krim

Black Krim comes originally from the Crimea. It was introduced to the wider world as late as 1990 by the Swede Lars Olov Rosenstrom. It is a large beefsteak-type tomato with chocolate-brown flesh, striped with dark green and blushed with smoky purple. Its taste is unique. Distinctly smoky, almost salty, with very meaty flesh, this is a no-nonsense

BLACK KRIM TOMATO

tomato for grown-ups. Black Krim is compact, relatively early cropping for a beef-steak tomato and it performs well in less-than-ideal conditions.

Brandywine

BRANDYWINE TOMATO

Have you ever noticed those tomato-shaped tomato sauce bottles in American movies and wondered why they are pink when we all know that tomatoes are red? Take a look at Brandy-wine and there is your answer. Brandywine was once the USA's favourite tomato. In the first half of the twentieth century it was a local legend, instantly recognisable and synonymous with flavour. What better variety to mould in plastic as a ketchup-squirting table decoration? Several strains of Brandywine are grown in its native USA, including yellow, red and black strains. Here we only see one of the many beautiful pink strains, the Sudduth strain.

Broad Ripple Yellow Currant

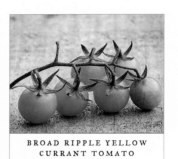

BROAD RIPPLE YELLOW
CURRANT TOMATO

Discovered growing in a crack in the footpath in the USA city of Indianapolis in the 1980s, this tiny cherry tomato has a bigger flavour than its size suggests. Broad Ripple Yellow Currant might be small in size but it certainly makes up for it in quantity and taste. The vines are big and sprawling, dripping with tiny golden fruits. It crops over a long season and makes a great garnishing tomato. Throw a handful of these little beauties over any dish and you will make it look instantly summery and fresh.

Costoluto Genovese

Costoluto Genovese means 'Genoese ribbed'. This tomato is extremely pretty, like a pillar box-red silken purse gathered up at the top with a green draw-string. It is probably very similar to the first tomatoes to reach Europe from the New World.

Green Grape

Another one of Tom Wagner's babies, Green Grape is a prolific yellow-green cherry tomato. At its best it is sweet and tangy with a hint of toast on the back palate. When it is grown in cool regions, however, it's just plain old sour.

GREEN GRAPE TOMATO

Green Zebra

A modern heirloom bred by Thomas 'Tommy Tomatoseed' Wagner. Green Zebra is a round, medium-sized tomato with an acid-yellow skin striped with bright pea-green. Green Zebra is a pleasure to grow, behold and eat. It has a sweet, tangy flavour that is very approachable and instantly likeable. The plants are very giving and because the fruits are green the birds mostly leave them alone. To tell when a Green Zebra is ripe, watch for the background colour of the skin to change from cold apple-green to a warm golden green. Give the tomato a gentle squeeze. If the flesh gives a little, it's ready to go.

GREEN ZEBRA TOMATO

Grosse Lisse

Ask an Australian to name a tomato variety and Grosse Lisse will be their answer. Australians have had a love affair with this heirloom variety for a century. Its origins are obscure. First listed by the French seed company Vilmorin in 1900 under the name Grosse Lisse ('big smooth' in French) and in England under the name Trophy not long thereafter, it is probably American in origin. Or maybe German. Either way, Australians are the only people on earth who obsessively grow Grosse Lisse as if their national pride depended on it.

Grosse Lisse is so familiar in Australia that it hardly needs description. It bears biggish, roundish, reddish, juicy/meaty tomatoes grow on a fairly compact vine. It is a good, middle-of-the-road tomato that does the job expected of it without distinguishing itself. Perhaps it's the perfect tomato for the nation that invented the tall poppy syndrome. If you want to experiment with something a little more interesting, try one of the other varieties listed.

Isis Candy

Isis Candy is a modern heirloom cherry tomato bred by Joe Bratka in the USA. It has unusual peach–orange, slightly fuzzy fruits borne in small clusters. When fully ripe Isis Candy has a distinctive fruity taste.

ISIS CANDY TOMATO

Jaune Flamme/Jaune Flammée/ Flamme/Jaune Flammé

The doyenne of all things tomato, Amy Goldman, says of this variety: 'This tomato can do no wrong [...] Unsurpassed in flavor and appearance [...] I could fill a whole tomato garden with nothing but Flammes.' I couldn't agree more. Usually known as Jaune Flammée in our part of the world, Jaune Flamme is a French heirloom variety passed on by the French tomato collector Norbert Parreira (whose

JAUNE FLAMME TOMATO

surname and home commune of Hellimer are misspelled in nearly every reference to this tomato on the internet; it's amazing how typos can go viral and morph into facts).

Jaune Flamme is an oval, medium-sized tomato, glowing orange inside and out. It has a sweet, punchy flavour. The plant is robust, generous, relatively early to ripen and it performs reliably even in heavy soils and cool summers. If you have room for only one tomato in your garden, make it Jaune Flamme.

Lemon Drop

Lemon Drop bears yellow fruits the size of a five-cent piece. They are sweet and tangy with a definite citrus note, just like the old boiled lolly of the same name. The plants are extremely productive over a very long season. This is a great tomato for small gardens and balconies.

LEMON DROP TOMATO

Radiator Charlie's Mortgage Lifter

This fantastically named variety was bred by Marshall Cletis Byles, nicknamed 'Radiator Charlie', in West Virginia during the Great Depression. By the 1940s Byles had perfected the strain and was able to sell the seedlings for a dollar each and pay off his $6000 mortgage.

This is a great tomato. Huge, fat and bloated like a pumped-up Grosse Lisse, the fruits beg to be eaten greedily. They have tomato-red skin with pink, meaty flesh. Juicy, well-flavoured and high-yielding for a beefsteak, this variety has everything going for it. Radiator Charlie's Mortgage Lifter gets called Mortgage Lifter for short, but it's not the only tomato with that title. Amy Goldman lists another fifteen varieties of Mortgage Lifter in her seminal book *The Heirloom Tomato*.

MORTGAGE LIFTER TOMATO

Russian Black/Black Russian

An Australian heirloom tomato passed on to the Diggers Club in 1992 by a gardener who knew it from Gippsland. A medium-sized fruit, round tending toward egg-shaped, with chocolate-brown skin and juicy flesh. Its flavour is mild and savoury, with just a hint of the smokiness of Black Krim. A good doer in the backyard, it crops fairly early in the season.

Tigerella/Tiger Tom

Tigerella is a small salad tomato, red with orange stripes, bred in England by Dr L.A. Darby around 1970. Tigerella was bred for glasshouse culture, a safer bet in England given the vagaries of their summer weather. It thrives in Australia's heat and crops very heavily here. The flavour is not top shelf, but it ain't bad either.

TIGERELLA TOMATO

Wapsipinicon Peach/Yellow Peach

This nineteenth-century American heirloom gets its mouthful of a name from the Wapsipinicon river in Iowa. Its fruits are soft, buttery yellow with fuzzy skin like that of a peach. They look a bit wan and ethereal, but bite into a fully ripe Wapsipinicon Peach and it will smack you in the mouth with its monster flavour. Sugary and packed with mouth-filling umami, you can still taste this variety in your mouth half an hour after eating one.

WAPSIPINICON PEACH TOMATO

Having said that, I feel the Australian strain of Wapsipinicon Peach has become bigger, yellower, smoother-skinned and blander in recent years. If you save your own seed, make sure you keep only seed from your best, truest plant. Wapsipinicon Peach ripens over a long season. Even after the vine has withered and died the fruits continue to ripen until the first frosts. This is a great tomato for pots and balcony gardens.

WILD SWEETIE TOMATO

Wild Sweetie

Wild Sweetie is aptly named. It resembles wild *S. pimpinellifolium* tomatoes, only with a superior flavour. The teeny-tiny, currant-sized fruits are surprisingly sugary with hardly any tang at all. They grow on big, rangy vines that scramble everywhere, cropping prolifically as they go. A single plant will bear hundreds of delicate trusses spangled with glossy red fruits, like garnet bracelets. Even after the vine has died off the fruits continue to ripen for weeks. Kids love foraging for these tiny treats and it is a wonderful variety for turning a courtyard or balcony garden into an edible jungle.

In the interests of balance I should point out that there are some pretty substandard heirloom tomatoes, too. **Stupice** is an early ripening Czech heirloom. Sadly, it is watery and insipid, as is the pretty, ferny-leaved Russian heirloom **Silvery Fir Tree**. In my opinion the French heirloom **Rouge de Marmande** isn't much chop either, despite effusive descriptions in seed catalogues.

The beautifully striped **Schimmeig Creg** (which means 'striped rock' in the all-but-extinct Manx language) is as hard and hollow as a tennis ball but with less flavour. Schimmeig Creg was bred by Tom Wagner, of Green Zebra fame. Why, you might ask, would an esteemed breeder such as Tom keep such an inedible variety going? Two reasons: the first is that Schimmeig Creg's hollowness make it ideal for stuffing. It's more like an 'edible box' than a 'fruit'. More importantly, however, it might come in handy one day for imparting its genes for firmness and hollowness. All open-pollinated vegetable varieties – even the yucky ones – are important for the genes they contain. Who knows what we will need those genes for in the future?

SCHIMMEIG CREG TOMATO

PERUVIAN HEIRLOOM POTATOES

POTATOES

If the tomato is the dazzling Queen of Vegetables, then potatoes are the mud-caked peasants. An undifferentiated lump of starch grubbed from the dirt was never going to enjoy the celebrity status of a glossy, bauble-like fruit. Yet to many people potatoes have a homely, rustic beauty all their own.

Potatoes are one of the few staple crops that are not a member of the grass family. Their importance to human nutrition can hardly be overstated. They are the third most important crop after rice and wheat. Whole cultures depend on potatoes for their nutrition. Indeed, potatoes have shaped human history at certain times; not a bad effort for an ugly tuber.

There are around 190 species of tuber-forming *Solanum* native to the Americas. They come from as far south as Argentina and as far north as the southern USA. The area where the greatest number of tuberous species overlap is in the region of Lake Titicaca in southern Peru and western Bolivia. It was here that the domesticated potato (*Solanum tuberosum*) first appeared. The domesticated potato is a natural hybrid, probably between the wild species *Solanum stenotomum* and *S. sparsipilum*. The potato is an *amphidiploid*, meaning it has four sets of chromosomes: two from each of its parents. This is twice the amount of genetic material found in most organisms, giving the cultivated potato enormous potential for genetic variation and adaptation.

Chuño is made by freeze-drying potatoes.

The oldest physical examples of potatoes come from a cave in Peru around 5000 BCE, although people might have eaten them since 8000 BCE. The potato's astounding genetic variability made it an ideal crop plant, since it was able to adapt to the diverse microclimates found over relatively small distances in Peru, from the tropical coastal strip to the warm inland valleys and subalpine grasslands high in the Andes. The cultivated potato evolved into two subspecies, *S. tuberosum* subsp. *andigena* from the northern Andes and *S. t.* subsp. *tuberosum* from Chile. The Andean subspecies preferred the seasonless conditions of the tropical highlands, while the Chilean subspecies adapted to the changing seasonal day lengths experienced at higher latitudes.

As the potato radiated from its centre of origin, new varieties were selected that were suited to local conditions and different uses. The Moche civilisation of northern Peru depicted amazingly realistic potatoes in their ceramics between the first and eighth centuries CE. By the fifteenth century, the great Inca civilisation united cultures from Columbia in the north through to Chile and Argentina in the south, assimilating many smaller cultures and many hundreds of potato varieties into their empire.

Inca society was fuelled by the potato. Potatoes were farmed at higher elevations (up to 4700 metres) and transported downhill on the backs of llamas to be traded for corn and quinoa farmed at lower altitudes. The Inca did not eat potatoes as chips, or mashed or boiled like we do. They processed their potatoes in some way, typically by making them into *chuño*. Chuño was (and still is) made at higher altitudes in the Andes where icy nights coupled with dry, sunny days create natural freeze-drying conditions. The potato varieties grown for chuño are slightly toxic but freeze-drying them removes the toxins and renders them edible. Chuño was traded over long distances and was able to be stored for long periods without any loss in quality.

The Spanish first took potatoes to their colony on the Canary Islands in the 1560s where, it is speculated, the two subspecies *andigena* and *tuberosum* crossed and gave rise to the familiar European strain of potatoes. Potatoes arrived on the

Europeans originally grew the potato for its ornamental flowers.

Spanish mainland and in the Spanish Netherlands (now Belgium) around 1570. The English might have brought potatoes back to Europe from South America a second time in the 1580s or 90s on one of Drake's or Raleigh's swashbuckling expeditions.

The potato made it to Ireland early on. Some stories attribute its arrival there to potatoes washed ashore from the wreckage of the Spanish Armada in 1588, others to Sir Francis Drake. It has also been suggested that they arrived there courtesy of Basque fishermen who used to put ashore in Ireland.

The Spanish adopted the Quechua word *papa* for potatoes. They also adapted the Taíno word for sweet potato, *batata*. The Spanish have used the two terms *papas* and *patatas* interchangeably for potatoes ever since. However, in England the term *potato* was used interchangeably for both sweet potatoes (*Ipomoea batatas*) and real potatoes, even though they are not related to one another. By 1600 John Gerard was the first to make a distinction between 'common' potatoes (sweet potatoes) and 'Virginia' or 'bastard' potatoes (true potatoes).

The frontispiece to the posthumous 1636 edition of Gerard's famous *Herball* depicts him holding a potato flower. This is interesting because the potato did not catch on immediately as a food source in Europe. It was thought to be poisonous, to arouse unwanted passions and to cause leprosy. It is true that the leaves, fruits and light-exposed tubers are poisonous but blaming potatoes for leprosy seems a bit over the top. In any case, it wasn't until food shortages in the mid eighteenth century that the potato began to gain acceptance in Europe, 200 years after its introduction.

By the end of the eighteenth century the potato had come to be seen as a food which the poor could subsist on perfectly adequately, though not fit for the tables of the affluent. Adam Smith wrote in his *Wealth of Nations* in 1776 that:

> The chairmen, porters, and coalheavers in London, and those unfortunate women who live by prostitution, the strongest men and the most beautiful women perhaps in the British dominions, are said to be, the greatest part of them, from the lowest rank of people in Ireland, who are generally fed with the root.

Thomas Malthus added in 1798:

> The lands in England […] would all bear potatoes; and Dr Adam Smith observes that if potatoes were to become the favourite vegetable food of the common people, and if the same quantity of land was employed in their culture as is now employed in the culture of corn, the country would be able to support a much greater population […]

The French almanac *Le Bon Jardinier* noted of potatoes in 1785 that 'the poor should be quite content with this food.'

If this has a faint 'let them eat cake' ring to it, it is not without reason. European society was undergoing massive restructuring. France was on the verge of revolution. In Britain the Enclosures were being ramped up, robbing the landless peasant class of its historical right to grow and glean food on common land. The poor, forced to move to urban industrial centres to seek work, became dependent on the cheap, abundant potato for their nutrition. The new industrialists grew wealthy off the back of their potato-fuelled labour.

With disturbing prescience Thomas Malthus wrote in 1806:

> […] nothing could be more detestable than the idea of knowingly condemning the labourers of the country to the rags and wretched cabins of Ireland for the purpose of selling a few more broad cloths and calicoes.

In this he foresaw the darkest chapter in the potato's history; the Irish potato famine of 1845–48.

The potato famine is called in Irish, chillingly, *an Gorta Mór*: 'the Great Hunger'. It was caused by several consecutive years of potato crop failure, resulting in the deaths of a million Irish and the flight of a million more refugees. But to call the Great Hunger a 'potato famine' is to tell only half the story, because this famine was caused not only by potatoes but by human greed and indifference to the suffering of others. It was the result of a shameful moral blight as much as the famous potato blight which customarily bears the blame.

In the nineteenth century the Irish were a subjugated people ruled by an Anglo-Irish landowner class. The Anglo-Irish landowners lived mostly in England, extracting handsome incomes from the beef and grain exported from their farms in Ireland. These absentee landowners rarely (in some cases, never) visited their farms and for the most part had no personal attachment to them. To them, their farms were simply businesses. They saw Ireland as a food mine that could have its bounty stripped and exported for their own private gain. There was no legal mechanism for putting any of Ireland's agricultural bounty back into the country itself, either in the form of food or social infrastructure. Nor did the landowners feel any sense of *noblesse oblige*.

The Irish farms were worked by Catholic labourers. Although they represented the majority of the Irish population, Catholics were prevented from owning land under British law. Therefore the labourers were obliged to rent land from the absentee landowners on which to live and grow their own crops to feed their families. This was known as the 'conacre' system. A class of so-called 'middlemen' administrated the conacre system, renting land from the landowners at a fixed rate and subletting it to labourers for their own profit.

The Catholic Irish labourers had no rights whatsoever. British law gave landowners all the rights but no responsibility toward the labouring poor who were, for all intents and purposes, their slaves. Hence a huge underclass of Irish farm labourers was locked into a cycle of poverty and dependence. In 1745 a Royal Commission into land laws in Ireland found that:

> It would be impossible adequately to describe the privations which [the Irish peasantry] habitually and silently endure […] in many districts their only food is the potato, their only beverage water […] their cabins are seldom a protection against the weather […] a bed or a blanket is a rare luxury […]

The Irish were the most destitute people in Europe. Yet, in the newfound spirit of capitalism, landowners and middlemen contrived to squeeze ever more profit and productivity from the workforce. Less time was made available for labourers to tend their own crops as landowners ramped up production on their farms. Less land was made available for conacre as more was turned over to grain and beef. A decreasing supply of conacre allowed the middlemen to charge extortionate rents for smaller and smaller tracts of marginal land.

There was only one crop that could give high enough yields to enable labourers to feed their families, with just a few acres of land and no time to spare: potatoes. Potatoes facilitated the Irish agricultural boom of the early nineteenth century, allowing the Irish population to swell to eight million. Ironically the potato itself did not have a starring role in this agricultural boom. It was merely the fuel for the farm labourers who grew the grain and beef for export.

The farm labourers grew their potatoes in so-called 'lazy beds'. These were raised beds mulched with seaweed and manure. They had no time for niceties like bringing in the potato harvest, let alone crop rotation. They just left the potatoes in the ground to grow, grubbing a few as needed for each meal. It was literally a hand-to-mouth existence. Potatoes gave exceptionally high yields, even on marginal land, with relatively little labour. In Ireland's wet climate potatoes produced six tons per acre compared with one ton of wheat or oats. However, potatoes were seen as the food of the poor so there was no demand for them. Grain and beef were more profitable commodities so the economics of the situation was perfectly simple as far as the landlords were concerned. More land had to be turned over to grain and beef production and as little as possible allocated to housing potato-eating peasants.

The greed of the landowners squeezed the already destitute Irish subsistence farmers even tighter. Their conacres, once mixed smallholding farms, became little more than tiny potato monocultures. The labourers could barely grow enough to feed the whole family. Menfolk began to travel to Scotland as seasonal 'guest' workers where they could earn extra money to pay their exorbitant rents and coincidentally reduce the number of mouths needing to be fed at home.

By the early 1840s Ireland was a net food exporter, producing record amounts of grain and beef. Yet a Malthusian catastrophe was just around the corner.

In 1845 a disease called potato late blight (*Phytophthora infestans*) arrived in Europe. It appeared first in the Netherlands, brought in with new potato varieties imported from the Americas. The blight destroyed portions of the Dutch and English potato crops but fortunately in those countries the poor had other food sources to fall back on. In Ireland, the working poor were totally dependent on potatoes for their nutrition. When the blight arrived in Ireland in 1845 it wiped out 40 per cent of the crop. This was a disaster, but things got even worse the next year.

The 'lazy bed' growing system coupled with a lack of understanding about fungal pathogens meant that diseased tubers were left in the ground to rot, inoculating the soil with blight spores ready to infect the following potato crop. In 1846 a devastating 90 per cent of the Irish potato crop was destroyed by blight.

The reason that such a huge proportion of the Irish potato crop was destroyed is that it was composed of just one variety of potato called, rather inauspiciously, **Lumpers**. Lumpers has no resistance to late blight. As potatoes are propagated vegetatively rather than by seed, every potato plant in Ireland was genetically identical to every other. If the Irish had grown more than one variety of potato, some of these might have had a degree of resistance to blight and the losses might not have been so high. They didn't. Ireland's potato crop was a single variety monoculture.

Faced with a catastrophe within their own borders you might think that the British government would have stepped in to provide aid to the poor. It did . . . kind of. First a 'work-for-the-dole' programme was set up, paying workers below-market wages to make unnecessary roads. This scheme was pretty clearly designed to fail and it quickly fell by the wayside. In 1847 – two years after the famine began – soup kitchens were set up but, again, these were soon abandoned.

It is fair to say that the man given the job of overseeing aid to Ireland, Charles Trevelyan, had little pity for the Irish peasants. He saw his job as ensuring that business as usual was maintained on behalf of the landowners. In 1846 he wrote: 'Our measures must proceed with as little disturbance as possible of the ordinary course of private trade', adding as an afterthought that 'the people must not, under any circumstances, be allowed to starve.' And yet they were. By 1848 Trevelyan had become more hardened towards the Irish, describing the famine as 'a direct stroke of an all-wise and all-merciful Providence'.

In contrast to Trevelyan's chilling indifference to the plight of the Irish was the response of the indigenous Choctaw people of the USA. In 1847 news of the Irish people's desperation reached the Choctaw. They knew first-hand what the Irish were experiencing. They had been evicted from their lands in Mississippi in 1831 and forced to march to a reservation in Oklahoma. Many Choctaw people died of hunger and exposure on that march, the infamous 'Trail of Tears'. Although the destitute Choctaw people had nothing, they decided to make a collection and give everything they could to help the starving Irish. They raised $170. The Irish people remember their humble gift to this day.

Meanwhile the government of the richest, most powerful nation on earth – Britain – continued to protect private business interests at the expense of the starving masses. Grain grown in Ireland was not redirected to feed the Irish people but continued to be exported in order to line the pockets of the absentee landlords. Food riots, during which the Irish peasants tried to prevent grain-laden ships from leaving Ireland, were put down by the British government. Grain was transported from farms to port under armed guard. The Irish were dying in their thousands yet they were still expected to pay their rents and taxes. Hundreds of thousands of people were evicted from their homes. Then, almost unbelievably, in 1847 the British government *raised* taxes.

It has been suggested by some commentators that the British government's response to the famine was, in essence, genocidal. This is a very compelling argument when you consider that by the 1850s up to a million Irish had died of starvation and disease within the borders of the richest, most powerful nation on earth, and a million more had fled to the USA, Canada and Australia as refugees. Perhaps the most telling commentary on the matter was in a statement made on the Irish famine by former British prime minister Tony Blair in 1997, which was carefully worded to give the impression of an apology while simultaneously avoiding any admission of guilt.

The Great Hunger was played out at the nexus between food security, economics and politics. Issues of food ownership and distribution, the complicity of government with private interests at the expense of the majority, and the unchecked rapacity of middlemen collided with terrible consequences. This couldn't possibly happen today, could it?

Lessons have been learned from the Irish potato famine regarding crop diversity and disease resistance. Yet, paradoxically, a tension exists between groups like the International Potato Centre (CIP), who are doing their utmost to preserve genetic diversity and make it widely available, and giant agribusinesses who want to dominate the sector with their own 'improved' (read 'patented') potato varieties and swallow up competitors, effectively *reducing* crop diversity. Stakeholders on all sides know that the ability to harness genetic material is the key to the future of food. However, their approaches to the ownership of genetic material are fundamentally different.

One can't help but draw a parallel with the eighteenth-century Enclosures in Britain. The Enclosures were a ruthless land grab which transferred the ownership of commonly held land to private interests. This story is playing out again in our own time, only it is not common land that is being grabbed but genes.

Happily, there are groups working to keep potato breeding in the public domain. The CIP is an international collaboration between scientists and farmers based in the potato's heartland, Peru. The CIP aims to alleviate poverty through giving the poor access to tuber crops, especially potatoes. They maintain germplasm of 4300 traditional potato varieties in their gene bank, they run traditional breeding programmes and, with the utmost caution, they conduct research into genetic engineering. More strength to their arm, I say.

VARIETIES

•

Potatoes are propagated vegetatively rather than by seed, so they don't get the adaptive benefits that come from sexual reproduction. As a result, heirloom potatoes tend to be a sickly bunch, prone to all manner of fungal, bacterial and viral diseases. Very few truly 'ancient' breeds have come down to us today. Most of the heirloom potatoes grown today actually date from the late nineteenth and twentieth centuries. Many modern commercial potatoes are patented and are grown under licence for a predetermined use, such as making French fries for a particular fast food chain or vegetable processor. Heirloom varieties might lack disease resistance from a commercial grower's point of view but this is not such a problem for home gardeners, who do not grow their potatoes in monocultures under contract. What heirlooms lack in disease resistance they make up for in the kitchen. There is a potato to suit every possible taste and recipe.

Banana

Yellow and banana-shaped, this early season Baltic variety is in many ways similar to the more familiar Kipfler.

Bintje

A very high-yielding Dutch potato from 1910 with medium, round-oblong, creamy yellow tubers. It is a very versatile variety in the kitchen.

BANANA POTATO

Bismarck

A Tasmanian heirloom from the 1880s, Bismarck has blocky cream tubers with purple eyes and white flesh. It crops early, making lovely new potatoes for Christmas.

Charlotte

A French-bred, smallish, creamy white potato with buttery flesh that is good for just about any use. Delicious and productive.

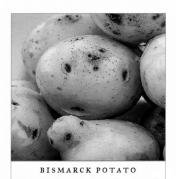

BISMARCK POTATO

Congo/Black Congo/ Purple Congo

A nineteenth-century potato with cylindrical tubers pitted with lots of deep eyes. The skin is purple-black and the flesh is bright, deep purple marbled with white. It is a prolific producer even in substandard conditions. Its mealy flesh cooks to an amazing lurid purple.

PURPLE CONGO POTATO

Desiree

A Dutch variety released in 1962 with flattened tubers with smooth pink skin and cream flesh. Desiree has fairly good disease resistance and is grown as a commercial variety so it is well known. Its waxy flesh is good for roasting, baking and potato salad but not much chop for making chips.

Kennebec

An American variety introduced by the US Department of Agriculture in the 1940s and still a very good potato. It is vigorous, disease resistant and heavy cropping. The tubers are very large, oblong in shape, with white skin and flesh. They have shallow eyes so they are very easy to peel, hence its popularity as a commercial potato for processing into chips. The flesh is starchy and nutty in flavour. It is a good all-rounder in the kitchen.

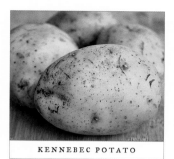

KENNEBEC POTATO

King Edward

First listed in the UK in 1902 when King Edward VII was on the throne, his namesake potato produces stout oval tubers of pale yellow with a bit of pink flush. The flesh is floury and good for mashing. For roasting in their jackets, King Edwards are second to none.

Kipfler

A 'Kipfel' is an Austrian pastry made from a sheet of dough rolled up and curved like a horseshoe – the parent of the French croissant. Kipfler potatoes resemble Kipfel pastries in their curved cigar shape and pale brown colour. They were the first 'boutique potatoes' to come on to the Australian scene and are still one of the most popular. They have waxy yellow flesh which holds its shape when cooked. The flavour is nutty and delicious. This is not a high-yielding variety but it is a gourmet's delight. Kipfler has a tendency to push its tubers up above the ground so keep topping them up with soil or mulch during the tuber-producing season to avoid green potatoes.

Nicola

A German potato first released in 1973. It is very reliable in the garden, having better disease resistance than many varieties. It produces large crops of tubers that are flattish and oblong with yellow skin and cream flesh suited to anything from baking to mashing. An excellent home garden variety.

Pink Eye

A Tasmanian heirloom from 1944. The tubers are blocky with numerous indentations, cream in colour, stained with rosy purple. The flesh is cream-coloured and waxy, excellent as a new potato.

Pink Fir Apple

In the old days a pine cone was called a 'pine apple'. The cone of a fir tree was a 'fir apple'. Fir cones are elongated and rosy pink when young, hence the name of this French potato variety from the 1850s, which is also elongated and rosy pink. Pink Fir Apple has yellow waxy flesh and a magnificent flavour. It is not especially heavy cropping but it is so delicious that it is worth growing all the same. It tends to be a bit knobbly, especially in heavily manured soil.

PINK FIR APPLE POTATO

Russet Burbank

A classic American French fry variety, Russet Burbank is the progeny of the Burbank potato bred by the prolific American plant breeder Luther Burbank in the 1870s. Russet Burbank has a pale brown, rough (i.e. russeted) skin, white flesh and large, oblong tubers.

Sapphire

Not to be confused with the pale yellow variety called Saphire, Sapphire is a purple potato. Its skin is dark purple and its flesh is purple at the core surrounded by a ring of white flesh. It cooks to a pale violet colour.

Snowflake

This American variety from the 1870s is remembered with great affection by old Victorian potato farmers. Snowflake has yellow skin with very white starchy flesh. Old timers say it tastes the best of all potatoes – which is a very big call indeed. Its tubers grow bigger and bigger the longer they are left in the ground, eventually becoming quite branched, making them impossible to peel mechanically. For this reason, and because of its susceptibility to root knot nematodes, Snowflake disappeared from Victoria's potato fields after the introduction of the Kennebec potato. Despite its former popularity, it is practically impossible to find Snowflake today. It is not to be confused with a potato of the same name released in the 1960s.

VIOLETTO DI FIRENZE EGGPLANT

EGGPLANTS

Have you ever wondered how a blobby, glossy purple-black vegetable came to have the name 'eggplant'? This paradox bothered me for years, until the day I found out about heirloom vegetables, when suddenly it all made sense. Like many heirloom vegetables, eggplants come in an astounding variety of shapes, sizes and colours. That includes varieties which are – you have probably already guessed – white and egg-shaped.

Some eggplants do look for all the world like eggs. Sometimes the only giveaway that they are a fruit and not an egg is the big, star-shaped calyx attached to the top.

Unlike most of the nightshade crops, which are native to the Americas, the eggplant (*Solanum melongena*) is an Old World plant. It was first domesticated in the India-Burma region, not from a local species but from *S. incanum*, which is a native of east Africa and the Middle East. How *S. incanum* got to Asia in the first place is not known. It may have hitched a ride with the very earliest human migrations from Africa, perhaps as a medicinal plant.

JAPANESE WHITE EGG EGGPLANT

The Egyptians, Greeks and Romans, who left us so many depictions and descriptions of vegetables, do not mention the eggplant at all. This suggests that it arrived in the Mediterranean region relatively recently. Eggplants are mentioned in Sanskrit and Chinese literature around 2000 years ago, and in Persian in the sixth century. The Arabs took them westward to Spain some time between the seventh and ninth centuries. By the eighth century eggplants had crossed Asia to reach Japan. Asia and the Mediterranean became the major centres of eggplant diversification, and diversify they have.

Eggplants display much more variation than their relatives the tomatoes, but unfortunately the overwhelming majority of varieties are unknown in Australia or, indeed, to Western horticulture. In our culture eggplants are still seen as slightly exotic. However, in parts of tropical Asia and Africa they are a staple, eaten almost daily.

VARIETIES

•

Eggplants come in just about any colour you can name. Purple-black is the colour we are most familiar with but there are also golden yellow, lime-green, brilliant orange, pillar-box red, blue-violet, rose-pink, dove-grey, magenta and bull's blood-red eggplants. Some are beautifully striped, or netted with a contrasting colour. In shape they can vary from blown-up party balloons to sausages to cricket balls, teardrops, spindle-shaped and even lobed and ridged like little pumpkins. In weight they range from pea-sized to over a kilo.

Most Eurasian heirloom eggplants belong to the species *Solanum melongena* but there are several other species that fit under the eggplant umbrella including *S. torvum*, *S. macrocarpon* and *S. aethiopicum*.

Black Beauty

An old standard black, glossy eggplant with fat fruits. It has great flavour but is quite light cropping and late, so it's not the best variety for gardeners in the southern states.

Casper

Casper is a French heirloom with white, medium-sized, elongated, tear drop-shaped fruits. The plants are compact, generous and bear early in the season. A good variety to grow in restricted spaces like balconies and courtyards.

CASPER EGGPLANT

Japanese White Egg

Japanese, white and egg-shaped as you might expect, with skin the texture of the finest eggshell porcelain. The pretty little fruits are richly flavoured with dense, silky flesh, and are produced in good quantities.

Kamo

A Japanese heirloom with black, round fruits the size of an orange, very tender and sweet. The plants are extremely ornamental, with black-purple stems and purple-green fuzzy leaves.

KAMO EGGPLANT

Listada de Gandía

A striking heirloom with white, pear-shaped fruits heavily striped with purple. They are borne early in the season. This is a very versatile eggplant, tender enough to be eaten raw when small, but solid enough to stand up to stewing when older. Often listed as an Italian heirloom, its origins are more likely Spanish, hence its Spanish name 'Striped of Gandia', Gandia being a town near Valencia. It was introduced into neighbouring southern France in the mid-nineteenth century.

LISTADA DE GANDÍA EGGPLANT

Long Purple

Also known by its Italian name **Lungo Violetto**, this nineteenth-century heirloom is the glossy, black-purple eggplant on which modern hybrids are based. It has the classic appearance, flavour and texture and is appreciated in cooler European climates for being quick cropping.

PINGTUNG LONG EGGPLANT

Pingtung Long

This lovely Taiwanese heirloom from Pingdong has pretty lavender-purple fruits with a metallic blue cast. The flesh is very creamy, without any bitterness, and the seeds are soft and not at all unpleasant. Pingtung Long is extremely robust, quick to crop and a good choice for cooler areas.

ROSA BIANCA EGGPLANT

Rosa Bianca

'White Rose' in Italian, is an heirloom bearing roundish, white fruits flushed with rosy purple. Pretty, mild in flavour and never bitter.

Slim Jim

A prolific little eggplant, great for home gardens. The fruits are slender, purple and up to 15 centimetres long, borne in dense clusters.

SLIM JIM EGGPLANT

Thai pea eggplant

These tiny eggplants are usually encountered floating in Thai curries or perhaps for sale in Asian grocers. Although we call them eggplants, they properly belong to a different species altogether, *Solanum torvum*. *S. torvum* is popular in South East Asian cuisine although it is native to Central and South America, unlike 'true' eggplants (*S. melongena*) which are Asian in origin. The 1-centimetre-wide, pea-like fruits have very thin flesh and a lot of seeds, and are borne in large clusters on big shrubs 2 metres in height. When fully ripe they turn yellow but just like true eggplants they are usually harvested young, before the seeds become hard and unpleasant. Thai pea eggplants taste bitter and slightly metallic, so they are a good foil to oily foods such as curries. Like most nightshades, Thai pea eggplants are borderline toxic so they should not be consumed in large quantities.

Turkish Orange

A Turkish heirloom derived from the African species *Solanum aethiopicum*. It bears highly orna-mental, glossy, orange, round fruits which look more like tomatoes than eggplants. Best harvested before they are fully coloured, the flavour is quite sweet for an eggplant, although with typical night-shade bitterness in the background.

TURKISH ORANGE EGGPLANT

Violetto di Firenze

'Violet of Florence' has tubby fruits of a dull smoky purple, with a purple calyx and lobed and ridged like a small pumpkin.

TOBAGO SEASONING CHILLI

CAPSICUM & CHILLIES

Capsicums are referred to as 'peppers' in the UK and USA but in Australia we like to call this vegetable by its scientific name: *Capsicum*. The name 'pepper' probably derives from the fact that chillies have a pepper-like spiciness. True pepper (*Piper nigrum*) is a tropical spice. It had to be imported at great expense to Europe, where it was extremely popular in medieval times, from Asia, where it was grown. Chilli peppers could be grown locally in Europe, costing a fraction of the price of true pepper. This might explain why capsicums caught on so quickly in Europe while their relatives the tomatoes and potatoes met with considerable resistance.

Capsicums are native to the American tropics. There are around thirty species in the genus *Capsicum* but only five are cultivated for food. The distinction between 'capsicum' and 'chilli' is a bit arbitrary as sweet capsicums are simply chillies that have been bred to be large, fleshy and devoid of heat. Sweet capsicums all belong to the species *Capsicum annuum*. So do many of the chilli varieties such as cayenne and jalapeños. Other chillies are descended from *C. baccatum* (ají chillies), *C. pubescens* (black-seeded rocoto chillies), *C. chinense* (habaneros) and *C. frutescens* (tabasco, bird's eye chillies and piri-piri).

Capsicums and chillies were first domesticated as early as 6000 years ago in Ecuador. They were traded across the Andes and established themselves throughout the American tropics and subtropics. Our word chilli (or chili or chile, as you prefer) comes from Nahuatl, the language of the Aztec, along with words like 'tomato', 'chocolate' and 'avocado'. Chillies arrived in Europe in 1493 after Christopher Columbus encountered them in the West Indies. The Spanish and Portuguese took them around the world on their trade routes and to their colonies in the tropics and subtropics, where they were eagerly embraced.

Chillies' claim to fame is their spicy heat. This comes from a chemical called capsaicin which tricks our pain receptors into thinking that they are burning. This trick is designed to stop mammals from eating chilli fruits. However, birds are insensitive to the capsaicin so they can eat them with impunity, carrying the seeds far afield.

Far from deterring humans, chillies are totally addictive for many of us. Part of the body's response to capsaicin is to release 'feel-good' endorphins in the brain. Once you get a taste for chilli, you always want more. Some cultures are hooked on chilli, eating it for breakfast, lunch and dinner. It defines their whole cuisines. Korean, Sichuan Chinese, South East Asian, Indian and Latin American cuisines wouldn't be right without lots of chilli. Latin Americans in particular are chilli connoisseurs. They grow dozens of different varieties for different culinary effects. From the giant green *poblano* chillies enjoyed for their subtle background heat, to the brain-searing *habaneros*, Latin Americans have a chilli for every imaginable use.

In our culture we think of chillies as a spice or garnish; something to be added to a dish in tiny quantities. In Latin American cuisines chillies sometimes form the body of a dish, as black *ancho* chillies do in the famous *chili con carne*. Using chillies in this way spread to Europe, where it was taken up with particular gusto by the Hungarians. Hungarians are mad about paprika. They have several distinct varieties: some hot, some sweet, some pungent, some which add amazing depth of flavour to a dish. They love paprika so much that they have a grading system for it, jealously keeping the best grades for domestic use. If you want to taste the best paprika, you have to go to Hungary. In Budapest's central market several aisles are devoted entirely to dried paprika. It is strung from the rafters and stacked high in baskets. Shopkeepers and their customers passionately discuss the comparative merits of the different kinds. It is like walking into a parallel, chilli-powered, universe.

CAPSICUM VARIETIES

•

There are dozens of heirloom capsicums. Many of them are quite different from the sweet bell pepper types we are used to seeing in supermarkets. Some are noticeably thin-fleshed, some are horn-shaped, some pencil-thin. They each have a different use in the kitchen so be prepared to find the right way to use each different variety.

Alma Paprika
A cherry variety with small, tomato-like fruits. They are thick-fleshed, ripening from cream to red via orange. They are nice eaten raw, being sweet with a modest chilli kick. They can also be dried and turned into paprika.

Golden Marconi
This variety produces brilliant yellow fruits somewhere between a bell pepper and horn pepper in shape. They are thick-fleshed and can be eaten fresh or used for frying or throwing on the barbecue. Golden Marconi needs a long, hot growing season to do well.

Jimmy Nardello
Red, horn-shaped fruits 20 centimetres in length are sweet and excellent for frying or throwing on the barbecue. This variety is named after the man whose parents brought it with them when they migrated from southern Italy to the USA in 1887.

PURPLE BEAUTY CAPSICUM

Purple Beauty
This could equally be called Black Beauty as the unripe fruits are such a dark shade of purple. The short, square bell-type fruits eventually ripen to red, but are sweet and crisp even during the purple stage.

Sweet Chocolate

A chocolate-brown bell pepper type bred by Elwyn Meader at the University of New Hampshire in 1965. The fruits are quite slender and relatively thin-fleshed but the flavour and sweetness are superb. Its quickness to crop and tolerance of cool weather are a bonus, too.

SWEET CHOCOLATE CAPSICUM

CHILLI VARIETIES

•

There might be dozens of capsicum varieties but there seem to be gazillions of chillies. Their hotness is measured in Scoville Heat Units (SHU). The highest capsaicin content is in the white pithy tissue around the seeds, called the placenta. Removing the seeds and placenta turns the heat down considerably.

Bhut Jolokia

One of the world's hottest chillies, with a SHU rating in the almost unbelievable region of 600 000–1 000 000. Probably a hybrid between *C. chinense* and *C. frutescens*, the so-called 'ghost chilli' produces a red, wrinkled, horn-shaped fruit to 5 centimetres long. Handle with extreme caution!

BHUT JOLOKIA CHILLI

Fatalii

An African cultivar with yellow, wrinkled fruits like an elongated Habanero. They have a fruity, citrusy flavour and are extremely hot.

Fish

Fish is unmistakable as both the plant and the fruits are variegated with white stripes and splashes. The smooth, torpedo-shaped fruits ripen

FATALII CHILLI

from green through red to brown. This 1870s heirloom from the Philadelphia-Baltimore region was traditionally grown by African-Americans and used in recipes featuring shellfish and turtle. The plants are well covered in dainty foliage, making this a very ornamental plant.

Habanero

Habaneros belong to the species *C. chinense*, which suggests they are from China, but in fact they are from South America like all other chillies. Habanero plants have soft, pale green leaves. The fruits have thin, waxy flesh and ripen to yellow, orange or red. They look like half-deflated beanbags. They have an unusual fruity flavour and are very hot with a SHU rating up to 350000.

Hungarian Hot Wax

Large, horn-shaped fruits have thick, waxy flesh, ripening through pale yellow to red. They are hot and sweet, good for pickling.

Jalapeño

There are many different types of Jalapeño chilli, named for the Mexican city of Xalapa. Jalapeños are straight, wedge-shaped, thick-fleshed chillies with not much heat. They are often served green and pickled in Mexican cuisine.

Joe's Long

Originally from Italy via Canada, Joe's Long produces glossy red, pencil-thin fruits up to 30 centimetres in length with mild heat. They look very pretty dried in a garland.

FISH CHILLI

HUNGARIAN HOT WAX CHILLI

JOE'S LONG CHILLI

Poblano

A very large, capsicum-like chilli from Puebla in Mexico. They are used fresh when green or dried when they ripen fully to red. Dried Poblano chillies, called *anchos*, are mixed with cocoa to make the Aztec-inspired dish *mole*. Poblanos are used fresh to make *chiles rellenos*, stuffed chillies, on account of their size. Poblanos have a pleasing background heat without blowing your head off.

POBLANO CHILLI

Red Cap Mushroom

Very pretty cherry-red fruits shaped like wrinkled, shrunken mushrooms, which grow on an open bush. This is a hot one, being a relative of the Habanero.

RED CAP MUSHROOM CHILLI

Thai Birdseye

Thai Birdseye chillies are the smooth red (or green) torpedoes of fire used in South East Asian cooking. Just 3 centimetres long, they not only contribute heat to a dish, but a lovely chilli flavour, for which reason they are often used in large quantities, seeded to reduce their heat.

CHAPTER SEVEN

THE

Amaranth

FAMILY

(Amaranthus cruentus)

Spinach and beets used to be considered members of the goosefoot family, or Chenopodiaceae. Today the goosefoot family has been subsumed by the Amaranth family, the Amaranthaceae, within which spinach and beets have been given their own subfamilies, the Chenopodioideae (try saying that ten times fast) and the Betoideae respectively.

This new superfamily is named for the genus *Amaranthus*. Several species of *Amaranthus* are grown as grain crops in Central and South America; others are grown as leafy vegetables in Asia. In Australia, they are grown as very old-fashioned ornamentals: *A. cruentus*, known as prince's feather, and *A. caudatus*, with the rather melodramatic common name of 'love-lies-bleeding'.

The amaranth family also includes samphire, which has long been enjoyed as a vegetable but has never been domesticated. Samphire is a halophyte – a plant adapted to salty environments. It is very difficult to recreate samphire's salt marsh habitat in your veggie patch without killing everything else growing in it. The amaranth family contains quite a lot of halophytes. Saltbushes are the best known, but the humble beet also began life as a beachside plant, washed with sea spray.

FAT HEN

SPINACH AND ITS RELATIVES — THE GOOSEFOOTS

The goosefoot subfamily (Chenopodioideae) is in many ways a gaggle of weeds. Good King Henry (*Chenopodium bonus-henricus*) and fat hen (*Chenopodium album*), also known as lamb's quarters or pigweed, are two of the many weedy members of this family. Good King Henry and fat hen are both edible, and they are not bad, though neither is a patch on true spinach.

Mountain spinach or orach (*Atriplex hortensis*) looks like the love child of spinach and fat hen. It is actually a kind of annual saltbush. It forms a rosette of dull green, triangular leaves with a mealy farina like that of spinach. The leaves can be harvested when young and tender and cooked like spinach. By the time the plant forms its tall flower stem, the leaves become a bit metallic-tasting. This acrid tang comes from oxalic acid, a chemical present in a lot of plants, including the members of the goosefoot family. I suspect that the domestication of spinach has been as much about reducing its oxalic acid content as improving its yields and curbing its propensity to bolt.

Orach is probably best thought of as an edible ornamental, grown in the flower garden rather than given dedicated space in the vegetable beds. It self-seeds rampantly so be prepared to remove 95 per cent of the volunteers (hoeing is the best way). There is an exquisite maroon-foliaged form, called 'Red Plume', which is definitely the one to grow.

The celebrity goosefoot-of-the-moment is quinoa (*Chenopodium quinoa*). It is one of the few grains that is not a member of the grass family. Quinoa is unique among grain crops. It is more energy-dense than other grains and it is the only known plant food that contains the full complement of amino acids needed for human nutrition. Quinoa is a native of Peru and Bolivia, thriving in the tough conditions of the high Andes. Along with the potato, quinoa has been a staple food for Andean subsistence farmers for 7000 years, giving them a means by which to survive from year to year.

Quinoa has recently become desperately fashionable in Western countries. Just like the clothes you wear and the music you listen to, eating quinoa *says* something about you in a way that eating, say, celery or spelt (*so* 2003!) does not. Maybe it advertises your environmental credentials or demonstrates your urbanity, or shows that you consider your body to be a temple into which no gluten/meat/dairy/non-organic food shall pass. In Western nations we don't eat quinoa to survive. For us it's a lifestyle food.

Increased demand for quinoa in Western nations is having interesting ramifications in Peru. It has caused the quinoa price to triple in just a few years, making it more attractive for farmers to sell their quinoa than to eat it. Quinoa farmers can afford television sets and educations for their kids for the first time, which is of course very positive. They can also afford Western-style processed junk food to replace traditional dietary items – like quinoa – which are healthy but, ironically, suffer from low status because of their association with poverty.

Quinoa, the wonder grain of the Andes.

Quinoa production from Peru has quadrupled in as many years as farmers flock to this cash crop and let others fall by the wayside. As farmers in other countries jump on the quinoa bandwagon (who can blame them?) international prices will be driven down. When this happens, what will happen to the Peruvian quinoa farmers' fortunes? When fickle Westerners lose interest in quinoa and latch on to the next must-have lifestyle superfood, what then?

We seem to be observing the transformation of an obscure Andean subsistence food into a global commodity before our very eyes. It's what happened to quinoa's compatriot, the potato, 200 years ago. Commodification comes with consequences, both good and bad.

The United Nations Food and Agriculture Organisation (FAO) declared 2013 the International Year of Quinoa. They believe that quinoa, with its unique nutritional profile and amazing adaptability to cultural conditions, has a big role in feeding the poor and, as the earth's climate changes and agriculture is forced to adapt, the rich, too. Stay tuned. It's going to be an interesting ride.

SPINACH

Spinach (*Spinacia oleracea*) is native to central and western Asia, the former Persian empire. It was probably brought into cultivation by the Persians in the sixth century. Unlike most Central Asian vegetables it seems to have travelled east before it went west. In the seventh century it was mentioned in Chinese texts as the 'Persian vegetable'. The Arabs were very keen on it, going to extraordinary lengths to grow it in their climate, since spinach hates heat and drought. Arabs introduced spinach to the lands within their expanding sphere of influence. Their word for spinach was *isab nikh,* which is reflected in the European names for spinach — *espinaca* in Spanish, *spanaki* in Greek and *spinacia* in Italian. The Moors introduced it to Spain in the late twelfth century. Spinach took another 200 years to creep north to France and England, where it made its first appearance as *spinoches* in the fourteenth-century English cookbook *The Forme of Cury,* appearing along-side old favourites like *caboches* (cabbages), *pasturnakes* (parsnips) and *rapes* (turnips).

Much has been made of spinach's famously high iron content. It seems that we owe this 'common knowledge' to Popeye, the hyper-masculine cartoon sailor from the 1930s, who would chug a can of iron-rich spinach and instantly grow huge muscles which would allow him to thwart his enemies. If only it were that straight-forward. Spinach is indeed high in iron – it contains 50 per cent more than meat, in fact – but other chemicals in spinach prevent the human body from being able to absorb it. Incidentally, the first time Popeye popped a can of spinach was in 1932, citing its vitamin A content, not iron, as the source of its healthfulness. Which all goes to show that we probably shouldn't be getting our nutritional science from a cartoon character. We don't need Popeye to tell us to eat spinach, anyway. Spinach tastes good. With its soft, melting leaves and subtle, earthy flavour, it is truly one of the most exquisite of all vegetables.

VARIETIES

•

There are two types of spinach: round-seeded varieties traditionally grown over the European summer, and prickly-seeded varieties, which are hardier and grown over winter. In reality, Australian summers are far too hot for any kind of spinach to grow well, but our winters are mild by European standards. Round- and prickly-seeded varieties seem to do equally well for us during the cooler months.

Amsterdam
A venerable European prickly-seeded heirloom noted for its robustness and resistance to bolting. It has bright green, flat leaves.

Bloomsdale Long Standing
A dependable smooth-seeded variety with very dark, glossy, heavily savoyed foliage. It was introduced by the oldest seed house in the USA, the D. Landreth Seed Company, which has been in operation since 1784. Bloomsdale Long Standing was first listed in 1826. The strain was given a freshen-up in 1925 and is still enormously popular today for its excellent earthy flavour and reliability.

BLOOMSDALE SPINACH

Giant Noble

A Dutch variety introduced in 1926, Giant Noble certainly lives up to its name. The plants can be 60 centimetres across and the huge, flat leaves remain soft as they age.

VIROFLAY SPINACH

Monstrueux de Viroflay

Literally 'Monstrous of Viroflay', the name is usually simply shortened to 'Viroflay'. This French variety from the 1860s has very large, very tender, flat leaves. When well grown they can be nearly the size of an A4 sheet of paper. The leaves remain tender and mild-tasting even when they are very old and large.

HEIRLOOM BEETROOTS

THE BEETS & CHARDS

The Betoideae subfamily is a small one. The only notable members are the beets and chards. Botanically speaking, beets and chards are the same species. They are both descended from a European and North African beachside plant, the sea beet (*Beta vulgaris* subsp. *maritima*). Swiss chard (*B. vulgaris* subsp. *cicla*), or silverbeet as we call it in Australia, was selected for its thick, tender stems while beetroot (*B. vulgaris* subsp. *vulgaris*) was selected for its swollen root (really a hypocotyl).

The earliest mention of a beet comes from eighth century BCE Babylonia. It was well known by the time of the classical Greeks. Theophrastus mentions it in the third century BCE and by 350 BCE Aristotle was already able to wax lyrical about a red-stemmed variety of chard. Beetroot came much later, sometime between the end of the Roman empire and the Middle Ages. However, by the sixteenth century beetroots were well known.

In the eighteenth century beetroot sired two interesting offspring. The first was the beautifully named mangelwurzel. The word mangelwurzel comes from German *Mangold* meaning chard and *Wurzel* meaning root. Mangelwurzels are giant beets which appeared spontaneously in the Rhineland in the 1750s. Mangelwurzels are humungous – easily five or six times bigger than beetroots, and either yellow or red.

Mangelwurzels are giant fodder beets.

They are primarily used as stock fodder, grown over the European summer to feed livestock during winter, but they are perfectly fine as human food, too. One root will feed a family of ten.

Beetroot's second baby was sugar beet. Sugar beet first appeared in the 1770s, the product of plant breeding in Germany in the search for a cheap, domestic source of sugar. At that time the British had a virtual monopoly on the sugar market, importing cane sugar to Europe from their colonies in the tropics. For which reason Napoleon took a strong interest in the sugar beet. He established an experimental sugar beet industry in France to reduce that country's reliance on British sugar. France is still the top producer of sugar beet today, with the USA coming a distant second. You might be surprised to learn that genetically modified sugar beet, made to resist the herbicide glyphosate, was released in the USA less than a decade ago.

You may not think you have ever eaten beet sugar, but if you fancy the occasional Belgian chocolate then you almost certainly have.

The process of extracting sugar from beets (which contain about 20 per cent sucrose) is not simply a case of squeezing them and refining the juice, as it is with cane sugar. With sugar beet it is quite an industrial process involving some pretty nifty chemistry. Don't bother trying it at home.

BEETROOT VARIETIES

•

When I was a boy in the 1970s, you could only get one variety of beetroot: tinned. While Americans insisted on a pickled cucumber in their hamburgers, Australian hamburgers were simply not complete without a round of beetroot peeking out from between the layers, loaded and ready to flop on to your lap and stain your best beige flares. It came as a revelation to me discover that a) beetroots do not exist pre-sliced in nature and b) that they are available in several amazing colours.

Albino/White

A Dutch heirloom with crisp, white roots. The flavour is very sweet and mild, lacking the earthiness of red beetroots. Eating one raw feels more like crunching your way through an apple than eating your greens. The best thing about white beetroot is that it does not stain your clothes. If only we'd known in the 70s, we could have worn our beige flares with impunity.

ALBINO BEETROOT

Bull's Blood

Bull's Blood has plush maroon foliage and stems, earning it a place in the ornamental garden. Its roots are medium-sized and globe-shaped, and are pale beetroot-red with indistinct white bands when cut in half. Bull's Blood beetroots are best eaten as soon as they are ready or they can become rather coarse.

BULL'S BLOOD BEETROOT

Burpee's Golden

Burpee's Golden was introduced in the 1940s by the famous (but rather unfortunately named) Burpee seed company in the USA. Its roots are dull orange on the outside but brilliant golden yellow on the inside. The foliage has yellow veins. The taste is very sweet and mild and lacks the 'dirty' flavour of red beetroot. Absolutely delicious and particularly good raw.

BURPEE'S GOLDEN BEETROOT

Chioggia

Chioggia is an unmistakeable Italian heirloom beetroot, originating around 1840 in the island town of the same name, just south of Venice. Cut a flattened pink Chioggia root in half and you will be amazed. Concentric rings of shocking pink and white are arranged into a perfect bullseye. Sweet and mild in flavour, this variety is very robust, fast-growing and extremely productive. Chioggia is chronically mispronounced in Australia. Why not impress your Italian friends by pronouncing it correctly: 'kyo-jya', *not* 'chee-ogg-ee-a'.

CHIOGGIA BEETROOT

Cylindra

As its name suggests, Cylindra has cylindrical roots like a carrot rather than the usual globe shape. They are perfect for slicing and pickling. In all other respects it is like any 'normal' beetroot.

CYLINDRA BEETROOT

Detroit

Detroit is not a single variety but a series of closely related strains. However, they are usually listed simply as 'Detroit'. Detroit is a beetroot's beet-root, with large, globe-shaped, smooth-skinned, black-red roots and red-veined foliage. The roots hold for a long time in the ground without becoming woody so they are good varieties to sow in autumn and harvest over winter.

DETROIT BEETROOT

SILVERBEET OR SWISS CHARD VARIETIES

•

Let's get one thing straight. Silverbeet and spinach are not the same thing. Australians have been calling silverbeet 'spinach' for generations but the two vegetables could not be more different. Spinach is definitely the aristocrat of the two, being finer in texture and more delicate in flavour than silverbeet. Spinach is more difficult to grow, more finicky about soil quality, water and temperature. Silverbeet might be less refined from a culinary point of view but it is also a whole lot easier to grow. It germinates quickly and reliably at pretty much any time of the year, tolerates all kinds of adversity including salty soils, mild drought and a degree of shade, and it is very generous with its crops. It is a great vegetable for beginners to practise their gardening chops on. But, without wanting to denigrate this workhorse of the vegetable garden, once you have mastered the art of growing silverbeet, it is probably worth setting your sights a little higher and moving on to more interesting crops, like spinach.

FIVE-COLOUR SILVERBEET

Five-Colour

Also known as rainbow chard, Five-Colour silverbeet is described by Diggers Club founder Clive Blazey as 'the poster child of the heirloom movement'. It's easy to see why. Rather than having classic white (read 'boring') stems, Five-Colour's stems come in every shade of glorious technicolour. One plant can be tangerine-orange, the next shocking pink, the next cadmium-yellow, the next screaming vermilion or blood-red or baby-pink or creamy lemon – all from the same packet of seeds.

Having raved about its appearance I feel compelled to inform you that Five-Colour tastes as silverbeety as any other silverbeet: not that interesting. It is so ornamental in the garden, however, and so easygoing, that it does no harm to have a few tucked in here and there as an emergency backup crop. Bear in mind that the colours muddy somewhat when cooked.

Fordhook

This variety is reputed to have been introduced in the 1750s, but like so many other heirloom vege-tables it is named after W.A. Burpee's family farm, Fordhook Farm, which suggests an introduction date in the late nineteenth century. When well grown this variety produces leviathan black-green leaves atop obscenely thick, flat white stems. A single leaf can supply enough greenery for a family meal.

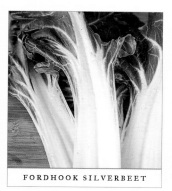

FORDHOOK SILVERBEET

Lucullus

Named after a Roman general famous for his extravagant eatathons, Lucullus was first introduced in seed catalogues around 1900. It is notable for its enormous, soft, heavily savoyed foliage and rounded, fleshy white stems.

Perpetual

Also known as perpetual spinach, this is the most spinach-like silverbeet. It has smaller leaves and thinner stems than other silverbeets, of a uniform apple-green colour. It is finer in texture and more subtle in taste than other silverbeets, so this variety is the gourmet's choice.

PERPETUAL SILVERBEET

CHAPTER EIGHT

THE Daisy FAMILY

(*Helipterum* and *Brachyscome*)

The word 'daisy' conjures up an image of a very particular kind of flower: one shaped like a little sun, with a ring of white petals surrounding a smiling yellow face. These sun-shaped flowers gave the daisy family its botanical name, Asteraceae, from the Greek word for a 'star' (think 'asteroid', 'astronomy' and 'astrology'). All members of the daisy family share this basic flower arrangement. Botanically speaking it's called a *capitulum*, Latin for 'little head'. The capitulum is made up of dozens of tiny, individual flowers crammed together. The round central cushion of the capitulum is called the 'disc'. If you look at the disc through a magnifying glass you will see that it is composed of tiny individual flowers, each with five weeny little petals and a bouquet of yellow stamens emerging from them. The disc is usually surrounded by a collar of what look like petals but are in fact specialised sterile flowers called 'ray florets'. Their job is to attract pollinators.

There is a lot of variation on the daisy flower theme. Sometimes it can be difficult to tell that a plant is a member of this family. Sunflowers, marigolds and our native everlasting daisies are pretty easy to spot. But some members of the family are less obvious. The herb yarrow has capitula so small and borne in such profuse clusters that it is easy to overlook the fact that they share the same basic daisy floral structure.

SUNFLOWER

Wormwoods (*Artemisia*) and their cousin tarragon have capitula so tiny and drab that we barely even register them as flowers. Artichoke flowers, by contrast, are so enormous and spiky that it difficult to imagine that they are related to daisies. But indeed they are. The artichoke's central disc has evolved into a giant, shaggy shock of electric-blue stamens. Artichokes' ray florets have disappeared entirely and instead have been replaced with the fleshy sepals that are so delicious to eat.

Lettuces are also members of the daisy family. Their flowers are more obviously daisy-like, being round, creamy yellow and decidedly daisy-shaped. You have to look very closely, however, as they are just a few millimetres across and only last for half a day.

Quite a few herbs are members of the daisy family. Many of those have lovely bucolic names like wormwood, southernwood, lad's love, camomile, tarragon, feverfew, yarrow, marigold, mugwort, dandelion, leopardbane, thoroughwort, tansy, goldenrod, sweet Joe Pye and snakeweed. The insecticide pyrethrum is also derived from a daisy, *Tanacetum cinerariifolium* (aka *Pyrethrum cinerariifolium* or *Chrysanthemum cinerariifolium*).

The daisy family has also given us a wealth of ornamental plants. Perennial daisies with large, colourful, ray florets are particularly loved by gardeners for

CAMOMILE

PYRETHRUM

creating solid banks of colour in late summer and autumn. Dahlias, echinaceas, achilleas, chrysanthemums and asters (after which the Asteraceae family is named) to name just a few. Echinops or globe thistles have flowers devoid of pretty ray florets but their spherical flower heads create an amazing visual impact in the garden, like electric-blue Christmas baubles.

HELENIUM

ECHINOPS

Some ornamental daisies are not grown for their flowers at all but rather for their foliage. *Senecio* is an enormous genus of daisies with foliage forms ranging from finely cut and ferny to succulent and cactus-like to huge and oar-shaped. Their flowers are generally inconspicuous and beige in colour, or at best small and yellow. One plant you would never pick in a million years as being a member of the daisy family is the string-of-pearls plant, *Senecio rowleyanus*. Its succulent leaves look like frozen peas threaded on to pendulous strings. It says 'seaweed' more than 'daisy' to the casual observer. A good indoor plant, the string-of-pearls plant had its heyday in the 1970s when a pot of it hanging in a mission-brown macrame hanger was the last word in interior design. It is a perennial favourite at school fetes and trash and treasure markets.

As you might expect from such a big family, a few members of the Asteraceae are badly behaved and spoil things for everyone. Dandelions and milk thistles are

SENECIO ROWLEYANUS

both members of the daisy family. They are annoying weeds in home gardens, but they are nothing in comparison with the South African boneseed or bitou bush (*Chrysanthemoides monilifera*) which has become a monster in Australia, consuming thousands of hectares of native coastal vegetation. In colder parts of the country ragwort (*Senecio jacobaea*) is problematic, being both thuggish and poisonous to stock. Thistles are the most heavily armed members of the daisy clan. Scotch thistle (*Onopordum acanthium*) is the symbol of the proud Scottish nation, credited with holding back invading Vikings. Both the Scotch thistle and its smaller sibling the spear thistle (*Cirsium vulgare*) are serious agricultural weeds in this country.

PRICKLY LETTUCE

LETTUCE

The lettuce (*Lactuca sativa*) was first domesticated by the Egyptians by 3000 BCE. Its nearest relative is the prickly lettuce (*L. serriola*), a Mediterranean native that has become a common weed of gardens, farms and urban environments around the world. Prickly lettuce is so common that you would recognise it instantly.

Whether the cultivated lettuce is descended from the prickly lettuce or they are sibling offspring from another, possibly extinct, ancestor is not known. In any case, prickly and cultivated lettuces can interbreed successfully.

The leaves of wild lettuces taste very bitter, so chances are they were originally domesticated either for their seeds, which yield an oil, or as a drug. Ancient lettuce varieties contained lots of milky white sap, the origin of our word 'lettuce', via Latin *lactus*, meaning 'milk'. This sap is narcotic, and lettuces throughout much of their history were eaten as a soporific to help induce sleep. The narcotic drug in lettuce is present in much smaller quantities nowadays since they have been bred to be less bitter and milky. However, I'm sure you'll never look at a lettuce the same way again.

We know the Egyptians grew lettuce as their art is awash with depictions of it. Lettuce was sacred to the Egyptian fertility god Min, and thought to be the source of his endless virility. Lettuces were offered to him in his temples and festivals. The lettuce cultivated by the Egyptians did not grow as a fat rosette in the way that modern lettuces do. Rather it was a tall plant up to a metre high like a very tall cos lettuce, with narrow, overlapping leaves.

The Greeks were sceptical about lettuce. They felt that it made men sleepy and took away their virility and desire. However by the third century BCE Theophrastus mentioned three different cultivars of lettuce. By the first century CE Pliny the Elder described nine varieties of lettuce. He also described the Roman upper-class custom of serving lettuce as an appetiser before a meal, giving birth to a culinary custom that is still practised today: a salad starter.

By Pliny's time, lettuces had been bred to grow shorter, leafier and less bitter. They had probably been persuaded to be less quick to 'bolt', too. Bolting – that is, producing a flower stem and going to seed – has always been a problem with lettuce because it become bitter and unpalatable when it starts to bolt. Bolting is hard-wired into lettuce's genes. Any sign of stress, such as a lack of water or temperatures over 30°C, is enough to tell the lettuce plant that the end is nigh and it had better get a wriggle on and reproduce itself. And reproduce themselves they can, each plant producing hundreds of tiny, lemon-yellow daisy flowers, each of which is loaded with a dozen or more seeds. A single lettuce plant can give rise to thousands of progeny. Each seed has its own individual parachute, just like those of lettuce's cousin the dandelion. With these, the seeds are dispersed far and wide on the wind. Lettuce seeds are usually either white or black, or occasionally brown or yellow. Seed colour is an important diagnostic tool for teasing apart the many heirloom varieties which look superficially similar.

The familiar heading lettuces are a recent development. The first hard evidence we have for them dates from the late sixteenth century, when they begin to appear in the paintings of the Dutch masters. The Dutch masters seemed to enjoy depicting vegetables as much as they enjoyed painting skulls, glassware and stern Calvinist burghers. Their paintings have been a great source of information on heirloom vegetables of all kinds.

Lettuce was first introduced to the Americas by Columbus around 1500, but like so many vegetables it was during the nineteenth century, when the USA became a melting pot of immigration, that lettuces really blossomed there. Unique strains brought by migrants from many lands began mixing with each other and with the descendants of the lettuces brought to the Americas by earlier waves of colonists. In many ways American heirloom lettuces, and indeed all vegetables, reflect American society itself.

VARIETIES

•

Lettuces fall into one of several categories according to how their foliage is presented. The oldest categories are the loose-leaf (or salad bowl) types and the cos (or romaine) types. Loose-leaf lettuces don't form a heart of any kind, simply growing as an open rosette. Their leaves tends to be quite soft and thin. Some are flat and smooth, others bubbly ('bullate' to botanists). Loose-leaf lettuces are the best cut-and-come-again lettuces, as they can be harvested leaf by leaf as required. Cos or romaine lettuces form tall heads of long, straight leaves with thick midribs. They tend to be very crisp in texture. They are usually harvested as a whole head but can also be taken leaf by leaf. They get their names from their ancient association with the Greek island of Kos and with the Roman Empire. Butterhead lettuces form loose hearts. Their leaves tend to be very soft and tender, gently folded around one another like a handful of scrunched-up silk. Butterheads can also be harvested leaf by leaf. Crisphead varieties are those which form dense hearts of tightly overlapping leaves. Crispheads are one-trick ponies. Once you've harvested the fully developed head, it's all over for them. Iceberg is the classic crisphead lettuce.

We usually think of lettuces as salad leaves, to be eaten raw. However, lettuces can also be cooked. The French sauté lettuce in butter along with fresh peas to make their classic dish *petits pois*. The Chinese stir-fry lettuce with garlic or add it to clear soups. The Italians throw quartered cos lettuces on the grill before dressing them with olive oil and vinegar or orange juice. There is no reason why you shouldn't cook lettuce, as long as you match your variety to your cooking technique. A loose-leaf variety thrown on a grill might come off a bit the worse for wear.

Amish Deer Tongue

A plain lettuce from the plain Amish people. No frills, no bright colours or proud swollen heads. Just no-nonsense green, flat, triangular leaves (hence Deer Tongue) with a substantial but gentle character. Amish Deer Tongue stands up well to cooking as well as eating fresh. First introduced around 1840.

AMISH DEER TONGUE
LETTUCE

Australian Yellow

Said to be an Australian heirloom, this is a very pretty lettuce with seersuckered foliage in a unique shade of chartreuse yellow. It is a big lettuce, heat- and cold-resistant and delectably soft even when the leaves reach full size. This is a truly wonderful variety.

Bunte Forellenschluss

This beautiful lettuce is mired in a bog of confusion. For a start its name barely makes sense. The name literally means 'mottled trout finish' in German. The 'mottled' part makes perfect sense because it has light green leaves heavily spotted with maroon. As for the 'trout' part, well, the beautifully speckled leaves do look like the sides of a trout. But 'finish'? In this context *schluss* probably means 'closing'. German speakers say a lettuce is *selbstschließend* when its foliage automatically closes inwards to form a pale coloured

BUNTE FORELLENSCHLUSS
LETTUCE

head without needing to be tied closed with string, as was the practice in former times. In English we would say 'self-blanching'. So Bunte Forellenschluss might be best translated as 'self-blanching mottled trout'.

The next source of confusion is this lettuce's provenance. It is widely sold as an Austrian heirloom, said to have been found in an old farm garden in Gänserndorf, Lower Austria; however it has long been grown in Germany, too, and offered by seed companies there as far back as 1866. Anyway, it's definitely an oldie.

There are several heirloom lettuces with spotty leaves and they get hopelessly mixed up in Australia, a situation exacerbated when seed companies make up their own names for them. I'm sure the reason they do this is to avoid their staff and customers having to get their tongues around names like 'Bunte Forellenschluss'. Yet German words like Edelweiss, Schnitzel and Schadenfreude roll off our tongues with relative ease; surely the name of a lettuce shouldn't scare us.

FORELLENSCHLUSS LETTUCE

The thing that all the spotty lettuces have in common is light green leaves spatter-painted to a greater or lesser degree with red flecks. This striking feature has distracted attention from some other obvious differences between them. True Bunte Forellenschluss is a loose butterhead lettuce with softly rumpled leaves. It is wider than it is tall. It is usually called simply Forellenschluss or Forellensalat in German. The lettuce we call simply **Forellenschluss** is a type of cos lettuce. It is taller than wide, with straight, narrow leaves. Called Grazer Forellenschluss in its native Austria, it was introduced in 1954 by the Thianich seed firm.

There is also **Speckled**, a North American spotty lettuce. Speckled is a tight, cabbagey butterhead lettuce pre-dating 1799, grown by a Mennonite family from Pennsylvania who took it with them to Canada, whence it entered horticulture. Its spots are finer and less distinct than the Forellenschluss types. There is also a spotted Russian lettuce, a Syrian one and a French one, called **Sanguine Ameliore**, which was released in the USA in 1906 as **Strawberry Cabbage**. You see what I mean about confusion. Luckily the spotty lettuces are all good ones so you can't go wrong with them. Not only do they look very pretty but they tend to be vigorous, slow to bolt and they tolerate heat well.

Celtuce / Asparagus lettuce

Celtuce is a Chinese heirloom, a lettuce that developed independently of European lettuces. It might be descended from those tall, ancient cos-like lettuces of the Egyptians because like them it has triangular overlapping leaves which grow on a tall stem. Unlike Western lettuces which have been selected for their soft, non-bitter leaves, celtuce was selected for its crisp, juicy stem. Harvested at

CELTUCE LETTUCE

around 40 centimetres in length, the stems can be sliced finely and eaten raw, but are at their best when they are steamed, braised or stir-fried. The delicate, slightly bitter lettuce flavour marries well with other subtle flavours like chicken, shellfish, mushrooms and bean curd. Several cultivars of celtuce are available, including a red form. Celtuce was introduced to France in the 1880s by missionaries returning from China, and to the USA in the 1940s, but it has never really taken off in Western countries. It's time that it did.

Flame

Flame is a relatively new open-pollinated, loose-leaf lettuce introduced in 1988. It has rumpled, pale green leaves which turn copper-red where the sun touches them. Very handsome.

Gold Rush

Gold Rush is an Australian heirloom with a great pedigree. It is said to be descended from lettuces brought to the Victorian goldfields by gold diggers – possibly Chinese – during the gold rush of the 1850s. The variety had been preserved by an elderly lady who passed it on to the Australian Seed Savers Network. They named it Gold Rush and passed it around to others. It is now grown around the world.

GOLD RUSH LETTUCE

Gold Rush is a lettuce with an afro. It forms big rosettes with very tightly curled leaves that form an impressive solid mass. The leaves are a distinctive pale green colour. Because this lettuce was developed in dry Central Victoria it shows good bolt resistance in dry weather.

Great Lakes

Great Lakes is an open-pollinated crisphead lettuce in the same vein as Iceberg. Its heads are looser and greener. Like Iceberg, it is heat-tolerant and does well over summer. However, like Iceberg, it needs optimum growing conditions to perform well.

Iceberg

Once the only lettuce you could buy in Australian groceries, Iceberg is an American heirloom

GREAT LAKES LETTUCE

crisphead lettuce dating back to the 1890s. It is a good lettuce for growing during the summer as it is heat-resistant and its crisp, white heads are beautifully refreshing. Iceberg's outer leaves are dull apple-green, fringed and torn at the edges. The head itself blanches white within its protective layer of outer leaves. In order to form a good solid head and not bolt to seed Iceberg needs careful watering. The head takes quite some time to form but once it does it needs to be picked and refrigerated immediately so that it doesn't begin to split and go brown.

Mignonette

Mignonette is a delightfully soft butterhead lettuce. It forms small cabbagey heads of melt-in-your-mouth leaves that are bright apple-green or bronze, smooth and rounded. The bronze strain was introduced first in the USA in the 1890s, with the green one following later.

MIGNONETTE LETTUCE

Oak Leaf

A super-duper loose-leaf lettuce for growing over summer, as it never seems to become bitter and resists bolting better than almost any other variety. Its rosettes are large with substantial but tender leaves lobed and scalloped like oak leaves. The terminal lobe is long and finger-shaped. There have been several iterations of Oak Leaf over the years. The earliest was introduced in France by Vilmorin in 1771. The strain we grow today is closer to the American Philadelphia Oak Leaf first released in the 1840s.

ROYAL OAKLEAF LETTUCE

Red Velvet

A vampish loose-leaf lettuce with glistening leaves of the darkest garnet red, ruffled like a flamenco dancer's dress. The leaves are as soft as silk velvet. A stunningly beautiful variety reintroduced by the American Seed Savers' Exchange as recently as 2002.

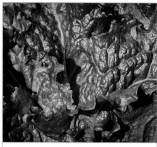

RED VELVET LETTUCE

Rouge d'Hiver

'Winter Red' in French, this is a handsome bronze dwarf cos. In spite of its name, this variety is equally good in winter and summer. A French heirloom listed by Vilmorin in 1885.

White Paris Cos / Blonde Maraichère

An eighteenth-century French heirloom cos which became the benchmark for all cos varieties. It is extremely crisp and juicy with massive, pale hearts surrounded by bright apple-green leaves. This is probably the variety taken by Thomas Jefferson back from Paris to be grown at his estate, Monticello.

ROUGE D'HIVER LETTUCE

Not to be confused (as it routinely is) with **Parris Island Cos**, an American variety named for Parris Island, South Carolina, introduced around 1950.

WILD CHICORY

CHICORIES & ENDIVE

In Anglo culture, chicory (*Cichorium intybus*) is known only as a slightly smug caffeine-free coffee substitute and a pretty useless 'herb'. In Italian culture things are different. They know that there is no substitute for real coffee and that chicories make great eating.

Chicory, also known as succory, is native to Europe and the Middle East. It is closely related to the dandelion and looks like it in many ways. Wild plants form a little rosette of toothed, dandelion-like leaves. However, instead of producing single, ground-hugging yellow flowers as the dandelion does, chicory puts up a tall scaffolding of wiry stems decorated with cornflower-blue flowers in the classic daisy form. These are the blue flowers commonly seen along southern Australian roadsides, dotted amongst the dry grasses in late summer.

From this tough roadside weed a suite of different cultivated plants was developed, making chicories very versatile in the kitchen. Why don't we see any of these interesting chicories on the market in Australia? There is just one reason: chicories taste bitter. Most Australian palates find bitterness totally unacceptable. Italians embrace it. They feel, as the Chinese do, that bitterness stimulates the appetite and gets the juices flowing. This explains why Campari, Aperol and Chinotto are so popular in Italy. Chicories are usually treated in some way to make them less bitter, either in the way they are grown or in the way they are cooked. Surely all those Italians can't be wrong about chicory. Maybe our palates need to grow up a bit.

Just like lettuces, there are loose-leaf and heading chicories, and some are grown for their stout roots, too. The Italians have bred an astounding variety of forms. Some have toothed green leaves like giant dandelions, some are bronze, some are red, some have spots or coloured veins. Some form tight heads like cabbages or have thick stems like celery. There are baby chicories for growing as cut-and-come-again salad crops. Each variety has its own use; some for eating fresh in salads, others for braising, others for grilling.

VARIETIES

•

Witlof or witloof

Also called Belgian chicory, witlof is a bit of a palaver to grow. It is a major investment of time and energy, which is why it is usually done by specialist growers who are set up especially for the task.

Here's how it is done. Witlof seeds are sown in spring and the plants are grown in the open ground to their full size over the course of summer. They look like big, messy dandelions. In autumn the plants have their leaves removed and their roots are lifted from the ground. The roots are packed into damp sand in crates, covered with a light-proof cover and put into warm, dark sheds for 'forcing' over winter. Forcing means placing a dormant plant indoors in warm conditions to induce it to resume growth out of season. After several weeks in the warmth and darkness of the shed, each root produces a single, white *chicon*; the torpedo-shaped cluster of leaf bases that is the part of the plant we eat.

Many Australian palates find witlof bitter and unpleasant. However in the Low Countries where witlof enjoys its greatest popularity (Belgians eat, on average, 7 kilograms per person per year), its fresh, bitter crispness is appreciated during the winter months as a foil to the stodgy cheesy, meaty foods that predominate in that season. Witlof is delicious in winter salads, especially when coupled with walnuts and walnut oil.

A field-grown witlof plant.

WITLOF CHICONS

Witlof is derived from the same wild ancestor as radicchio, but it has been selected for big, thick roots that produce big, tight chicons. The old story about witlof's origin is that it was accidentally discovered by a farmer in Schaerbeek during the Belgian Revolution in 1830, when he stored chicory roots in sand in his cellar, or threw them into his barn. It is said that conditions were mild that year and the chicory roots sprouted and so witlof was born.

It's a nice story but in fact, witlof was deliberately developed as a forcing crop in 1851 by Frans Breziers, head gardener at the Brussels Botanical Gardens. Ten years later the new crop hit the marketplace in Brussels and became a sensation. Belgian farmers turned their fields over to the new 'white gold' and never looked back. They could command a premium price for supplying scarce fresh winter vegetables of a kind that ordinary people could not grow at home.

Pan di Zucchero/Sugar Loaf

Sugar Loaf is chicory's answer to cos lettuce. Out of a rather tousled green rosette it produces a 40-centimetre-long, 10-centimetre-wide head of very densely packed, self-blanched leaves, like a giant witlof. This Italian heirloom is a good one for grilling or braising.

RADICCHIO

•

Strictly speaking radicchios are red-coloured, heading chicories. Radicchios only attain their dramatic contrasting colours of icy white and wine-red when the heads are 'blanched'. This means that light is excluded from them for a few weeks, causing the cells to grow big and juicy, and allowing the green pigment chlorophyll and bitter-tasting chemicals to dissipate. On a commercial scale this is done in forcing sheds or with black plastic covering the rows of plants. At home, you can do it by putting a ceramic mixing bowl, metal bucket or if you are lucky enough to have one, an old-fashioned terracotta forcing pot, over the developing heads. Or you can use the ancient method and dump a bucketload of manure on them. It doesn't matter what you use so long as light is completely excluded for a couple of weeks. The outer leaves will inevitably go slimy, but they are easily removed to reveal the lovely pale heart.

Radicchios are cold-climate crops. They grow through the summer but need to feel some chill in autumn and winter in order to colour up well and form a head. Expect to see quite a lot of variation in seedlings. Some individuals will form heads better than others.

VARIETIES

•

Orchidea Rossa & Palla Rossa
'Red orchid' and 'red ball', respectively, are round, cabbagey radicchios that are pretty reliable to grow.

Rossa di Treviso
'Treviso red' is a famous Italian eighteenth-century radicchio that has spawned a whole tribe of minor variations ('precoce' – early, 'tardivo' – late, 'svelta' – slender, etc). They are all variations on the basic theme: a 20-centimetre-tall, torpedo-shaped

PALLA ROSSA RADICCHIO

head of green leaves heavily stippled with red, which turn darker bronze as the cold weather advances in winter. Protected inside its jacket of outer leaves, the head becomes dark wine-red with green-white midrib and veins.

The really beautiful red and white, octopus-like Treviso radicchios seen for sale in Italy are grown by forcing them in a similar fashion to witlof. The technical know-how for forcing radicchios was taken to the Veneto in the 1860s by, no surprise, a Belgian agronomist who was familiar with the brand-new way of cultivating witlof. From him, the Italians learned how to lift the mature roots and force them in dark sheds. The Italian varieties are forced not in sand boxes but with their roots suspended in water at around 15°C, warm enough to start the dormant plants into growth. It's too much of a faff to do at home, but plants are easy to blanch in the garden with an upturned bowl or something similar.

Rossa di Verona

'Veronese red' is a mid-twentieth-century variety descended from Rossa di Treviso. It has the same glorious red wine colouring with bright white veining, but its heads grow in tight round balls rather than Treviso's torpedo shape. This is the familiar radicchio commonly seen in supermarkets.

VARIEGATA DI CASTELFRANCO RADICCHIO

Variegata di Castelfranco

'Variegated of Castelfranco' has pale green leaves with dark red flecks a lot like the Bunte Forellenschluss lettuce. When blanched, the heads turn a pearlescent shade of ivory-yellow spotted with blood-red. They are absolutely beautiful to behold, tender and delicious.

Incidentally, Variegata di Castelfranco, Rossa di Verona and Rossa di Treviso have been given protected *Indicazione Geografica Protetta* (IGP) status. Even though those varieties have been known since the eighteenth century, it is now illegal to sell them as 'Treviso', 'Verona' or 'Castelfranco' unless they are grown in specific parts of Italy, under the watchful eye of a governing body. It is true that the growers in those regions produce a superlative product. Yet one has to wonder if radicchios forced in dark sheds in the official IGP region taste significantly different from radicchios forced in dark sheds anywhere else in the world? Is the rarefied concept of 'terroir' also at work in dark, temperature-controlled sheds, on plants with their roots suspended in water instead of growing in soil? Call me sceptical, but I doubt it. It is interesting to note that the witlof growers of Belgium produce an equally good product that is not geographically protected.

ENDIVE

•

When Australians talk about 'salad' in generic terms, we think of the basic ingredient as lettuce. When the French talk about 'salad', they are just as likely to mean endive.

The endive (*Cichorium endivia*) is very closely related to chicory. Endives resemble loose-leaf lettuces in their growth habit. There are two basic categories of endive. One has finely cut foliage, collectively termed the curly endives or *frisée* (French for curly). Endives with entire leaves are called broad-leaf or Batavia endive, or *escarole*.

Like chicories, endives are very bitter and are usually blanched by covering the fully developed rosettes with dinner plates for a couple of weeks to exclude the light. This results in a tangy-bitter, pale-coloured salad that goes well with fatty ingredients. Hence its routine appearance in French *salades composées*, which almost always feature some kind of fatty protein such as lardons or goat cheese.

Frisée and escarole are rarely sold by variety in this country, although there are many in existence.

CURLY ENDIVE

WILD ARTICHOKE

ARTICHOKES

If you want to impress your friends, grow artichokes. Unlike their neat little relatives the lettuces and radicchios, artichokes look like thistles on steroids. With their ragged, silver leaves a metre in length topped with electric-blue, spiky flowers the size of dinner plates, artichokes never fail to impress.

Artichokes look like thistles on steroids because that is exactly what they are. They are descended from the wild cardoon (*Cynara cardunculus*), a spiky little thistle from dry, rocky hillsides around the Mediterranean. Selective breeding has produced two edible crops from this ancestral plant; the artichoke (sometimes given its own species name, *Cynara scolymus*) and the cultivated cardoon. Both of them are much larger than their parent.

The cultivated cardoon is still widely grown in Mediterranean Europe and North Africa for its edible leaf stems. Its flower buds are very small and spiky.

Cardoons form leaf rosettes of huge proportions; two metres wide by one and a half high is quite normal. The stems can't be eaten straight from the plant. They must first be blanched by either hilling up soil around them to exclude light, or by wrapping them in cardboard or black plastic for a few weeks until they lose their bitterness. It's not uncommon to see blanched cardoons for sale in markets in southern Europe. They look like bunches of giant white celery but they taste just like artichokes. They are delicious braised with butter and garlic.

Artichokes and cardoons contain an interesting chemical called cynarine which alters taste perception, making other foods taste an odd sort of saccharin-sweet. At the same time, the sap itself tastes incredibly bitter. Artichokes lend these unique sweet-bitter flavours to the Italian liqueur made from them, called Cynar.

VARIETIES

•

Artichokes are propagated from seed, so there is naturally quite a bit of variation amongst siblings from the same seedling swarm. To obtain the best, most true-to-type artichoke plants, you will need to grow out the seedlings for a year, select the best few to be divided and replanted in your garden, and discard the inferior ones. The temptation is to keep all of the seedlings. However, you will notice that the inferior ones really are inferior. They can be brutally thorny and the buds may be small and tough. The good ones have big buds, soft foliage and a harmless indentation where a sharp thorn would normally sit on the bud scales, making picking and preparation much more enjoyable.

Green Globe
Long popular in France, this robust variety has very large, round, fleshy buds suitable for stuffing.

Imperial Star
This artichoke is probably the youngest 'heirloom' in this book, released in 1991. Imperial Star has big, globe-shaped, green, thorn-free buds that hold well on the plant. The really interesting thing is that the buds are borne in the first growing season after sowing. This is a big advance because it means

GREEN GLOBE ARTICHOKE

that this variety can be grown as an annual. That is great news for gardeners in warm climates where the lack of winter cold usually means that artichokes don't survive to their second year and so never set a crop. It's also great news for artichoke-lovers who have limited space because you no longer have to have a devote a massive, permanent patch to the plants in order to grow your favourite treat. Because it is an annual, it is possible to grow Imperial Star in your normal vegetable beds, starting with fresh seedlings every year and throwing them out at the end of the cropping season, as you would with any other annual vegetable. Of course if you are able to leave Imperial Star plants in the ground to grow on, they will remain productive for several years, like any other artichoke.

Imperial Star is the result of breeding done by Wayne Schrader and Keith Mayberry at the University of California Cooperative Extension. It is subject to Plant Variety Protection for eighteen years so that the developers can recoup their costs. After that, it becomes open source. No seed saving for now, then.

Violetta di Chioggia

An Italian heirloom with medium-sized, oblong buds of attractive dark purple. This colour changes to olive-green when cooked. The plants are quite compact. Yet another vegetable named after the Italian town of Chioggia. They are certainly proud of their veggies there. Remember: it's pronounced 'kyo-jya', not 'chee-ogg-ee-a'.

VIOLETTA ARTICHOKE

JERUSALEM ARTICHOKES

If you have ever wondered why botanists and gardeners insist on using scientific names for plants instead of simply using their common names, Jerusalem artichokes provide the answer.

Like many plants, Jerusalem artichokes' common name is irritatingly imprecise, for they are neither artichokes nor from Jerusalem. On the other hand, their scientific name, *Helianthus tuberosus*, does tell us something useful about them. *Helianthus* comes from Greek *helios*, meaning the sun, and *anthos*, a flower. *Tuberosus* is Latin for 'bearing tubers'. This tells us exactly what this plant is: a tuber-bearing sunflower.

So where on earth did the 'Jerusalem' part of the name come from, given that the plant is a native of North America? It seems to be a corruption of the Italian word for sunflower, *girasole*, which does sound an awful lot like Jerusalem. The artichoke part of the name is probably just due to the similarity in flavour of the tuber to the heart of a true artichoke.

Unfortunately this fascinating lesson in semantics is about the most useful thing the Jerusalem artichoke has to offer. As a garden plant it is incredibly rapacious and weedy. In the kitchen it is fairly limited. These are the very reasons why, each winter, gardeners who had a bucket of Jerusalem artichokes foisted on them the previous winter – and were foolish enough to plant them – visit the same dubious act on other unsuspecting victims. Permaculturists, I'm looking at you.

Jerusalem artichokes are the vegetable equivalent of a chain letter. They should be destroyed as soon as you receive them. Do not under any circumstances plant them or they will take over your garden, if not your life. Don't believe me? I guarantee that you will, after you have eaten your hundredth bowl of Jerusalem artichoke soup, sealed your hundredth jar of Jerusalem artichoke pickles and *still* have a hundred buckets of tubers left to foist on unsuspecting friends. And I haven't even touched on the indelicate subject of flatulence.

You have been warned!

YACON

•

The yacon (*Smallanthus sonchifolius,* syn. *Polymnia sonchifolia*) is the South American cousin of the Jerusalem artichoke. It is built along pretty similar lines: it is a tuber-bearing sunflower. However, unlike its rampant North American relative, the yacon really *should* be more widely grown.

Yacon is grown for its large, crisp-fleshed tubers. These look very much like dahlia tubers, and indeed the two are distantly related. Yacon tubers are usually eaten raw. They have a very sweet, slightly resinous taste like carrots and a refreshing crispness not unlike water chestnuts. The whole experience is very much like eating a nashi pear; delicious!

Yacon tastes the sweetest when allowed to sit on a sunny windowsill for a few days after being dug.

Yacon has attractive foliage.

GREATER BURDOCK

Greater burdock (*Arctium lappa*) is a delicious, underrated vegetable. Known to lovers of Japanese food by its Japanese name *gobō*, burdock is considered no more than a weed in most of the northern hemisphere. It is commonly seen growing on forest margins, in meadows and on waste ground in Europe, where nobody takes much notice of it.

In Japan, however, people get very enthusiastic about it. There, burdock is cultivated for its cylindrical, brown taproot, which can grow to an impressive metre in length and be ramrod-straight. Markets in Japan are seldom without rows of handsome burdock roots, neatly bundled and displayed with pride. Burdock roots are slightly woody in both texture and flavour. They have a pleasing crunch and an earthy pungency – there is no vegetable like them. In Japan burdock roots are stewed, pickled or stir-fried in sesame oil to make more-ish *kinpira gobō*.

In nature burdock is a biennial plant. It forms a rosette of huge, triangular, felted leaves in its first growing season. Then it goes dormant over winter before returning in the spring and sending up a 2-metre-tall, multi-branched flower stem, like some kind of elaborate ham radio antenna system. Each branch ends in a small, purple, thistle-like flower, or burr. The outside of each burr is covered in bristly hooks, which, when the seed is ripe, attach themselves to the fur of passing wildlife. This system of little hooks attaching themselves to animal fur – specifically his pet dog's fur – gave the Swiss electrical engineer George de Mestral the idea for Velcro in 1941.

WATANABE BURDOCK

Although a biennial in the wild, burdock is cultivated as an annual. It is best sown direct in the spring, for harvest in late summer and autumn. Burdock needs a very deep, well-worked soil to produce its longest, straightest roots. Few of us can provide topsoil a metre deep, but don't be put off. Short, gnarly burdock roots taste just as good as long, straight ones. There is nothing more nurturing on a crisp autumn evening than a hotpot of burdock, pumpkin, eggplant, tofu and shiitake mushrooms simmered in miso and garnished with a big handful of *katsuobushi*.

There are several named selections of *gobō* in Japan, some of which are available through seed merchants in Australia. **Watanabe** is earlier cropping with shorter, thicker roots. It is suitable for a late summer sowing for harvest over winter. **Takinogawa**, a favourite in Japan, crops later and its roots are longer.

SALSIFY & SCORZONERA

Salsify (*Tragopogon porrifolius*) and scorzonera (*Scorzonera hispanica*) are related root crops in the daisy family. Both are Mediterranean biennials grown for their carrot-like roots.

Salsify has white roots which bleed a milky sap when cut. Salsify is sometimes called oyster plant on account of its faintly oyster-like taste. If you think that sounds revolting, don't be put off. It is not at all overpowering. Boiled and buttered, salsify is delicious. If left to overwinter in the ground, salsify produces edible young shoots the following spring, which look like leek foliage (porrifolius means leek-leaved). These shoots are called 'chicons', just like the shoots of witlof. Salsify is naturalised in parts of Australia. If you have ever seen giant dandelion 'clocks' growing by the side of the road in late summer, that is salsify.

Scorzonera is similar to salsify but it has broader foliage and roots which are darker coloured and rough on the outside but white on the inside. Scorzonera has a sweet, mild flavour. A few selections of salsify and scorzonera are available occasionally, such as Salsify **Mammoth Sandwich Island** and Scorzonera **Russian Giant**.

MAMMOTH SANDWICH
ISLAND SALSIFY

CHAPTER NINE

THE

Amaryllis

FAMILY

NAKED LADIES

(Amaryllis belladonna)

The onions formerly had a family in their own right, the Alliaceae. Nowadays they have been demoted to a subfamily within the Amaryllis family, the Amaryllidaceae. This has won them lots of interesting relatives. For a start, there are the beautiful 'naked ladies' or belladonna lilies (*Amaryllis belladonna*) after which the family is named. Daffodils and jonquils, nerines, clivias, hippeastrums, agapanthus, snowdrops and snowflakes are all members of the Amaryllis family. By now you will have noticed that this is a family of bulbs. A bulb is an organ made from modified leaf bases, used for storing water and food, which allows the plant to tough out periods of drought. Many members of the Amaryllis family come from Mediterranean and semi-arid climates. These climates feature mild, moist winters and fierce, dry summers; hence Amaryllids' adaptation to growing during the winter months and hiding below ground during summer. Onions, garlic and leeks are no exception to this, adapted to lives on the rocky shores of the Mediterranean, the sands of the Middle East and the steppes of Central Asia.

The onion branch of the Amaryllis family, the Allioideae, contains only a handful of genera, of which the onion genus *Allium* is by far the largest, comprising somewhere between 250 and 800 species, depending on which botanist you ask. *Allium* species all contain sulphurous compounds which give them their characteristic

GLOBEMASTER ALLIUM

oniony odour. Many of the ornamental alliums are extremely beautiful, with spherical flower heads made up of hundreds of tiny flowers. Interplanted with grasses and perennials, they bring a unique texture to the ornamental garden.

Onions, garlic and leeks are native to those parts of the world where agriculture was first practised. They are some of the earliest crops grown by humankind. There is a famous biblical reference to onions, leeks and garlic in Numbers, in which the Israelites, who have subsisted in the desert on nothing but 'manna from heaven' for forty years, bemoan: 'We remember the fish which wee did eate in Egypt freely: the cucumbers and the melons, and the leekes, and the onions, and the garlicke.' You can hardly blame them when you consider that manna was probably a kind of aphid-like scale insect.

It has long been thought that the workers who built the pyramids in 2500 BCE were given rations of garlic, onions and radishes, based on contemporary inscriptions, as well as comments made 2000 years later by that legendary exaggerator Herodotus. It is a matter of some conjecture whether the 'garlic, onions and radishes' referred to in the hieroglyphic inscriptions were vegetables or in fact minerals used in the construction of the pyramids. Arsenate minerals smell of onions and garlic when they are heated. It has been suggested that different arsenate compounds used in the construction were referred to by their smells to help workers identify them. This hotly contested theory certainly makes more sense of the fact that the ledgers show that the 'onions' and 'garlic' bought during the construction were fabulously expensive.

Whatever the case, there is no doubt whatsoever that the Egyptians grew and loved onion and garlic plants. Pliny the Elder tells us that Egyptians valued them so much that they would swear an oath on them. That's serious respect.

In Mesopotamia, onions, leeks and garlic were grown by the Sumerian civilisations. Babylonian recipes dating from 1700 BCE make frequent use of leeks, onions and garlic to flavour dishes of gazelle, goat and pigeon. If you think Mrs Beeton's and Mrs Alexander's cookbooks are heavy, spare a thought for the Babylonians – their recipes were written on clay tablets.

Alliums have long been thought to heat the blood, inflame the passions and get the juices flowing. In his description of the corrupt church Summoner in his fourteenth-century *Canterbury Tales*, Geoffrey Chaucer wrote: 'Well loved he garleek, oynons, and eek lekes. And for to drinken strong wyn, reed as blood.' By which he meant that the Summoner was a hard-living man, adding that he was lecherous, bearded and red in the face, had a nasty skin complaint, and children were frightened to look at him. Perhaps it is no wonder that the alliums are eschewed by some cultures. High-caste Hindus, Jains and followers of certain strands of Buddhism do not partake of alliums.

Besides the major crops of onions, garlic and leeks there are several minor allium crops, too. Chives (*A. schoenoprasum*) are a popular herb in European cuisine, loved for their delicate onion flavour and edible purple flowers. Garlic chives (*A. tuberosum*) have flat, garlic-flavoured leaves used in Asian cookery. They are a traditional accompaniment to the Thai dish *pad thai*. In China the flower stems of garlic chives are used in stir fries. Both chives and garlic chives have very pretty edible flowers, but they self-seed like crazy. Be sure to dead-head them before the seeds drop.

Ramsons (*A. ursinum*) and their North American equivalent ramps (*A. tricoccum*) are harvested from the wild when they shoot in the springtime and eaten as seasonal delicacies. The plant called society garlic (*Tulbaghia violacea*) is a South African native. It is sometimes sold in nurseries as an edible plant but, while it won't kill you, it is not very palatable, tasting like a rather rank, insipid garlic chive. Its best use is definitely as an ornamental.

By the way, the insidious onion weed is not, in fact, an allium but a member of the related genus *Nothoscordum*.

NERINES

TROPEANA ROSSA LUNGA ONION

ONIONS

My grandmother used to say that if you've got an onion and a cup of water you can make a meal. She would know, having fed a family of six during the Depression and war years. Onions make anything taste hearty and mouthwatering. Just the smell of an onion frying in a pan is delicious, before any other ingredient is added.

The bulb onion (*Allium cepa*) probably originated in Central Asia, a hotspot for alliums (and tulips, too). Like so many ancient crops its wild ancestor is unclear. The most likely contender seems to be *A. vavilovii* from Iran and Turkmenistan, although this could be an ancient cultigen itself. Perhaps the original ancestral onion is extinct.

Onions were already cultivated in Mesopotamia and Egypt by the third millennium BCE. Onions routinely appear in Egyptian art and entombed with mummies, both *inside* the mummies as a preservative and alongside them as a meal for the afterlife. Onions are mentioned in Indian writings by the fourth century BCE.

By Greek and Roman times there were already several cultivars in existence. The Romans took onions all over their empire. Onions really hit their straps in the Middle Ages, when there was a blossoming of cultivars in the disparate climates of Europe; some adapted to hot Mediterranean climates, others to the mild summers of northern Europe.

Christopher Columbus took onions to the Americas in the late fifteenth century, the pilgrim fathers did so again in the early seventeenth century, and so did subsequent waves of migrants. Today the USA boasts an amazing range of cultivars. Bulb onions made it fairly late to north Asia, where the native bunching onions were, and still are, a more important ingredient in the cooking of that region. In South East Asia, where the influence of Hinduism, Arab trade and European colonisation are felt, bulb onions are more pervasive.

Where does the future of onions lie? In 2008 scientists in New Zealand engineered a 'no cry' onion by switching off the gene that makes the enzyme that causes our eyes to water when we cut into one. They feel that this modification is a great leap forward as it will also 'enhance' the 'health and flavour profiles' of the onion. They hope to see these genetically engineered 'no cry' onions on our supermarket shelves within a decade.

Now come on, people. Have we become so effete that we can no longer endure the horrendous inconvenience of our eyes watering while we chop an onion? Onions have been causing this reaction for nigh on 5000 years and we seem to have coped all right until now. Is it really so awful that we need to resort to genetic engineering? Secondly, do we really need to 'enhance' the 'health and flavour profiles' of what is already a very healthy and flavourful vegetable? The onion ain't broke. Please let's not try to fix it.

VARIETIES

•

Onions fall into several broad categories according to their hotness and keeping qualities. Some onions are meant for immediate consumption, others will store for up to a year. Some onions are mild and sweet, suitable for eating raw; others are very pungent, perfect for cooking. It's important to match the onion to its final purpose.

Onions are very sensitive to photoperiod (day length). They will only form bulbs when the days are of a certain length. Onions' day length requirement varies from variety to variety. 'Short-day' onions form bulbs when the days are around ten to twelve hours in length. These are the best varieties for gardeners in 'northern' Australia, which in this context actually means any garden north of about Canberra. 'Intermediate-day' onions form bulbs when days are around thirteen to fourteen hours in length, so these varieties are better suited to gardens in southern Australia. 'Long day' onions need days fifteen hours or more in length in order to form bulbs so they are only suited to very southerly gardens – southern Victoria and Tasmania, in effect. Be sure to choose a variety suited to your summer day length or you will not get bulbs.

AILSA CRAIG ONION

Ailsa Craig

A Scottish heirloom named after a geographical feature, not a person, Ailsa Craig was introduced in 1887 by the head gardener to the Marquis of Ailsa in Ayrshire. It is an awe-inspiring onion, popular with exhibition growers in the UK because it produces enormous, globe- or slightly turban-shaped onions with satiny, straw-coloured skin. When well grown the bulbs can be significantly bigger than grapefruits, well on the way to soccer-ball-sized. Two-kilogram bulbs are not unheard of. Ailsa Craig is a long-day onion so unfortunately it is only suited to very southern parts of Australia. Its flesh is mild and sweet but it does not store for long periods, so after you have shown off your giant onion to your friends it is best to eat it fairly promptly.

Australian Brown

This variety is immensely popular in the USA yet, despite its name, virtually unknown in Australia. It was introduced by the American seedsman W. Atlee Burpee in 1897 from brown Spanish onions imported from Australia by C. C. Morse, another American seedsman. Australian Brown is an intermediate-day onion. It has globe-shaped bulbs with pungent, yellowish flesh wrapped in thick, copper-brown skins, which make for good storage.

Barletta

A small, round, white onion that is good for eating fresh and pickling. It is a short-day variety so it's good for northern Australia or as a spring-sown onion in southern parts.

Borettana

Borettana is an Italian heirloom onion with golden, flying saucer-shaped bulbs traditionally used for pickling, but wonderful for gentle cooking, too. An intermediate-day variety suited to southern Australian gardens.

Gladalan White

This is the classic white onion seen in Australian groceries. It has round, greenish-white bulbs with a good oniony flavour. It is a short-day variety which does well in northern states or from a spring sowing in the southern states.

Pukekohe/Creamgold

A New Zealand heirloom, this is the classic brown onion seen in groceries. It has globe-shaped bulbs, ever so slightly flattened, with thick, copper-brown skin and dense, pungent cream-coloured flesh. Creamgold stores well for long periods. It is an intermediate-day onion suited to the southern states.

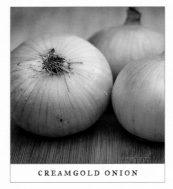

CREAMGOLD ONION

Rossa Piatta d'Italia

'Red Flat of Italy' was listed by Vilmorin in 1885. It has the classic Italian 'cipollini' shape, like a little flying saucer. It is a mild, sweet onion but sturdy enough to stand up to cooking.

Tropeana Rossa Lunga

This famous Italian heirloom from Tropea in Calabria has been awarded Protected Geographical Indication (*Indicazione Geografica Protetta*) just like its famous compatriot, Parmigiano Reggiano cheese. This is a bit tiresome because it means that when this onion is grown outside the Tropea

TROPEANA ROSSA LUNGA

area it cannot legally be called a Tropeana Rossa Lunga (literally 'Red Long from Tropea'). You will have to think of a different name if you want to grow it and avoid being thrown in the slammer. 'Pink Torpedo' might do. Whatever you call it, this variety is pretty unmistakeable. The bulbs are 15 centimetres long and spindle-shaped, with silky red-violet skin. The flesh is crystalline white with each layer covered in a magenta film.

These onions were probably taken by the Phoenicians to Calabria and they have been grown around Tropea ever since. A festival is held in their honour at harvest time each July, during which town squares are decked out in hanging bunches of red bulbs and the air is thick with the smell of onions cooking. Tropea Rossa Lunga is sweet and tender, good for fresh eating, roasting and barbecuing. It is not cut out for long storage, however.

Rossa Lunga is not the only red onion grown in Tropea. Its cousin, **Tropeana Tonda** ('Round from Tropea') is, in fact, distinctly heart-shaped with a slightly flattened top and a pointy bottom. Coming from the Mediterranean region, they are both intermediate day onions.

The Tropea onions are credited with a raft of health benefits including, predictably, curing erectile dysfunction. I can scarcely think of a vegetable that is *not* credited with curing erectile dysfunction. So eat your greens, chaps.

White Sweet Spanish

A large, round Spanish onion with exquisite pearly white skin. Sweet and juicy for eating fresh and quite a beauty to behold. An intermediate-day variety.

SHALLOTS

•

The vegetables which many Australians persist in calling 'shallots' – those leafy, green-topped, white-bottomed onions bought in thick bundles – are categorically not shallots. They are spring onions. That is, they are either baby bulb onions or Asian bunching onions. True shallots, or *eschalots* as some clever gourmets call them to show that they know the difference, are a distinct race of bulbing onion. Their bulbs are small, usually about the size of a walnut, matte copper or purple in colour, and either squat and squared off at the corners or long and torpedo-shaped. Shallots have a unique flavour that is simultaneously mild and sweet but warm and oniony.

GOLDEN SHALLOT

Shallots and spring onions are not good substitutes for one another in cooking. They do different things.

True shallots' defining feature is that a single 'set' (a small bulbil used for propagation) planted in the winter or spring will divide into a clump of a dozen or so small bulbs over the course of the growing season. This is different from a 'normal' bulb onion which will only form a single, large bulb. Hence shallots are known as the Aggregatum group of *Allium cepa*, 'aggregatum' meaning the onions that 'group together'. 'Potato' or 'multiplier' onions are also members of the Aggregatum group.

Although there are several heirloom varieties of shallot, they are usually sold only by colour in Australia. Golden or red. Take your pick. If you start your shallots from seed rather than sets you are almost certainly growing one of the F1 hybrid shallots such as Picador.

The Egyptian onion or tree onion (*A.* × *proliferum*) is a hybrid of the bulb onion and the bunching onion. Egyptian onions resemble shallots except they are 'topsetting', meaning that they produce tiny bulbils where the flowers should be. When the 60-centimetre flower stems dry out at the end of the growing season, they topple over, and the bulbils take root and grow into a new clump. Year by year Egyptian onions can move quite a distance from where you originally planted them, hence their nickname 'walking onions'.

WELSH OR BUNCHING ONIONS

•

Welsh onions do not derive their name from the country of Wales, but from the Germanic word *welsch*, which loosely means 'foreign' (in the sense of something that is non-Germanic in origin). The term 'welsh onion' refers to the Asian bunching onion, *Allium fistulosum*, which is Siberian and East Asian in origin. Welsh onions are called bunching onions because they grow in clumps, like shallots. However, they do not form prominent bulbs. Both the white and green parts of bunching onions are used. Each has a distinct flavour so it is common to see Asian recipes calling for only the white or green part of the onion, or using both in different stages of the recipe. Several cultivars of bunching onion are available in Australia now, many of them Japanese in origin, such as **Ishikura**, **Tokyo Long White** and **Natsuguro**. Several red varieties are available, too.

ISHIKURA BUNCHING ONION

JAUNE DE POITOU LEEK

LEEKS

Leeks (*Allium ampeloprasum*) are native to the eastern Mediterranean basin. They were grown by the Egyptians as early as 2000 BCE and by the Mesopotamians, too. Leeks buried with Egyptian mummies have been carbon dated at around 3500 years old. These might have been interred as a meal for the deceased in the afterlife, suggesting how highly the Egyptians thought of leeks.

Leeks caught on with the Greeks and Romans, too. Pliny the Elder tells us that Emperor Nero was excessively fond of them, earning himself the nickname *porrophagus*: 'leek-eater'. Nero ate leeks several times each month in the belief that they improved his voice. What a shame they didn't have any effect on his penchant for cruelty and despotism. The Romans took leeks with them across their empire. By the Middle Ages they were popular throughout Europe. Medieval cookbooks are full of recipes for them.

The earliest cultivated leeks had narrow leaves and a thin stem with a swollen bulb at the base, much like their close relatives the so-called Russian or elephant garlics, and the *kurrat* leeks still grown in the Middle East. Unlike their ancestors, modern leeks show almost no bulbing at the base and their leaves are wide and soft. Generations of selective breeding has given us leeks with very stout 'shanks': the name given to their long edible 'stems'. The shank of a leek is not a true stem, but a bundle of overlapping leaf bases. Many leeks in existence today are descended from an extinct heirloom variety from Rouen in France, called **Gros Court** – 'Fat Short' in English. This monstrous variety was reported to form enormous stems a whopping 30 centimetres wide at the base. It was used in breeding a new generation of leeks by the Vilmorin seed house, passing on its thick shank to its progeny such as Musselburgh and Monstreux de Carentan.

The leek is a symbol of the proud Welsh people. How it came to be so is uncertain. There are several legends used to explain it, all of them military-themed and all involving hats. In the oldest, Wales' sixth-century patron, St David, told Welshmen to wear leeks in their hats to distinguish friend from foe in a battle against the Saxons. In an almost identical version of the story from a century later, the Welsh King Cadwaladr instructed his soldiers to do the same thing, also in a battle against the Saxons. Later versions mention the Welshmen wearing leeks in their hats in battle against the French in Crécy in 1346 and at Agincourt in 1415. The daffodil is a more recent floral symbol of Wales. Interestingly, daffodils are called 'Peter's leeks' in Welsh.

Leeks are not a fast-growing crop. It takes between five and nine months for a good thick shank to develop. This is a long time for a plant to take up space in the vegetable garden. Leeks earn their place thanks to their resistance to cold. In northern Europe where leeks enjoy their greatest popularity, seeds are sown in early spring and reach full size before the onset of winter, when they can be harvested as needed during the lean months.

The shank of a leek does not grow long and white by itself. This is the result of careful cultivation. Leek shanks need to be blanched by having light excluded from them during growth. The blanching process is begun when leek seedlings are transplanted. They are placed as deep as possible into the soil, with just their green tips showing above the surface. As they grow taller, soil is drawn up around them bit by bit, a process called 'hilling' or 'earthing up'. If you don't make any effort to blanch leeks' shanks they will come out short and mostly green. They are still edible, of course, but not as tender and nice as those which have been blanched.

VARIETIES

•

There were dozens of varieties of leek in cultivation during their heyday in the nine-teenth century. Exhibition leek growers developed their own strains and jealously guarded their secret cultivation methods, such as growing them in tall terracotta pipes in order to produce astonishingly long, thick, shanks. These secret techniques ensured their leeks the best chance of winning at the local agricultural show. A beautifully dressed brace of leeks, with decoratively plaited leaves and roots trimmed to perfection, is quite a sight to behold.

These days far fewer varieties are available, but there are some beauties nevertheless.

Bleu de Solaise
A French heirloom leek with beautiful blue foliage that takes on violet purple tones in frosty weather.

Gros Jaune de Poitou
A French heirloom with yellow-green foliage, hence 'Big Yellow of Poitou'. This is an early leek best harvested in autumn from a spring sowing.

King Richard
A more recent open-pollinated leek which naturally forms slender shanks up to 30 centimetres long before the leaves fan out, alleviating some of the need for hilling up. It is not as cold-hardy as some older varieties but it is quick growing. It is probably best sown in spring for summer and autumn harvest.

Monstreux de Carentan
A French heirloom bred by Vilmorin in France. It is capable of producing very thick shanks, 5 centimetres or more in diameter, though it needs a lot of water to do so.

Musselburgh
A Scottish heirloom developed from seed obtained from the French seed house Vilmorin, and first cousin to Monstreux de Carentan. Musselburgh was introduced in 1834 and named for a town near Edinburgh (now practically a suburb of it).

Musselburgh is noted for its robust nature and, in cold climates, its ability to stand in the ground through harsh winters unaffected. It remains a very good leek.

The Lyon/Prizetaker

A late nineteenth-century English heirloom which, when well grown, can approach a metre in height with thick shanks.

KING RICHARD LEEK

EARLY PURPLE GARLIC

GARLIC

Garlic (*Allium sativum*) is a very old cultigen — a plant created by human, rather than natural, selection. It has long been thought to be descended from a bulb that grows wild in Turkey, Iran and Central Asia, *Allium longicuspis*. However, like most kinds of domesticated garlic, *A. longicuspis* cannot flower or set seed. *A. longicuspis* might not be a wild species at all, but an even more ancient cultigen domesticated by a culture long since gone. It is possible that both cultivated garlic and *A. longicuspis* are descended from one or more of the garlic-scented wild alliums from the eastern Mediterranean such as *A. tuncelianum* from Turkey or *A. truncatum* from the Levant, though recent phylogenetic studies have thrown these suggestions in doubt, too. The origins of garlic are truly a mystery. Perhaps its wild ancestor is already extinct.

Most kinds of domesticated garlic are unable to reproduce themselves sexually or to travel long distances without the aid of humans because they cannot flower or set seed. Many varieties of garlic routinely send up flower stems but, in all but a handful of varieties, these terminate in a cluster of tiny bulbils where the flowers should be. Garlic is truly a domesticated plant that relies completely on humans for its survival.

Still, garlic hasn't done too badly in the 6000 or so years we've been growing it. From its dry homeland, garlic has spread far and wide, hitchhiking with humans. It has adapted to a wide range of climates and latitudes and has been embraced by dozens of cultures for uses as diverse as a medicine to expel worms from the bowels, an aphrodisiac and a vampire repellant. And, of course, as food.

The 'flower' stems of hardneck garlics are tender and delicious.

People seem to either love garlic or hate it. Garlic has come to define some international cuisines by its presence (e.g. Korean and French cuisine) and others by its absence (e.g. Japanese and British cuisine). Cultures which do not eat it tend to look down upon those which do. The Japanese once referred to Koreans pejoratively as 'the garlic eaters'. In 1818, the Englishman Percy Shelley wrote in a letter from Naples:

> There are two Italies [...] The one is the most sublime and lovely contemplation that can be conceived by the imagination of man; the other is the

most degraded, disgusting, and odious. What do you think? Young women of rank actually eat – you will never guess what – garlick! Our poor friend Lord Byron is quite corrupted by living among these people, and in fact, is going on in a way not worthy of him.

Shelley's disgust sums up the attitude of non-garlic-eating cultures toward those who do eat it. It is something that foreigners, the uncouth and the poor indulge in, and frankly beyond the pale. Fine by me. More for the rest of us, I say. Because people who do eat garlic *really* love it and think that those who don't are missing out.

The oldest preserved garlic plants come from Copper Age Palestine, dated to 4000 BCE. The Egyptians depicted it in their art as long ago as 3700 BCE. Sumerian recipes include garlic in dishes with gazelle, pigeon and goat by at least 2300 BCE. Garlands of garlic were entombed with the boy pharaoh Tutankhamun in 1325 BCE, together with a breathtaking hoard of gold. Like the mummified remains of his body, Tutankhamun's garlic is desiccated and fragile but otherwise looks exactly like the garlic we know today.

The Greeks and Romans grew garlic, too. Just about every Greek and Roman commentator mentions garlic at some time, usually as a medicine. Pliny the Elder

EARLY PURPLE GARLIC

recommends it for every malady you can imagine, from toothache to epilepsy to shrew bites and consumption. Garlic has long been seen as a panacea.

Meanwhile in Asia, Chinese documents show that garlic was being cultivated there by 2000 BCE. The Indus Valley civilisation grew garlic but it doesn't get another mention in that part of the world until an Indian Ayurvedic medical manual from the second century BCE.

There are dozens of garlic varieties which fall into one of two categories: hardnecks and softnecks. Hardneck garlics (*Allium sativum* var. *ophioscorodon*) are so called because they develop a flowering stalk up the middle of the bulb which, when dried, forms a pencil-like hard core in the bulb. As it grows, the flowering stalk emerges curved over like a swan's neck, at which point it can be picked and eaten like asparagus. If left on the plant, it will eventually straighten and open into a cluster of tiny bulbils. The bulbils can be eaten or used for propagation but they take several years to form a full-sized bulb, so it is better to pick them off and eat them at the swan's neck stage. There are several kinds of hardneck garlics including purple stripe garlics, turban garlics, the hot-flavoured Asiatic garlics, porcelain garlics, the big-flavoured rocamboles and handsome creole garlics. The creole garlics are the best varieties for areas with warm winters, but also the hardest to come by. Although they are properly hardnecks, creole garlics rarely flower so you might see them listed as softnecks.

True softneck garlics (*A. sativum* var. *sativum*) are so called because they do not form flower stalks and therefore lack the hard central core of hardneck garlics. When dried, the stem of softnecks is quite floppy and pliable. Therefore, softneck garlics are the best varieties for plaiting. There are two kinds of softneck garlics: the multilayered artichoke garlics and the neat, pearly silverskins.

In general hardneck garlics produce 6–12 large individual cloves per bulb. They have a hot, pungent flavour. Softnecks are milder in flavour and produce 10–20 cloves per bulb, a few large ones around the outside of the bulb and many smaller ones in the centre. Hardnecks do not keep as long as softnecks so if you want to be self sufficient for garlic it is a good idea to grow some of each kind, using up the superior hardneck varieties first before moving on to the longer-keeping softnecks. As a rule, softneck garlics perform better than hardnecks in areas with mild winters but they also require a longer growing season.

VARIETIES

•

There are said to be somewhere in the vicinity of 600 garlic varieties. However, many of them are barely distinguishable from one another. It is more than likely that there are just a few genetically distinct varieties, each represented by several locally developed strains. You are just as likely to see garlics listed by descriptors like 'Early Purple' in Australia. Sometimes a variety purchased one year does not resemble a variety sold under the same name the following year. A fair bit of substitution goes on. Sorting out which varieties are grown in Australia would take years of field trials. Take any varietal name you see with a grain of salt. The best advice is to road-test a few varieties. When you find one that grows well for you, hang on to it and propagate your own.

Inchelium

An American artichoke garlic found on the Coleville Indian Reservation at Inchelium in Washington state USA. It has cream, violet-streaked skin and a mild flavour.

Korean Red

An early-ripening Asian-style hardneck with purple-blotched outer skin and red-brown cloves. The flavour is big and warm but not too hot. Koreans are major garlic aficionados so if they like this variety then it must be good.

PRINTANOR GARLIC

Printanor

A famous French artichoke softneck garlic with dirty white skins and beige-pink cloves in multiple layers. Some cloves can be very large and others very small. Its flavour is warm but mild.

Red Italian

There are two garlics that bear this name. One is a spectacular Italian rocambole garlic with a pink-white bulb and bright red-purple skin on each individual clove. Its cloves are very large and, like all rocamboles, they peel easily and have a big, rich flavour. The other Red Italian is the exact opposite: a mild-flavoured softneck. Don't get them confused.

Rojo de Castro

A handsome Spanish creole garlic with satiny, purple-red cloves that store very well. It does well in areas with mild winters (most garlics don't).

Rose du Var

A French silverskin softneck with pretty pink cloves in fat clusters, surrounded by a white skin. They are mild in flavour.

Spanish Roja or Spanish Red

A rocambole variety with pale purple skin and copper-brown cloves. This variety has very large cloves that are easy to peel. Its flavour is rich, warm and mellow.

Russian or **elephant garlic** is not a true garlic but rather a kind of leek (*A. ampeloprasum*). It is very pretty, bearing big globes of mauve flowers in late summer, on tall, stiff stems. It has an insipid, garlic-onion flavour that is inferior to true garlic in the kitchen. Russian garlic's saving grace is that it keeps for longer than real garlic, so it can be used to fill the short gap experienced when last season's true garlic has withered and sprouted in the cupboard but the new season's garlic crop has not yet been harvested. A word of caution: Russian garlic is the onion family's answer to the Jerusalem artichoke. Once you have it in your garden it will pop up everywhere unannounced, upon which you will feel obliged either to eat it or to pass it on to unsuspecting friends. Save yourself and your friends the trouble by not growing it in the first place.

CHAPTER TEN

Odds

AND Ends

(*Oxalis tuberosa*)

Some of the best-known vegetables don't belong to the big vegetable families.

They are not orphans, however. Within their own plant families, their 'vegetable' status makes them the exception to the rule, rather like the child of a long line of doctors who ran away to join the circus. These nonconformists are lumped together in this Odds and Ends section, for no other reason than that they don't belong anywhere else.

GREEN ASPARAGUS

GREEN ASPARAGUS

ASPARAGUS

Asparagus (*Asparagus officinalis*) is an odd vegetable. It is one of the few vegetables routinely grown as a perennial crop. Unlike most veggies, which are unlikely to live past four months of age before coming to the end of their usable lives, asparagus crowns can remain productive for upwards of twenty years. The edible part of the asparagus plant is unique, too. It is the tender shoot tips as they emerge from the underground rootstock in spring that are prized for their fresh, springy flavour.

Finding asparagus a family niche has given botanists a lot of trouble over the years. It has been considered a member of the lily and butcher's broom families at various times. Recently it has been given its very own family, the Asparagaceae. This has got it a whole tribe of exciting new relatives, including aspidistras, lilies-of-the-valley, bluebells and yuccas.

Asparagus plants are either male or female, not bisexual as many plants are. In botanical-speak we say they are *dioecious*. Dioecious comes from two Greek words, *di* meaning 'two' and *oikos* meaning 'household'. This term dates back to the eighteenth century when the classification of plants was determined by the arrangement of their sex organs (i.e. the flowers). The male parts of the flower were thought of as 'husbands' and the female parts the 'wives'. Hence a plant can have 'two households': a situation whereby the husband and wife live apart on separate plants (not a bad idea, I hear you say).

Female asparagus plants bear pretty red berries which self-seed rampantly if permitted. Female asparagus spears tend to be thinner but more woody as they need greater rigidity in order to bear the weight of the berries.

Male asparagus plants have thicker spears which are, counterintuitively, more tender than the skinny female spears since male plants don't have to bear the weight of a crop of berries. For this reason asparagus breeding is primarily concerned with developing F1 hybrid strains with a high proportion of male seedlings in a population.

Many home gardeners start their asparagus plants from mature crowns. However, starting from seed is much more economical. Regardless of whether you start with crowns or seed you must wait for three growing seasons before you can begin to harvest spears. Mature crowns take three years to recover from transplant shock and re-establish themselves. Baby seedlings hit the ground running but take three years to reach full size. When you consider that a single crown costs more than twice the price of a packet of 100 seeds (which come up like weeds if the seed is fresh), the choice is obvious. You'd be mad to start with crowns.

In Australia the asparagus we see is green or occasionally purple. People who visit Europe in the springtime are always amazed by the prevalence of white asparagus. White asparagus turns up everywhere – in breakfast, lunch and dinner, even in ice cream and schnapps. White asparagus is not a specific variety. It is white because it has been blanched. That is, it has been covered with soil and black plastic to exclude sunlight. In the absence of light the spears do not produce the green pigment chlorophyll, and remain white. They are harvested by cutting their stems below ground.

In my experience white asparagus is stringier and more bitter than green. Think about it: when you prepare a normal green asparagus spear, which part do you remove because it is too tough and bitter? The white base. The asparagus plant deposits more woody lignin fibres in the below-ground portion of the stem to help brace the above-ground portion. When asparagus spears are blanched, they think they are still below the ground so they deposit more woody fibres, and cannot make sugars because they cannot photosynthesise.

White asparagus is blanched under black plastic.

VARIETIES

•

It has to be said that, like Brussels sprouts and sweetcorn, F1 hybrid asparagus are much more predictable than their heirloom counterparts, which show an exasperating degree of variation within each variety. Growing asparagus is a big investment of time. It takes three years before you can even harvest your first crop and the plants live for several decades. So you want to be certain that your asparagus plants are going to be large, vigorous and uniform at the *beginning* of the process. You don't want to discover that half of them are stringy, straggly runts three years down the track. For these reasons the F1 hybrids are a better choice than the heirlooms. You might choose to grow heirloom asparagus for ethical or historical reasons, but looking at asparagus from an objective horticultural standpoint, the F1 hybrids are superior, even for home gardeners.

Connovers Colossal
An American heirloom from 1885. Connovers Colossal became the dominant variety in the UK during the twentieth century.

Mary Washington
An old standard from the USA with long, narrow spears (mostly).

Précoce d'Argenteuil
A French heirloom with green spears tipped with purple.

Violetto d'Albegna
This Italian heirloom produces purple spears. It is very weak-growing and disease-prone, and has been comprehensively superseded by modern purple hybrids. All purple asparagus turn green when cooked.

EVER RED RHUBARB

RHUBARB

Good old rhubarb. It is such a reliable plant that it is easy to take it completely for granted. You might be surprised to learn that before rhubarb found a place in every backyard as a kind of 'common man's fruit' it had an interesting history as a luxury good.

There are sixty species in the rhubarb genus, *Rheum*. They are plants which like the cold, being native to the steppes of Central Asia, the Himalayas and Mongolia. Rhubarbs were originally valued not for their edible stems but for the medicinal value of their roots. The Chinese have been using rhubarb roots in their pharmacopoeia for a very long time. They call it *da huang*, 'big yellow', because of its thick, bright yellow roots. Rhubarb roots contain what herbalists delicately refer to as a powerful 'purgative'. That's a laxative to you and me.

There was obviously a big market for laxatives in Europe at one time, as Europeans used to value rhubarb root very highly indeed. Ruy González de Clavijo, the Spanish ambassador to the court of the Turko-Mongol ruler Timur at the Silk Road city of Samarkand, wrote in 1405 that the best merchandise Samarkand had to offer came from China. As examples he listed silks and satins, rubies, diamonds, pearls, musk and, of all things, rhubarb. The English merchant Anthony Jenkinson writing from Bukhara in 1558 said that 'from the countries of Cathay is brought thither in time of peace and when the way is open, musk, rhubarb, satin, damask, with divers other things.' Rhubarb roots were evidently very highly valued if they were mentioned in the same breath as diamonds, satin and musk.

It wasn't until the seventeenth century that Europeans began using rhubarb as food. Garden rhubarb (*Rheum* x *hybridum*) is of hybrid origin, most likely descended from *R. rhabarbarum*. Selection work has probably concentrated on producing a crop earlier in the springtime and enhancing the redness of the stems. Incidentally, there is no difference in flavour between red and green rhubarbs. Colour is not an indicator of 'ripeness' in the way that a red tomato is ripe and green one is not. No rhubarb tastes sweet without the addition of lots of sugar. Red rhubarb certainly looks prettier on the plate than green, but all rhubarbs taste pretty much the same. Red rhubarbs tend to go greener during hot weather, the best red colour appearing in cooler spring and autumn weather. Conversely, green rhubarb won't go red. Ever. If you particularly want red rhubarb, you need to buy a variety that is reliably red to start off with.

One thing everybody knows about rhubarb is that its leaves are poisonous. Well . . . probably. In fact, confirmed cases of rhubarb poisoning are scant. Like the maligned oleander bush, rhubarb has been the victim of Chinese whispers. Just about every Australian of a certain age claims to know a friend of a friend of a friend who died after stirring a cup of tea with an oleander twig, but where are the published cases to back these claims up? Surely if there was an epidemic of oleander or rhubarb-related deaths then some reports would make it into the coronial or medical literature or, at the very least, the tabloid news? I wouldn't go eating rhubarb leaves any time soon, but it is quite possible that the risk of death from them has been overstated.

Rhubarb is not the only edible member of its family, the Polygonaceae. Buck-wheats (*Fagopyrum*) are important grain crops in certain regions; one of the few grains that is not a member of the grass family. The strangely perfumed Vietnamese mint or laksa herb (*Persicaria odorata*) is a favourite ingredient in South East Asian cooking, indispensable in Vietnamese cuisine. Tangy sorrels (*Rumex acetosa* and *R. scutatus*) are popular in France. Less distinguished rhubarb relatives are the big dock weeds (also *Rumex* spp.), the pernicious little weed sheep's sorrel (*Rumex acetosella*), and the nightmarish mile-a-minute vine (*Fallopia baldschuanica*) and Japanese knotweed (*F. japonica*).

VARIETIES

•

Rhubarbs are propagated either by division or by seed. Don't bother with the seed-grown ones as they are usually substandard. They are cheap for nurseries to produce but the seedlings more often than not come up green and quite short in the stem – not what most people are looking for in their rhubarb. Make sure you get big divisions of true-to-type plants. You will pay more but they are better value.

Ever Red

This variety has very long, uniformly crimson stems, which keep their colour pretty well during hot weather. It gives useful crops during the winter.

Glaskins/Glaskins Perpetual

At its best a medium-sized greenish red rhubarb that crops over a long season. Unfortunately this variety has been propagated from seed for years in Australia and most plants are inferior. Colours, stem size and cropping season are all variable. Be wary.

Silvan Giant

Named for Silvan, an old rhubarb growing area in Victoria's Dandenong Ranges, this variety produces very tall, brilliant red stems. Its best season is spring but it continues to produce more or less throughout the year.

Victoria

An old standard bearing big crops of thin stems. They are red at the base shading to green at the top, like tourmalines. Not the reddest rhubarb but a great producer.

Wandin Red

This variety is named for Wandin, right next door to Silvan, in Victoria's Dandenong Ranges. Wandin Red bears only a few stems per clump, but when well grown the stems are nearly a metre long and as thick as your wrist. They are dusky raspberry-red from top to bottom and have a distinctive satiny skin. The leaves can be enormous. Wandin Red continues to give a small crop through winter. To get the biggest stems you need to feed and water it heavily.

WANDIN RED RHUBARB

IPOMOEA TRICOLOR

THE MORNING GLORY FAMILY

Mention the name 'morning glory' and most people will immediately think of a rampant weed with pretty flowers. The term 'morning glory' means different things to different people. Depending on where in Australia you come from it could refer to *Ipomoea indica, I. cairica, I. alba* or *Convolvulus arvensis*. They all have ephemeral flowers which open in the morning and die by midday, hence their shared common name. *Ipomoea indica* and *I. cairica* are responsible for suffocating areas of disturbed bushland and *Convolvulus arvensis* is a weed of pastureland.

These three have earned themselves a place on the noxious weed list. *I. alba* is not listed as a noxious weed in any jurisdiction but it is not making itself very popular, either.

There is more to the morning glory family (Convolvulaceae) than just weeds, of course. There are some beautiful ornamental plants like *Ipomoea tricolor*, *Mina lobata*, *Convolvulus sabatius* and *C. cneorum*. And you might be surprised to hear that there are some vegetable members, too.

KANG KONG

Sometimes called ong choy, water convolvulus or simply 'morning glory', kang kong (*Ipomoea aquatica*) is – no surprise – a morning glory that grows in water. It grows abundantly in rice paddies and waterways in South East Asia and is a common vegetable in the cuisines of that region. Kang kong has bright green, hollow stems and narrow, pointy foliage. It is used steamed, boiled and stir fried. It does not have a distinct flavour but its texture is simultaneously crunchy and slightly slimy. Its flowers are a pretty pale mauve.

KANG KONG

SWEET POTATO

Sweet potatoes (*Ipomoea batatas*) are native to Central and South America. We tend to think of them as second-class vegetables but sweet potatoes are very important staple crops in Polynesia, Asia and Africa.

In Australia we sometimes call sweet potatoes by their Māori name, *kūmara*. Polynesian cultures have a long association with sweet potatoes. They were grown in the Cook Islands by 1100 CE and New Zealand by 1250 CE. This raises an interesting question: how did they get to New Zealand and the Pacific Islands from South America such a long time ago? Presumably the Polynesians, those master seafarers, collected sweet potatoes directly from South America on one of their epic boat voyages and then took them island-hopping around the Pacific. The Māori in particular have a strong relationship with with their kūmara. They traditionally grew at least three cultivars of small kūmara but these were supplanted by bigger cultivars brought by American whalers in the nineteenth century, sweet potatoes being a popular crop in the steamy southern states of the USA.

Sweet potatoes come in lovely colours. Most popular in Asia are the purple-fleshed varieties which pop up alongside azuki beans and taro in mealy-textured Asian sweets. The Japanese grow a purple-skinned, yellow-fleshed variety often seen for sale roasted as a snack by street vendors, as well as one with white skin and purple flesh.

BEAUREGARD (BACK) AND NORTHERN STAR (FRONT) SWEET POTATOES

There are dozens of sweet potato cultivars in existence, but in Australia we commonly see only three. The most common is the American-bred **Beauregard**, with stout pinkish roots with orange flesh. **Kestle** is an Australian-bred variety with slender cream-coloured roots. **Northern Star** is also Australian bred with purple-skinned, white-fleshed roots. Sweet potatoes bear pretty mauve flowers just like any morning glory, but they rarely flower outside tropical latitudes. There are several ornamental varieties of sweet potato grown for their beautiful coloured foliage rather than their edible roots. This foliage may be black, burgundy, fluoro yellow or copper orange, and has an amazing retroreflective quality. These gorgeous foliage plants are very easy to grow from cuttings, but unfortunately their propagation is circumscribed under the *Plant Breeder's Rights Act*, which takes all the pleasure out of it.

CORN SALAD

•

Corn salad is unfamiliar to many people in Australia. You might see it called by its other English common name, lamb's lettuce, or by one of its many European names: *Feldsalat* or *Rapunzel* in German, *veldsla* in Dutch, *valerianella* in Italian or in French, *mâche*, which is pronounced, rather unfortunately, 'mush' (not 'mashay' as I have heard in several fine dining establishments).

CORN SALAD

Whatever you call it, corn salad is a lovely little ground-hugging plant with square rosettes of soft-but-crunchy, bright emerald-green leaves. Their taste is often described as 'nutty', which seems a bit overstated to me. I would describe it as a fairly nondescript 'plant' flavour. Nevertheless, eating corn salad in a winter salad is a very pleasant experience and always seems like a special treat.

Its scientific name *Valerianella locusta* gives us a clue to its family connections; *Valerianella* means 'little valerian', valerian being a medicinal herb to which it is closely related. *Locusta* means a locust or prawn, possibly a reference to this plant's ability to self-seed so rampantly that, like a plague of locusts, it can completely engulf an emerging grain crop. Corn salad was a weed of wheat fields in the days before herbicides, hence the 'corn' in corn salad. It still makes a nuisance of itself in colder, wetter parts of Australia. Not a great deal of selective breeding work has been done on corn salad so it remains to all intents and purposes a glorified weed. However, a bit of corn salad popping up here and there in your garden in winter is very welcome indeed.

OCA

Another unfamiliar vegetable, oca is a kind of oxalis which forms edible tubers. As you might expect, its scientific name is *Oxalis tuberosa*. The oca plant forms a mop of calf-high, hairy, clover-like leaves. Beneath the ground, the 10-centimetre-long tubers are shiny red, pink, yellow or white, resembling fat grubs. Don't let this turn you off. Raw oca is crunchy like a carrot, both sweet and tangy at the same time, with a faint passionfruit overtone. Boiled, it tastes like sweetcorn with a squeeze of lemon juice. Delicious.

Oca comes from the high Andes, where it is an important staple crop. Oca needs cool summer temperatures to thrive. It particularly hates warm nights. It is only really suitable for gardeners in cool tablelands climates and southern coastal areas. Oca languishes anywhere where summer nights are sticky. It is just not as adaptable as its compatriot the potato.

OKRA

Not to be confused with oca, okra (*Abelmoschus esculentus*) is a member of the Malvaceae family along with hibiscus, hollyhocks, cotton (*Gossypium* spp.) and the old-fashioned rosella (*Hibiscus sabdariffa*). Shrubby plants up to two metres tall bear the finger-like pods, hexagonal in cross-section, after yellow flowers which resemble its relative the hibiscus.

OKRA

Okra pods contain a mucilage which gives them a slimy texture when cut. They have a mild taste a bit like zucchini. Okra is particularly appreciated in tropical Africa and India. It could be native to either, but it is difficult to tell as it has been cultivated for such a long time. Okra travelled with African slaves to the southern states of the USA where it is used for making the classic Creole dish, gumbo, in which the okra is cooked down so that the slimy sap turns into a thick sauce for meat or seafood.

There are several varieties of okra including dwarf varieties, some with very thick pods, short pods or long pods. They are rarely seen in Australia. More usually they are sold by colour: green or burgundy.

WARRIGAL GREENS

This is the only Australian native plant that could truly be considered an heirloom vegetable. It has been grown in Europe since the eighteenth century and it is not uncommon to see it for sale at markets there. Here in its native country barely anybody takes a scrap of notice of it. Australians encountering Warrigal greens for the first time in a European market think it is something terribly exotic, not realising that it grows wild on our beaches.

Warrigal greens or New Zealand spinach (*Tetragonia tetragonioides*) is a member of the pigface family (Aizoaceae), native to beaches not only in Australia but also South America and New Zealand. Warrigal greens no doubt have a long, unrecorded, history of human use. However it was first taken into horticulture by Joseph Banks on James Cook's *Endeavour* voyage in the 1770s.

Warrigal greens is a sprawling perennial which grows to around one metre in width. Its vine-like stems bear fleshy, triangular leaves which can be cooked and eaten like spinach when they are young and tender. The leaves contain noticeable levels of oxalic acid, a chemical also present in true spinach. They need to be boiled to remove this acrid-tasting chemical, and the boiling water discarded. This cooking step is especially important for people prone to kidney stones.

In spite of being native to the salty, sandy beach environment, Warrigal greens grow and crop beautifully in rich vegetable garden soil. It is a useful plant to have tucked in here and there to provide emergency greens when there is a gap in the supply of 'normal' greens.

WARRIGAL GREENS

GROWING
YOUR OWN

Don't believe the television gurus. Growing your own vegetables is *not* easy. It is actually quite difficult. But so is driving a car, playing a musical instrument or knitting a jumper. Most of you can do one or more of those things, I'm sure, so there is no reason why you can't learn to grow your own veggies, too. Just like parallel-parking a car or playing the bassoon, the more you practise gardening the easier it becomes. After a few years it becomes second nature: intuitive and effortless. It's at that point when gardening stops being an oppressive chore and starts being a sublime pleasure, a drug.

Some misguided souls believe that if they buy the right products it will make them better gardeners. They think that if they own the most expensive secateurs, the shiniest hand-forged spade or the most rustic-looking trug it is tantamount to being a good gardener. It is not. Becoming a better gardener is not about what we buy. It is about what we *do*. It is about modifying our behaviours, not consuming more stuff.

True gardening is not an activity for the impatient or those who want instant gratification. Gardening is a process, not an end-point. By its very nature, gardening takes time, both in the day-to-day and in the long term. Don't let this turn you off.

Time in the garden is time well spent. I guarantee that you will never regret a single second you have spent in your garden, unlike time sitting in a car or in front of the telly. The act of gardening is time-enriching as no other activity is.

Our society finds failure and disappointment difficult to stomach. Gardening is a wonderful tonic to this because it teaches us patience and humility. Gardening is an imprecise science and failures are commonplace. Each garden's climate, soil and aspect is unique and it is only by trial and error that we learn how to work with them. Making mistakes is an important part of learning to garden. It cannot be skipped over. So my advice to you is this: relax. Leave society's ridiculous enjoiner to do everything perfectly all of the time behind you. I hereby give you permission to make mistakes. Embrace them; they will make you a better gardener.

One last word in your ear. There are several one-stop-shop, messianic garden cults out there which promise all the answers to all the questions if only you follow their one true path. They look very seductive to starry-eyed new gardeners. By all means look at what they have on offer and take what you need from them, but *do not* feel the need to jump on the bandwagon, boots and all. There is absolutely no need to conform to someone else's arcane theory about having beds in the shape of Buddhist symbology, or stirring your water in a particular direction, just to keep up with the greener-than-thou folks next door. Measure your success by the quality of your produce, not by whether you are adhering to a set of holy scriptures. Listen to your plants – they will tell you what they want. Listen and find out what works for them and for you, too. Garden for your *plants*, not to live up to the expectations of other humans. That's the true path to happiness.

TOP FIVE TIPS

Here are my top five tips for growing vegetables well. Think of them as jumping-off points for your own ideas.

I.   Feed the soil, not the plant.

This is the golden rule of organic gardening. If you look after your soil, everything else will fall into place: plant nutrition, pest and disease resistance, uniform germination, optimum yields, efficient water usage. *Everything*. Feeding the soil comes down to one thing: adding organic matter to it. Simply put, the more organic matter you add to the soil, the better.

2.   Feed the plant as well!

Foliar feeding is one of the secret weapons of organic gardening. Foliar feeding means applying dilute liquid fertiliser to the foliage of the plant. Plants can absorb nutrients directly through their leaves. Foliar feeding increases activity of beneficial bacteria on the leaf surface, which also aids plant nutrition. Foliar feeding encourages bigger, healthier leaves. Leaves are the solar panels which power plants, so the bigger the better.

3.   Set your sights low.

The old saying 'You have to crawl before you can run' applies doubly to gardening. I frequently meet eager-beaver greenhorn gardeners who set up gardens way beyond their skill level. In the first flush of enthusiasm they plant out vast tracts of land with every kind of fruit tree and vegetable known to horticulture, only to find they have neither the technique nor the time to look after it all. They feel overwhelmed and are forced to beat a retreat, pegging back what they have begun to something more manageable, sometimes giving up completely. Don't let this happen to you. Please trust my advice and *set your sights low to begin with.*

If you begin your gardening journey modestly, your successes will outnumber your failures. You will feel your confidence grow. As you become more skilled you will be hungry for more victories. Little by little you can expand your gardening repertoire. If you get really good at it you might be allowed to join the hallowed ranks of those legendary gardeners of yore, like your Nan or old Mario up the street, in that great Veggie Valhalla in the sky.

4.   Little and often.

If you do one small job every day, you will find that you can keep on top of things in the garden. It almost doesn't matter what job you choose – sowing one packet of seeds, thinning one row of seedlings, pulling out ten weeds, spending ten minutes watering, applying one watering can of foliar feed, mulching two tomato plants. Even just standing and plotting, smugly enjoying your own prowess (a personal favourite). As long as you spend a little bit of time in your vegetable plot each day, you will keep ahead of the game.

And now for the most important tip of all:

5.   Just do it.

Stop procrastinating and get out there into your garden. Stop poring over sexy gardening mags, perving at dreamy websites and leafing through tempting catalogues. The best thing you can do to succeed in the garden is to go outside and get your hands dirty. Right now. I don't care what the weather is like. I don't care that it will be dark in half an hour or that you have emails needing to be answered. Good gardens are earned with two ingredients alone: physical labour and time. Gardens are not theorised into existence or purchased online.

While we're on the subject of going online, I feel it is my duty to tell you that blogging does not count as gardening. If you spend more time blogging about your veggie patch than actually slogging in it, you need to change your settings. One of these days I'm going to have a bumper sticker made: *Real gardeners slog, not blog.* Want one? You'll have to earn it.

THE NUTS AND BOLTS OF GARDENING

There are hundreds of excellent how-to-grow books on the shelves already, so I'm not going to be too prescriptive in this section. What I want to do is to make you aware of the most important considerations in vegetable growing, and get you asking yourself the right questions as you embark on your gardening journey. Really, the basics are pretty simple: vegetables like the best of everything. If you give them plenty of sunshine, buckets of water, excellent soil and lashings of food they will repay you in spades.

SITE

•

Most vegetables need to grow in full sun. This means that they must have *at least* six hours of direct, unobstructed sunshine each day during their growing season. Vegetables are very uncompromising on this point. When you are planning your food garden it is of critical importance to choose the sunniest spot possible. Wherever that spot is – it could be your front yard or slap-bang in the middle of your rose garden – that's where your veggie garden has to be sited. Keep in mind that the sun's path is lower across the sky during winter (in the southern states) and that nearby trees will grow and cast more shade as they gain height.

There are a handful of vegetables which tolerate or even appreciate partial shade in summer (beans, silverbeet, lettuce and salad greens) but none will tolerate full shade. 'Partial shade' means half a day of unobstructed sunshine accompanied by half a day of shade, say on the eastern side of a fence. It can also mean the bright, dappled shade cast by a tall deciduous tree. 'Full shade' means the gloomy, dark shade produced by dense evergreen trees, under the eaves of a house or on the south side of a building. Unfortunately no vegetables will grow in full shade, at least not the kind dealt with in this book.

If you live on a very windy, exposed site or next to the sea it is extremely beneficial to create some kind of shelter for your vegetable garden. This can be done in all manner of ways, either using plants (making sure that they don't cast too much shade or create root competition) or with some kind of hard landscaping like fences or walls. Your shelter doesn't have to be expensive, so long as it helps to cut down on desiccating winds or salt spray.

SOIL

•

Have you ever thought about what soil is? I mean, *really* thought about it? Soil is much more than just 'dirt'. It is a complex biochemical cocktail of fungi and bacteria, tiny animals and plants, humus, air and water all set in a matrix of finely crushed minerals. A teaspoon of good, organic soil contains millions of living organisms.

While rainforests and coral reefs have captured our collective imagination as beacons of biodiversity, soils are in fact the most complex and diverse ecosystems on the planet, a fact we are only beginning to grasp. Just as the Daintree rainforest looks totally different from the Amazon rainforest, so the soil community in your front garden can be totally unique and distinct from the soil in your back garden.

Soil is an important carbon sink, storing a significant proportion of the earth's carbon. All terrestrial foods are derived from soil, from your morning coffee to your meat and three veg for dinner. The earth's gossamer-thin layer of soil is, without a word of hyperbole, this planet's life support system. Without it we will perish, so it is worth looking after.

I could write volumes on the subject of soil improvement, as hundreds of excellent authors have done before me. However, everything ever written about soil improvement can be summarised in this one piece of advice: *you can add any amount of organic matter to any soil type and it will always improve it*. It's quite that simple. Just keep adding organic matter to your soil and it will sort itself out.

We humans are arrogant enough to think that we are the dominant species on earth. Well, I've got news for us: fungi and bacteria own and run this planet. Fungi and bacteria live on our skin, inside our bodies, and in the air we breathe. They live in and on plants and animals, alive and dead, and even in seawater. Bacteria are able to live on the hydrothermal vents in the black abyss of the ocean, in boiling hot sulphur springs and even inside the frozen rocks of Antarctica. Fungi and bacteria live literally everywhere. Including in soil. And that's a good thing. Because fungi and bacteria are in no small part responsible for plant nutrition.

Fungi are able to break down once-living things into their component chemicals (this is why the earth is not twenty storeys deep in dead brontosauruses and every other animal and plant that ever lived – thank you fungi). Plants can't do this for themselves. However, what plants do very well is make sugars – carbohydrates – out of thin air and water, using solar energy. Mushrooms and toadstools are only the fruiting bodies of fungi. The main body of the fungus organism grows underground as a network of very fine threads called a *mycelium*. When you see a cute little mushroom pop up you might not realise that the organism that produced it could be the size of a football pitch hidden away underground. Special soil fungi form *mycorrhizal* associations with plant roots. They attach to the roots, receiving sugars made by the plant in exchange for the chemicals they extract from organic matter in the soil. They effectively act like an enhanced extension of the plant's root system. The majority of terrestrial plants have formed these beneficial mycorrhizal relationships with fungi. One of the rare exceptions to this is the cabbage family, which does not form mycorrhizal associations.

Bacteria are able to extract chemicals such as nitrogen directly from the air and from minerals in the soil, rendering them available to plants. Legumes have special nodules on their roots which are little houses for bacteria to live in. *Rhizobium* bacteria colonise the nodules and supply nitrogen directly to the plant. We can give plants as much fertiliser as we like as gardeners, but it is only a drop in the ocean compared with what bacteria and fungi can do for them. The very best thing you can do for your plants' nutrition is to create soil conditions that are appealing to fungi and bacteria. This basically comes down to a moist, well-structured, highly organic soil. So yet again, the more organic matter you add, the better.

SOIL TEXTURE

•

Have you heard the old saying 'Clay breaks your back but sand breaks your heart'? Never a truer word was spoken. Understanding your soil texture is an important step in knowing how to improve whatever soil Mother Nature has given you. Nobody has perfect soil. We all have to do things to it to achieve the holy grail: a well-structured, humus-rich, fertile loam.

Soil texture is a rather vague term used to refer to how it feels in the hand. It tells us what proportion of sand, clay and silt our soil is composed of. It is important to know this so you have an idea of which areas you need to do the most work on to obtain a good vegetable-growing soil.

An easy way to check your soil texture is to put a couple of handfuls in a screw-top jar, top it up with water, give it a good shake and then let it settle out for a few days. The heavy sand particles will sink to the bottom, the silt particles will settle in the middle and the clay particles on top.

Sand and clay respond in different ways to the application of water, organic matter and fertilisers. Sand heats up quickly and and clay stays cold for longer. Fertilisers leach from sand quickly; clay retains them better but it can be airless as well. It's swings and roundabouts.

SOIL STRUCTURE

•

Soil structure is the term used to describe how soil particles – clays, sands, silts and humus – bond together into aggregates. A well-structured soil is crumbly, like instant coffee granules. That means it is full of air, drains freely and allows plant roots to grow through it effortlessly. If you clench a well-structured soil in your fist it will form a ball, but you should be able to tease that ball apart again easily with your fingers.

A well-structured soil makes growing vegetables effortless. It fixes lots of problems and makes plants very happy. Good structure is almost more important than fertility to plant growth. Make it your holy grail.

pH

•

One of the most important things to understand about your soil is its pH. This is required learning, so brace yourself for a chemistry lesson.

The concentration of hydrogen ions in a solution is measured using the pH scale. In lay terms, the pH scale is used to measure how acid or alkaline a solution is. The pH scale runs from 0–14, with values from 0–7 being acid, 7 being neutral and values from 7–14 being alkaline. The pH scale is logarithmic, not linear. Don't be fooled into thinking that 6 and 8 are near enough to 7. They are not. A pH of 6 is ten times more acid than 7 and a hundred times more acid than 8.

It is important to understand pH is because it affects the soil chemistry, which in turn affects plant nutrition. At certain pH levels, some elements become chemically locked up so that plants cannot access them, even if there are plenty of them in the soil. For example as pH gets lower, molybdenum gets locked away. Molybdenum deficiency causes whiptail in cauliflowers, a condition in which foliage becomes very narrow and deformed, and heads are either very small or absent altogether. By raising the pH you can make the molybdenum that is in the soil available and fix that problem. So to cure whiptail in your caulies, don't automatically reach for the sodium molybdate; check the pH first – your soil might just need a bit of lime to release the molybdenum already present in it.

Most vegetables prefer a pH range of 6.5–7. A few, such as brassicas and peas, prefer a slightly higher range, up to 7.5. Others, such as potatoes, prefer things slightly more acid, down towards 6. As a rule of thumb, the closer you are to the 6.5–7 range, the better it is for most crops.

The majority of Australian soils are too acid for vegetables and need some remediation. Making soil more alkaline is easy with the addition of garden lime or dolomite. Making soil more acid, in those few parts of Australia that have alkaline soils, is much more difficult. Applying sulphur helps in the short term but adding organic matter is the only thing that really helps in the long term.

Testing soil pH is simple. Buy a pH test kit from a gardening supplies shop and test your soil several times per year. It will change the way you garden.

ORGANIC AMENDMENTS
AND SOIL CONDITIONERS

•

Whatever soil you have to start with, adding organic matter to it will improve it. Doing this allows water to penetrate the soil better and the soil to retain it for longer. Organic matter buffers against fluctuations in temperature and pH. It optimises the cation-exchange capacity of soil, improving the soil's ability to retain nutrients and make them available to plants. It creates ideal conditions for the growth of beneficial fungi and bacteria, which are essential for plant nutrition. It allows air to penetrate clay soils and glues sandy soils together, making soil structure more amenable to root growth. It's no wonder gardeners wax lyrical about compost. Homemade compost is the magic bullet which fixes everything. If you are able to make your own compost, do.

Compost is the magic bullet which fixes everything.

Not everyone can make their own compost, however. Proper composting takes up quite a lot of space, requires a lot of room to store the ingredients until you are ready to compost them, and needs quite a bit of physical strength to construct and turn the heap. Not everyone has the space or energy for it. Luckily there are some good alternatives. At the top of that list are worm farms. Worms process organic matter such as food scraps and manure into a light, uniform soil conditioner in the form of 'castings' (a delicate term for poo). Worm farms are ideal for even the smallest backyard. Most households only produce half a bucket of apple cores and potato peelings each day – not nearly enough material to make a full-blown compost heap, but perfect for fuelling a worm farm. Bear in mind that worms are living animals. They need to be fed, watered and looked after. They're not an enormous amount of work compared with a dog or a budgie, but you can't completely ignore them either.

A quick but expensive way to add organic bulk to your soil is to buy in organic materials such as pre-composted manure and mushroom compost. This is a good way to get bulk into your soil quickly, but be a bit circumspect. Mushroom compost can be very hot and alkaline, and can contain a lot of salt. So don't overdo it. Manures are good as long as they are well-composted; otherwise they can be too hot and full of weed seeds.

One of the easiest ways to put organic bulk into your soil is to grow your own *in situ*. Green manures are crops grown for the express purpose of cutting them down in their prime and incorporating them into the soil. Different green

Growing green manures is an inexpensive way to condition soil.

manure crops have different benefits – legumes add nitrogen to soil, mustards help to discourage soil-borne diseases. All add carbon and bulk to the soil.

Be very cautious about buying the stuff sold as 'garden soil' from landscaping suppliers. More often than not it is a random concoction of leftover fill and under-cooked organic matter such as raw fowl manure or chipped up municipal waste (often called 'euky mulch' because of its high content of eucalyptus wood and leaves). Bought 'garden soil' can vary wildly in its quality and composition. I have personally had experience with bought 'garden soils' that were variously gluggy and airless; dusty and hydrophobic; so full of nitrogen that they heated up to 60°C and burned the plant's roots; so lacking in nitrogen that they caused nitrogen drawdown and made all the plants go yellow; had a pH as low as 4 or as high as 9; so salty that they formed a white crust on the surface; and so full of weed seeds that I spent the next six months digging out couch and sheep's sorrel. I'm not saying there aren't good products out there, but in my experience they are very few and far between. If you are going to buy 'soil', ask to see each individual batch before you buy it. Smell it, hold it in your hands and test its pH before you get your credit card out.

This points to one incontrovertible fact: the best way to obtain good garden soil is to make it yourself.

TO DIG OR NOT TO DIG?

•

Gardeners often hold strongly divergent views on this subject. Traditional vege-table gardening once advocated annual digging – preferably double digging to two spits in depth (that is; to the depth of two spade blades) – in order to incor-porate manures and compost. Many organic gardeners argue that digging destroys soil structure and disturbs soil life, and must be avoided at all costs. But organic gardeners are by no means an undifferentiated bloc. Some organic growing systems, notably the biointensive system, *do* advocate regular double digging in order to incorporate large amounts of organic matter at depth. Critics from the other camp label this environmental vandalism, yet biointensively grown produce speaks for itself. So who should you believe?

The Royal Horticultural Society conducted a trial of digging versus not digging a few years ago. It found, totally unsurprisingly, that both techniques have their benefits and their drawbacks. Digging was found to be a great way to incor-porate large amounts of organic matter quickly and to a good depth, but that it did indeed compromise well-structured soils. Not digging was found to be beneficial in maintaining already well-structured soils, but it was noted that few gardeners have such a soil in the first place. On balance, the RHS advocated the use of both techniques, as and when necessary. I'm inclined to agree with them.

In nature, plants die and decay, returning the nutrients they have pulled from the soil back to it. But gardens are not nature. They are managed landscapes and growing vegetables is the most intensive form of gardening there is, because we are always taking nutrients out of the system for our own consumption, in the form of produce. Sometimes we need to recharge the soil quickly for the next crop. The best way to do this is often to dig.

Don't dig when it is not necessary, but equally, don't *not* dig just to prove some ideological point. Digging is something you do, or abstain from, for your plants' benefit, not your own.

NO-DIG GARDENING

•

No-dig gardening is different from 'not digging'. No-dig gardening is a way of making highly organic soil from scratch by, in essence, constructing a special kind of compost heap from straw and manure and planting directly into it. There is much to recommend no-dig gardening if your soil is of very poor quality (e.g. very compacted or rocky) or if you lack soil entirely (such as on paved surfaces). No-dig beds are very rich and high in organic matter. Some crops such as brassicas and potatoes respond well to them but others like carrots and onions are less happy in such rich conditions.

No-dig beds are a great way to start building your soil. However, it can get expensive bringing in manure and straw season after season, especially if you want to grow lots of veggies. Once you have developed a half-decent soil you will probably want to start using it as you gain more skill.

TIME

•

One of the most important ingredients in building good soil is time. Time is every bit as important in creating soil as the physical inputs you add to it, such as organic materials, fertiliser and water. Time is needed to allow the tiny animals, plants, fungi and bacteria living in soil to build up their numbers and to do their awesome work of breaking up clods of clay, gluing together sand particles, digesting dead animals and plants, breaking down minerals, aerating the soil and distributing humus throughout it. Regardless of what kind of soil you start with, in my experience it takes around three years of constantly topping up organic matter, adjusting pH and applying water to bring soil to an ideal state for vegetable gardening. There are no shortcuts.

Unlike physical inputs such as manures, mulches and water, time cannot be bought with money. It can only be bought with patience. As a gardener, when I see a well-structured, fertile soil I know that someone has had to work for it and wait for it. A well-structured garden soil is evidence of patience and commitment – it's a badge of honour.

WATER

•

Vegetables are made of water and very little else. A tomato, for example, is composed of 90 per cent water and only 10 per cent solids (hardly worth eating, when you think about it). Therefore, if a tomato plant produces 10 kilograms of tomatoes, that crop contains 9 kilograms of water, or 9 litres. That's a whole bucket of water. The tomato plant itself is also composed mostly of water. If you think about the physiology of a plant, it is not much more than a bundle of very thin drinking straws – capillaries – wicking moisture from the soil through its roots and passing it out through the pores in its leaves. Therefore it takes quite a lot of water to grow a tomato crop, most of which the tomato plant 'wastes' by letting it evaporate out of its foliage.

How much water do you need to grow vegetables, exactly? Well, how long is a piece of string? Water requirements vary considerably according to the quality of your soil, weather conditions, the vegetable variety in question and its stage of growth. Basically, however, the answer is 'lots'. Vegetables are anything but drought tolerant.

Vegetable plants need to remain turgid at all times. This means that they need to absorb more water through their roots than they transpire through their leaves, otherwise they wilt. When you water the soil until no more water will soak in and then wait until the excess water has drained away (which might take a day or so), you create a condition whereby the soil is charged with as much water as it can hold in the form of a film on the surface of each soil particle, yet simultaneously contains the maximum amount of air it can hold in the spaces between the soil particles. This condition is called 'field capacity'. Drought-tolerant plants can function at 25 per cent field capacity or less before they start to feel the pinch. But not vegetables. At anything south of 50 per cent field capacity, vegetables quickly reach 'permanent wilting point', which means that the roots cannot supply the top of the plant with sufficient water to maintain turgid. When vegetables reach this stage they can't function properly and they begin to die.

To avoid reaching permanent wilting point you need to keep your soil's field capacity between 50 and 100 per cent. How on earth do you do that? Basically, by watering it. Lots. Enough so that your soil is constantly moist to the touch and your plants never wilt.

There are all kinds of fancy contraptions available to help sense soil moisture, and to regulate and automate irrigation. They take the guesswork and labour out of watering. But also the fun. One of the pleasures gardening has to offer is the act of *growing* your plants – tending them, interacting with them and getting to know their needs. It is not drudgery. It's a pleasure. Why on earth would you relinquish such fun to a computer or automatic irrigation system?

By the same token, keep in mind that watering is something you do for the plant's benefit, not your own. Overwatering is just as bad for plants as underwatering. Roots are designed not only for water uptake but also for gas exchange. For breathing, in other words. If you apply so much water to your soil that it excludes all of the tiny air pockets between the soil particles, then your plants will quite literally drown. When soil is free draining, water percolates down through the spaces between the soil particles and pulls fresh air in behind it. So when you water, you not only provide plants with moisture, but also with air.

One of the easiest ways to be fooled into overwatering is to trust your tomatoes. Tomatoes, and beans for that matter, droop their leaves as a normal response to hot sunshine. By drooping their leaves downwards these plants reduce the surface area exposed to the sun. It doesn't necessarily mean that they are thirsty. Feel the leaves. If they are nice and turgid even though they are hanging downwards, everything is fine. If they feel limp, however, the plant really has wilted and needs water urgently.

What is the best way to water? Well, I hate to say it but overhead watering is best, in my experience. Watering with an in-line dripper hose is inarguably more efficient if you're trying to conserve water, but overhead watering is better for the plants themselves, especially in dry inland climates. Overhead watering with a sprinkler or hand-held trigger nozzle raises humidity around the plants allowing them to open their leaf pores without suffering dehydration stress. They are able to grow bigger, healthier leaves, which in turn improves their performance. Leaf crops grow larger, juicier leaves when watered in this way. Other crops' foliage area is also increased, allowing them to produce bigger fruits, stems or roots.

I'm not advocating watering in a wasteful way, but in a way which gets the best growth from plants, as opposed to barely keeping them alive, which is utterly pointless. I am of the opinion that using water to grow your own food is a legitimate use of that scarce resource. To me it is ironic that if your hobby involves consuming fossil fuels – four-wheel driving, jet-skiing, or trail bike riding for example – then it's seen as no problem: use as much fossil fuel as you like. Yet people who want to use reticulated water to grow their own food are looked upon as profligate at best and criminal at worst.

FEEDING

•

Feeding is an important component of vegetable gardening. Vegetables strip-mine the soil of nutrients and those nutrients need to be replaced with fertilisers.

Plants make most of their own food from the sun. But there are certain elements they need in order to do this and it is your job as a gardener to see that they get them. Plants need relatively high levels of three macronutrients: nitrogen, phosphorus and potassium. Nitrogen is responsible for good leaf growth; potassium enhances flowering and fruiting, and builds strong cell walls (with the disease resistance that brings); and phosphorus is just good for everything as it is an essential component in plants cells and necessary for cell division.

Plants also need a variety of micronutrients: iron, calcium, magnesium, manganese, sulphur, boron and molybdenum, to name a few. Plants need these in smaller, sometimes only tiny, quantities, but when they are deficient your plants will let you know. For example, a common problem with tomatoes is blossom end rot, whereby the bottom of a tomato fruit goes brown and dies. It looks for all the world like a fungal disease but it is in fact a calcium deficiency. Add calcium to your soil and the blossom end rot quickly clears up.

Organic fertilisers such as blood and bone and manures contain varying amounts of these nutrients, but none of them is 'complete'. That is, none of them supplies all the macro- and micro-nutrients necessary for plant growth. Just as with humans, plants need a varied diet to make sure they get all their nutritional requirements. There is not space here to go into the detailed chemical analyses of different organic fertilisers, which, incidentally, can vary significantly from batch to batch, but this is something worth looking into it when you use them in your garden. A useful, all-round, complete-ish organic fertiliser can be made by adding 80 grams of sulphate of potash to one kilogram of pure blood and bone. Most commercial blood and bone mixtures actually already have a few chemical fertilisers added to them to make them 'complete'.

Foliar feeds such as manure tea and fish emulsion tend to contain a high proportion of macronutrients, especially nitrogen. By contrast, seaweed extracts and compost tea have very little in the way of 'food' but are good tonics because they contain trace elements, which plants only need in tiny amounts. They also contain organic compounds which help to bolster plants' immune systems. You can tailor your foliar feeding regime to suit your plants' needs.

Now that we have looked at organic fertilisers, I need to have a word with you on the squeamish topic of chemical fertilisers. First, let's be absolutely clear: *all* fertilisers, including organic ones, have chemicals in them. Compost, blood and bone, and manure have chemicals in them just as much as fertilisers that come in a box. When we talk about 'chemical' fertilisers what we really mean is fertilisers which come in the form of water-soluble mineral salts.

Unfortunately, the word 'chemical' has become very negatively loaded, as if 'chemical' is a byword for poison. It is true that some chemicals are extremely bad for us and for the environment. But many other chemicals keep us alive – oxygen and iron to name two. Chemicals *per se* are not 'bad'. Unfortunately many of us have a knee-jerk reaction when we hear *that* word, regardless of how benign a particular chemical is. Look up the chemical *dihydrogen monoxide* on the internet and you'll see what I mean.

Artificial fertilisers made from soluble mineral salts have several drawbacks. They can be very damaging to soil structure when used exclusively or in the long term. They can be very bad for beneficial fungi and other soil life if they are allowed to build up in the soil. However, artificial fertilisers have some useful attributes, too. First of all, you know exactly what's in them. They are consistent and precise in their ingredients and concentration, allowing gardeners to prescribe them to their plants with a high degree of accuracy. Artificial fertilisers are quickly and easily absorbed by plants.

Like humans, plants need certain nutrients – chemicals – to live and grow. Whether they get these in the form of 'organic' fertilisers or 'chemical' fertilisers makes little difference to the plant, as long as they get them.

Don't rule out the occasional judicious use of chemical fertilisers from your gardening repertoire. They can be very useful when they are used in a sparing and targeted way. Don't slather them on willy-nilly or you will ultimately ruin your soil. However, if your plants have a specific nutritional deficiency then chemical fertilisers are often the most efficient way to fix it. For example, boron deficiency causes broccoli heads to become hollow in the middle and rot from the inside out. You could try to fix this deficiency with organic fertilisers but you don't know how much (if any) boron is present in your manure or compost. On the other hand, you know exactly how much of it is present in a 'chemical' fertiliser, allowing you to apply it in a targeted way to fix the problem.

If you live in a cold climate you may experience times during winter and early spring when nothing in your vegetable garden seems to budge. One or two foliar applications of a balanced 'chemical' fertiliser at this time will often get the plants moving again. This might mean the difference between being able to harvest food from your own garden, or having to buy it from the supermarket, grown half a world away. Which would you rather?

A good way to think of chemical fertilisers is as plant *medicines* rather than plant *food*. Imagine this: as a human you get 99.9 per cent of your nutrition from good, wholesome food. If you are lacking something in your diet or feeling a bit low, you might pop the odd vitamin pill. Perhaps your doctor has even prescribed you iron supplements because you are not getting enough iron from your diet. Popping the occasional vitamin pill does not undo all of your good work eating a proper diet, does it? It doesn't turn you into a chemical-dependent junky. It's merely an adjunct to your normal diet. It is the same with plants and chemical fertilisers. On 99.9 per cent of occasions you feed your plants with proper, wholesome food – composts, manures, organic foliar feeds. If you give them the occasional chemical fertiliser, that does not somehow 'undo' all of your good organic gardening. Think of chemical fertilisers as a pep-up, not as a basic diet, and you won't go wrong.

MULCHING

•

Mulching is an important organic gardening technique. Mulch is a layer of organic matter applied to the soil surface in order to assist water uptake and retention, suppress weed growth, encourage biological activity near the soil surface, add carbon to the soil and insulate it against fluctuations in temperature and humidity.

Theoretically you can use pretty much any organic (i.e. formerly living) material for mulch. In practice, some mulches are much better suited to vegetable gardening than others. Different kinds of mulch need to be applied in different ways in order to do the jobs listed above properly. Bulky, airy mulches such as straw need to be applied deeply, by which I mean 20–30 centimetres deep. Any shallower and they won't suppress weed growth, retain water or cool the soil properly. Fine-textured products such as worm castings and daggy wool – yes, daggy wool; dags make great mulch! – can be applied much more thinly, just 5 centimetres deep. Chunky products such as corn cobs, peanut shells, coir chips and homemade compost can go on somewhere in the middle, perhaps 10 centimetres in depth. Woody mulches such as euky mulch are not suitable for vegetable beds as they tend to be hydrophobic (water-repellent) and cause nitrogen drawdown. That is, they suck nitrogen out of the soil.

Mulch needs to be applied differently according to which crop is being mulched. If you are starting vegetables from seeds, especially very fine seeds such as carrots, parsnips and lettuce, it is important not to have mulch too close to the row or it can smother the seeds before they germinate. Heat-loving crops such as tomatoes, pumpkins and watermelons don't like to be mulched too early; wait until the soil has warmed up fully before applying mulch or your mulch will only serve to keep the soil cold. In cold climates you might be better off not mulching them at all. Onions hate deep, humid mulches around their necks, while perennial crops such as rhubarb and asparagus like it packed on nice and deep. Potatoes benefit from having straw mulch topped up regularly during the growing season so that the developing potatoes are not exposed to light.

Never apply mulch to dry soil – mulch will keep soil dry just as well as it keeps it moist. Never apply mulch to cold soil, as it will keep the soil cold for longer. If you notice plants going yellow after you have mulched, it is probably a case of nitrogen drawdown. Mulches which are naturally low in nitrogen will draw it out of the soil as they begin to decompose. This is easily fixed by applying some high-nitrogen fertiliser such as blood and bone to the soil or giving a foliar feed and soil drench of high-nitrogen liquid fertiliser.

Coffee grounds can be used for mulch, if you produce enough of them, but don't expect them to keep slugs away. This irritating urban myth refuses to die. Think about it: if coffee grounds really kept slugs at bay, some enterprising individual would collect them from cafés around the country, repackage them and sell them to professional market gardeners. Nobody is doing that, because professional gardeners know they don't work. Don't believe me? Then do an empirical study on it at home. Don't believe everything you read on the internet.

CROP ROTATION

•

Crop rotation is the process of circulating crops between vegetable beds so that they do not grow in the same soil in consecutive years. When a crop is grown in the same soil year after year, crop-specific pathogens can build up in the soil, such as potato scab or verticillium wilt in tomatoes. Mineral deficiencies can also develop, weakening the crop's immunity to disease. The idea with crop rotation is to stay one step ahead of pests, diseases and nutritional deficiencies.

There are different schools of thought on crop rotation. The simplest system advocates three rotation beds and divides vegetables according to how each bears its crop – root crops, fruiting crops, and leaf and stem crops – because members of these groups have similar soil and nutritional needs. Root crops prefer low nitrogen levels, leaf crops prefer high nitrogen, and so on. Sometimes a fourth, fallow bed is added to this system. The most elaborate rotation system advocates six beds and divides vegetables into family groups. Under this system, potatoes, a root crop, belong in a rotation group together with tomatoes, a fruiting crop, because they are both members of the nightshade family and as such are prone to similar soil-borne diseases.

The fact of the matter is that crop rotation is not a perfect science. Each different crop rotation system has its own strengths and weaknesses. Applying crop rotation in the real world, as opposed to theorising about it, is not always straightforward. My advice is not to tie yourself in knots if your tomatoes end up in the same bed two years running or your zucchini find themselves cheek-by-jowl with your carrots occasionally. It is enough to be aware of why rotation is a good idea and do your best to apply it as far as possible.

GERMINATING SEEDS

New gardeners often feel that getting seeds to germinate is a totally hit and miss affair, sometimes resulting in runaway success and other times in unmitigated failure for no fathomable reason. It seems as if germinating seeds should be the most natural thing in the world, yet at the same time it seems totally bamboozling and arcane. In fact, seed germination is very predictable once you know what factors are involved.

Why would you bother with the palaver of germinating your own seeds in the first place when it is so easy to buy seedlings? For one thing, only a tiny, tiny fraction of heirloom varieties are available as seedlings. If you want to try some of the more interesting heirloom varieties you will need to propagate them yourself from seed. Propagating from seed is also much more economical than buying seedlings. A punnet of half a dozen broccoli seedlings, enough for one household crop, costs more to buy than a packet of 200 seeds, which is enough for a five-year supply. You'd be mad not to grow your vegetables from seed.

Have you ever thought about what a seed is? You might not realise it but a seed is a time-travel device. Seed are the means by which plants travel from one generation to the next, sometimes over vast stretches of time. Desert plants in particular have seeds which lie dormant for decades, even centuries, waiting for the right time to grow. In 2005 a date palm seed was excavated from a Judean desert fortress and carbon dated at 2000 years old. Amazingly, the seed germinated and grew into a baby date palm when it was sown in a pot and watered.

Seeds are also the means by which plants travel in space, from one place to another. Orchid seeds are as fine as dust and can blow considerable distances before reaching their destination. Coconuts can float for hundreds of kilometres across oceans before finally washing ashore and germinating.

Probably the best metaphor for a seed is a computer flash drive. A flash drive is a small package containing a lot of information. It can sit in your desk drawer for years without doing anything. When you take the flash drive out of your drawer and plug it into a computer, you give it the correct conditions to unpack its digital information, which could be a document, an application file or whatever. Similarly, a seed can sit happily in a drawer for years. When it is eventually given the correct conditions it unpacks its information. The information contained in a seed is stored in the form of DNA. It is a set of working plans for making an elegant, solar-powered, self-replicating machine out of nothing but air, water and a tiny amount of chemicals mined from the soil: a machine called a *plant*.

What are the special conditions that will make a seed unpack its contents and grow into a plant? It comes down to three main factors: temperature, moisture, and light. Not just any amount of moisture, temperature and light, but a specific combination of all three.

SOIL TEMPERATURE

•

Like Goldilocks' porridge, the soil temperature needed to induce germination has to be not too cold, not too hot; just right. Different vegetables have different ideas about what 'just right' is. Spinach seeds germinate within a range of about 5–20°C. If the soil is too cold or too warm the seeds are programmed to remain dormant. Watermelon seeds germinate within a range of about 20–35°C. You can already see that there is not much overlap between spinach and watermelon's version of 'just right'. If the temperature is good for sowing watermelons it is likely to be too hot for spinach. Each species of vegetable has its own temperature preference for germination. The majority of vegetables, however, will germinate when the soil temperature in the range of 20–24°C.

Soil temperature is much more stable than ambient air temperature so don't bother looking at the weather forecast to try to gauge soil temperature. For example, in spring the air temperature might be 16°C one day and 27°C the next, falling to 10°C at night, but the soil temperature will remain constant at 19 °C. The best way to keep tabs on soil temperature is by using a specially designed soil thermometer. Buy one – it will be one of the most useful pieces of gardening equipment you've ever owned. I have always found that the cheaper glass thermometers are more reliable than the expensive ones with a dial face.

MOISTURE

•

To stimulate germination, the soil needs to be moist enough for the seed to absorb water from it. Water softens the seed coat, allowing the seedling to swell up and break through it. It is wise to remember is that a new seedling is a baby. Babies are not able to go out looking for water themselves, they need to have it provided for them. Germinating seeds need to be kept consistently moist and not allowed to dry out between waterings. But equally, you don't want your baby to drown, so don't keep it permanently waterlogged. Finding the correct soil moisture level is once again a case of 'not too little, not too much'. Watering little and often is the key.

PHOTOPERIOD

•

Some seeds are sensitive to the length of the days. They know if the days are getting longer or shorter and will only germinate at a time which suits them. Some species' seeds can germinate in both lengthening and shortening days, but respond differently according to the season. For example, long-day onions like to be sown in the dying days of late autumn while short-day onions like to be sown during the waxing days of early spring. If you sow them at the wrong time, they will germinate but they won't form bulbs.

LIGHT AND DARKNESS

•

Light helps some species' seeds to germinate, especially small seeds such as lettuce and celery. A common cause of these varieties failing to germinate is that they have been sown too deeply, where light can't reach them. Make sure you cover small seeds with only the thinnest layer of soil at sowing time. Large seeds such as beans and corn tend to germinate equally well in light or dark.

FRESHNESS AND VIABILITY

•

Vegetable seeds have a limited shelf life, or 'viability'. This varies a great deal between species. The seeds of members of the carrot family are notoriously short-lived. Parsnips, in particular, are pretty well useless after their first year so don't bother storing them for longer than one season. Onions' viability plummets after one year, too. At the other end of the scale, lettuce seed is good for six years when properly stored. Most varieties have a viability of around three years but fresh seed always germinates better than older seed.

The best place to store seeds is somewhere dark with a stable temperature and humidity. A screw-top jar containing a silica gel sachet in the door of the fridge is a good place. The worst place to store seeds is on a shelf in the garden shed, where they are exposed to wide fluctuations in temperature and humidity. Fluctuating temperature and humidity compromises seed viability.

SOAKING AND CHITTING

•

One trick for encouraging prompt, uniform germination is to soak seeds overnight in tepid water before sowing them. This is the easiest thing in the world and it makes such a difference. Seeds with a hard seed coat (such as legumes and spinach) or a corky seed coat (such as beetroot and chard), or seed which is very desiccated (such as sweetcorn) especially benefit from being soaked. Soaking seeds helps to soften the seed coat, rehydrate the seed's contents and break its dormancy. Members of the carrot family (carrots, parsnips, celery and celeriac) also benefit from soaking as they are prone to poor germination due to drying out in the soil after sowing.

Soaking seeds in water before sowing aids germination.

In some countries it is possible to buy 'chitted' seeds. Chitting means to pre-germinate seeds by putting them between pieces of damp kitchen paper and keeping them warm indoors until their seed root appears, at which point they are planted into the garden. The benefit of this is that you can ensure even germination, but the downside is that you must sow them very carefully so as not to damage their fragile seed roots. On balance, it is probably not worth the risk.

Chitting seed potatoes is quite another matter. Seed potatoes benefit a great deal from being pre-sprouted before planting into the garden. To do this, place your seed potatoes 'rose end'-up (that's the end with the most eyes on it) in egg cartons and put on a sunny (yes, sunny) windowsill. They will go green and the eyes will swell into sturdy purple shoots. When the shoots are a centimetre or so in length, the seed potatoes are ready to plant into the garden.

Chitted potatoes ready for planting.

DIRECT SOWING VERSUS SOWING INTO POTS

•

Some vegetables resent having their roots disturbed. Root crops such as carrots and parsnips fork and knot together if they are disturbed as seedlings. Asian greens such as bok choy and choy sum bolt if their roots are disturbed. Beans have very fragile roots which rot easily if they are disturbed. Crops such as these are best sown directly where you want them to grow. There is no benefit in raising them in pots and transplanting them.

When sowing crops directly, it is beneficial to sow them more densely than needed and then thinning the seedlings out to their required spacing as they grow. Thinning seedlings can feel a bit brutal, but it is very important for the health and productivity of the remaining plants.

While some crops hate being raised in pots and transplanted into the garden later, other crops respond to it very well. The brassica and nightshade families have no problem with it at all and cucurbits are generally happy, too, as long as you are gentle when transplanting them. This is good news because it means you can start them early in pots before their spot in the veggie garden is ready to receive them, or before the soil is sufficiently warm.

Direct-sown seedlings ready to be thinned to the desired spacing.

Some seedlings thrive in pots; others do not.

TRANSPLANTING

There are a few tricks to transplanting seedlings into the ground successfully. They are not technically difficult but it is important to actually *do* them. They will contribute greatly to your success.

The most important thing, which can hardly be overemphasised, is to *water in newly transplanted seedlings properly*. When a seedling is transplanted, no matter how much care you take, its root system is compromised by exposure to the air and general jostling around. When the seedling is planted in its new hole, even if the soil is very moist and even if you have firmed the seedling in with your hands, there will still be tiny pockets of air around the roots which prevent the plant from taking up moisture. The plant will invariably go into shock, taking longer to recover, or in the worst cases, dying. To prevent this happening, it is vital to settle the soil particles around the roots by watering the new plant in properly. Watering in provides immediate moisture to the plant but more importantly, it expels air from the soil, allowing fine soil particles to come into contact with the seedling's fine feeder roots. This allows the seedling to take up moisture present in the soil and maintain its turgidity. It doesn't matter if it is pouring with rain when you transplant your new plants, you still need to water them in properly in order to expel air pockets.

When I say water them in 'properly', what do I mean? Well, it varies a bit according to soil type, but in a well-worked soil you need to apply water until you've saturated the soil and any further water that you apply pools on the surface briefly. At this stage it means you've expelled the air pockets around the plant's roots, which is the point of the exercise. If you're not sure, err on the side of overwatering. Try counting to twenty as you water each new plant in. That usually does the trick.

Watering new transplants in with a dilute seaweed solution helps them to recover more quickly. By 'dilute' I mean 1–2 teaspoons of seaweed extract mixed in a 9-litre watering can of water. Seaweed extract is not food, it is a tonic. You only need to take a small amount of a tonic for it to do its job. Think of it this way. If you are feeling a bit delicate after a night on the tiles, do you take one Berocca or do you down the whole packet? It's exactly the same with freshly transplanted seedlings. They are feeling delicate, not ravenous.

Moving backwards a step, two other important things to take care of when transplanting new plants are the size of the planting hole and the planting depth. The planting hole should not be the bare minimum size needed to cram the root-ball in. It needs to be at least a third as large again as the rootball, in order to give the roots nice soft soil to grow into while the plant becomes established. The sides and bottom of the hole need to be broken up to allow the roots to penetrate easily. This is especially important in clay soils, which can be made impenetrable to roots when a trowel or spade smooths the clay surface during digging. Whatever you do, remember that you are digging the hole for the plant's benefit, not your own, so do it properly!

Once you have prepared the perfect hole, the plant needs to be transplanted at the correct depth. As a general rule, this means planting it at the same depth it was in its pot. You might need to transplant the plant slightly proud of the soil surface to allow for it to settle after you've watered it in. Having said that, there are some vegetables which can be planted deeper than they were in their pots, to allow them to form bigger root systems. Tomatoes are a classic example. They are able to form roots along the length of their stems, wherever they come in contact with soil. Tomato seedlings may be set deeper than they were in their pots, with the first pair of leaves at ground level. You can also do this with all the other nightshades, brassicas, cucurbits, corn and leeks, which need to be set very deep in order to develop a nice white shank. Don't try it with anything in the daisy, carrot or amaranth families or you will almost certainly kill them.

GROWING ON

•

To obtain the sweetest, lushest crops, it is important that vegetables are grown quickly. 'Growing a plant quickly' means to grow it at the fastest possible rate without any interruptions to its development (more on this later). To achieve this, a plant needs optimum soil temperature, pH, nutrient availability and day length, consistent ambient temperature, water supply and sunshine. In a greenhouse, all of these factors can be controlled, which is, of course, why commercial nurseries grow their plants in greenhouses. The optimum growing conditions achievable in a greenhouse mean that it is possible to get the fastest growth from plants, which in turn means the highest turnover. However, field-grown produce always tastes better than greenhouse-grown, perhaps because the complex phytochemicals and sugars which give vegetables their flavours are produced in response to being exposed to the stresses of the outside world: high UV levels from full sun, fluctuating temperature and humidity, and bioactive soil.

AVOIDING CHECKS IN GROWTH

•

If the stresses of the outside world become too much for a plant, they can stunt its growth. 'Avoiding checks in growth' is a rather esoteric gardening term which means that a gardener should not let a plant have its growth interrupted by being exposed to very adverse conditions. Adverse conditions can be things outside a gardener's control such as unseasonably hot or cold weather. However, more often they are things within the gardener's control such as letting a seedling become pot-bound, unnecessary root disturbance from careless handling, transplanting seedlings on a 40°C day, not watering a newly transplanted seedling in, or watering developing plants erratically. Some vegetables are particularly sensitive to checks in their growth. Fast-growing Asian greens hate having their roots disturbed and will usually show their displeasure by bolting as soon as they are transplanted. For this reason it is best to sow them directly where they are to grow. If cauliflower seedlings are allowed to become pot-bound before they are planted out, they are liable to punish the gardener by forming golf ball-sized heads, just as if they were still imprisoned in their tiny pots. If tomatoes are not kept evenly moist during fruit development, their fruits will crack. Learning to prevent checks in growth is a great way of developing a deeper understanding of your garden, because it requires you to think about how to get the best performance from your plants.

SOIL TEMPERATURE

•

Correct soil temperature is crucial for good plant growth. In fact, it is more important than the air temperature. Soil temperature is more stable than ambient temperature and less prone to fluctuation. In northern Australia, soil temperatures are more or less constant throughout the year. In southern Australia soil temperature rises steadily as the days lengthen and declines steadily as the days shorten, even if the weather itself is a bit erratic.

Vegetables come from many different corners of the world and have adapted to grow under different seasonal conditions. It should not come as a surprise that they have specific soil temperature requirements, to which gardeners must adhere. Planting tomatoes too early is a classic way to check their growth. Tomato plants will only make active growth if the soil temperature is somewhere north of 18°C, preferably closer to 21°C. If they are transplanted into colder soil, they will not die outright but they will just sit there and languish, subject to root rots and slowly losing their will to live. It is much better to keep tomato seedlings in their pots until the soil is warm enough. This way when you transplant them they hit the ground running, growing away quickly without a check to their development. Ultimately you get an *earlier* crop. In Melbourne the received wisdom is to plant out tomato seedlings on Melbourne Cup Day. This is a useful mnemonic for Melbourne city but in the mountains around Melbourne, conditions are very different. There can still be the occasional frost and even snow flurry in October and soil temperatures are still in the mid teens so there is no guarantee that the soil will be warm enough to receive tomato seedlings by Melbourne Cup Day. It's worth checking with a soil thermometer before you transplant.

DAY LENGTH

•

If you live in southern Australia you will know the feeling of elation when daylight savings kick in in the spring, and the feeling of gloomy grogginess as they end in autumn. This is what it feels like to be sensitive to day length, or what horticulturists call photoperiodism. Plants, being solar-powered gadgets, are finely attuned to day length. They know when the days are getting longer or shorter and they respond to this in their growth patterns.

Many of us have had the experience of planting coriander seedlings only to have them bolt to seed immediately. If this has happened to you, then you almost certainly planted your coriander in the springtime. Coriander is very sensitive to the lengthening days of spring. It is programmed to set seed as soon as it senses the days reaching a certain length. If you had held off planting your coriander until after the summer solstice, which falls around 22 December, then the coriander would sense the shortening days, which are imperceptible to us, and respond by making big, leafy rosettes which would grow right through until the following spring.

Coriander, like many vegetables and herbs, has a biennial lifecycle. Brassicas, members of the carrot family, the amaranth family and most of the the daisy family are all biennials. Biennials are programmed to germinate as the days begin to shorten in the late summer, grow into as big a plant as possible during the short days of autumn and winter, flower as the days begin to lengthen again the following spring and set seed and die around the summer solstice. Biennials set their clocks by sensing the changing day length. You can use this knowledge to your advantage by sowing at the right time for the right effect. In the case of coriander, if you want lots of leaves, then sow it in late summer so that it doesn't bolt immediately to seed. However, if it is the coriander's seeds you particularly want, then of course you can sow it in the springtime so that it *does* bolt and produce seed quickly.

Garlic is programmed to sprout during the shortening days of autumn and make leaf growth over winter and early spring. After the spring equinox, around 22 September in the southern hemisphere, garlic senses that the days are longer than the nights, and it 'knows' to start forming a bulb. By the summer solstice the garlic has formed a bulb and is entering dormancy to escape the summer drought. Without these changes in day length, garlic doesn't form a bulb properly.

SAVING YOUR OWN SEED

This is a whole subject in itself. There is a handful of excellent books on the topic which explain it in much more detail than I have space to do here.

Seed-saving is a fun thing to do but it carries some responsibility at the same time. When you save seeds from an open-pollinated vegetable you are part of the unbroken chain of people who have maintained that vegetable throughout many generations. That is why we call these open-pollinated vegetables 'heirlooms'. They are precious things handed from one generation to the next. You wouldn't entrust your grand-father's gold watch to somebody who didn't know how to look after it. It's the same with heirloom seeds. They are precious and need to be looked after responsibly. If you are interested in seed-saving, become a member of a seed-saving network.

The main responsibility of seed-savers is to keep strains true to type and to maintain their vigour. If the gene pool of a strain gets too narrow, it can result in a phenomenon called inbreeding depression. The gene pool needs to have suffi-cient diversity to maintain the vigour of the strain. However, this diversity has to be balanced with ensuring that the strain remains true to type. The majority of individuals in a population should display all of the characteristics that are a feature of that variety. Any individuals which are the wrong colour/size/shape/flavour or lack vigour need to be discarded, or 'rogued out', before their genes get passed on. Always select the best, healthiest and most true-to-type plants in a population to save your seed from, not the dregs of the crop.

Try to think about improving the strain bit by bit each generation so that the strain is the best it can be, whether it is a glorious tomato or a humble lettuce. It doesn't matter if your strain morphs into something different over time, as long as that thing is *better* than what you started with – bigger, tastier, or better suited to your local conditions. In this way you can develop your own locally adapted heir-loom variety. It *does* matter if you allow your strain to get worse – weaker growing, less tasty, or the wrong colour and shape. If these things are happening then you are doing heirlooms a disservice by saving seed.

If you don't constantly try to improve your vegetable strain each generation that you grow it, its quality and vigour will inevitably decline as it degenerates into a race of either puny weaklings or a brutish ancestral version of itself. Eventually it will cease to show the characteristics that attracted you to it in the first place. Domesticated vegetables cannot maintain their varietal integrity for long without human help. So if you are saving your own seed it is critically important to run a ruthless eugenics programme. If you don't have the time, inclination and patience to take care of these matters then think twice about becoming a seed-saver. Sloppy strains of open-pollinated seed give all heirloom vegetables a bad name.

There is no shame in buying your seed from a reputable seed company if you cannot save your own. But seed companies must be accountable for the quality of the seed that they sell. Insist that all seed you buy is true to type and that each indi-vidual batch of seed is germination-tested to ensure its viability and vigour. If these simple conditions are not fulfilled, take your custom elsewhere.

FURTHER READING

There are a great many books on how to grow vegetables; some of them are more useful than others. Listed below are a few which I find myself coming back to again and again. Some of these books are hard to find, but don't let that put you off; they are well worth reading.

Ashworth, S. 1991. *Seed to Seed*. Seed Saver Publications. Iowa, USA.

Blazey, C. 1999. *The Australian vegetable garden: What's new is old*. New Holland Publishers. Sydney, Australia.

Deppe, C. 2000. *Breed your own vegetable varieties: The gardener's and farmer's guide to plant breeding and seed saving*. Chelsea Green Books. Vermont, USA.

Fanton, J. & M. 1993. *The Seed Savers' Handbook*. Seed Savers Network, Australia.

McFarlane, A. 2010. *Organic Vegetable Gardening*. ABC Books, Australia.

Michalak, P. 1995. *Lothian Succesful Organic Gardening: Vegetables*. Lothian Books. Melbourne, Australia.

Pollock, M. (Ed.) 2004. *The Royal Horticultural Society Fruit and Vegetable Gardening in Australia*. Dorling Kindersley Australasia. Melbourne, Australia.

ACKNOWLEDGEMENTS

My heartfelt thanks to all the people who assisted in the production of this book. To chef Annie Smithers, whose homegrown produce appears in a good many of my photographs, immediately prior to being served up in her restaurant. Thanks also to the Diggers Club for giving me the opportunity to photograph dozens of heirlooms at Heronswood and the Garden of St Erth. Particular thanks to Lou Larrieu, former Trials and Production Manager at the Diggers Club, and to Diggers' founder Clive Blazey for sharing their amazing knowledge of heirloom vegetables. Thanks to my wonderful publishing team at Lantern for making the process so enjoyable, and to my mum and dad for their boundless love and encouragement. Finally, to my lovely Lizzie, who kept calm and carried on while I buried my head in books.

L A N T E R N

Published by the Penguin Group
Penguin Group (Australia)
707 Collins Street, Melbourne, Victoria 3008, Australia
(a division of Penguin Australia Pty Ltd)
Penguin Group (USA) Inc.
375 Hudson Street, New York, New York 10014, USA
Penguin Group (Canada)
90 Eglinton Avenue East, Suite 700, Toronto, Canada ON M4P 2Y3
(a division of Penguin Canada Books Inc.)
Penguin Books Ltd
80 Strand, London WC2R 0RL England
Penguin Ireland
25 St Stephen's Green, Dublin 2, Ireland
(a division of Penguin Books Ltd)
Penguin Books India Pvt Ltd
11 Community Centre, Panchsheel Park, New Delhi — 110 017, India
Penguin Group (NZ)
67 Apollo Drive, Rosedale, Auckland 0632, New Zealand
(a division of Penguin New Zealand Pty Ltd)
Penguin Books (South Africa) (Pty) Ltd, Rosebank Office Park, Block D,
181 Jan Smuts Avenue, Parktown North, Johannesburg, 2196, South Africa
Penguin (Beijing) Ltd
7F, Tower B, Jiaming Center, 27 East Third Ring Road North,
Chaoyang District, Beijing 100020, China

Penguin Books Ltd, Registered Offices: 80 Strand, London, WC2R 0RL, England

First published by Penguin Group (Australia), 2014

1 3 5 7 9 10 8 6 4 2

Text copyright © Simon Rickard 2014.
Photography copyright © Simon Rickard 2014.
Illustrations copyright © Getty Images except for pages 121 and 269 from The Bridgeman Art Library 2014

The moral right of the author has been asserted.

Cover design by Emily O'Neill © Penguin Group (Australia)
Text design by Emily O'Neill © Penguin Group (Australia)
Illustrations from Album Vilmorin, Paris, 1850
Cover photograph by Simon Rickard
Author photograph by Elizabeth Pogson
Typeset in Adobe Caslon by Post Pre-Press Group, Brisbane, Queensland
Colour separation by Splitting Image Colour Studio, Clayton, Victoria
Printed and bound in China by C & C Offset Printing Co. Ltd.

National Library of Australia
Cataloguing-in-Publication data:

Rickard, Simon, author.

Heirloom vegetables/Simon Rickard.
9781921383069 (hardback)
Includes bibliographical references and index.
Vegetables--Heirloom varieties.
Vegetable gardening.
635

PENGUIN.COM.AU/LANTERN